> *"The concept of Queen is to be regal and majestic.*
> *Glamour is part of us, and we want to be dandy."*
>
> —FREDDIE MERCURY

Streatham Hill 2015

"Their music was incredibly original in blending hard rock and pop in a way that had never been done before … obviously they wrote a lot of catchy tunes that will probably be around forever. They seem to be the band that kind of created that rock/pop anthem that you hear at every sports arena. So, yeah, I think they're a fairly pinnacle band."

—GEDDY LEE, RUSH

"I think that they had an amazing sound. It was completely unique and nobody could duplicate it, in the same way that the Four Seasons had their own sound, in the same way the Beatles had their own sound. Queen had a sound that people loved, and it was undeniable."

—NEIL DIAMOND

"What I really like about them is they just didn't give a shit. They're so ridiculous.… And musically they really are phenomenal. Freddie Mercury was just a beautiful singer, and they all are so great as musicians and have so many great moments where it's like, oh my God, here's a band that didn't hold back."

—WAYNE COYNE, FLAMING LIPS

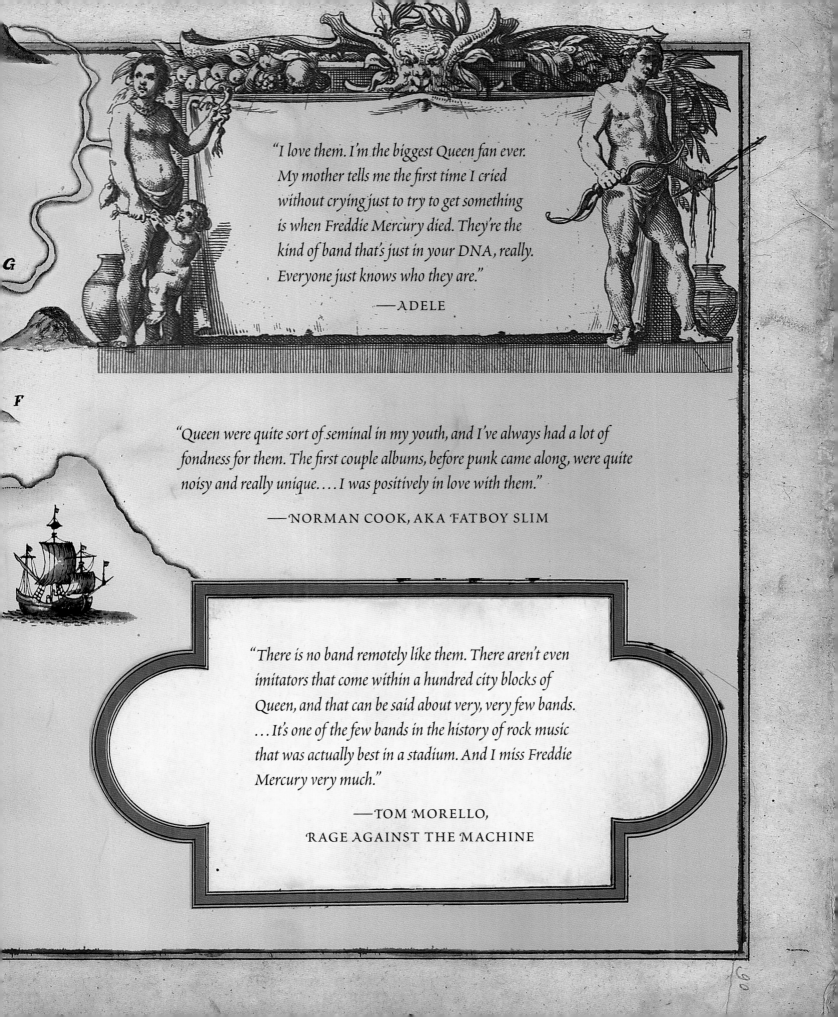

"I love them. I'm the biggest Queen fan ever. My mother tells me the first time I cried without crying just to try to get something is when Freddie Mercury died. They're the kind of band that's just in your DNA, really. Everyone just knows who they are."

—ADELE

"Queen were quite sort of seminal in my youth, and I've always had a lot of fondness for them. The first couple albums, before punk came along, were quite noisy and really unique.... I was positively in love with them."

—NORMAN COOK, AKA FATBOY SLIM

"There is no band remotely like them. There aren't even imitators that come within a hundred city blocks of Queen, and that can be said about very, very few bands. ...It's one of the few bands in the history of rock music that was actually best in a stadium. And I miss Freddie Mercury very much."

—TOM MORELLO,
RAGE AGAINST THE MACHINE

QUEEN

THE ULTIMATE ILLUSTRATED HISTORY OF THE CROWN KINGS OF ROCK

Voyageur Press

by

PHIL SUTCLIFFE

—— *with* ——

PETER HINCE   MICK ROCK

REINHOLD MACK   BILLY SQUIER

—— *and* ——

ROBERT ALFORD   ANDREW EARLES

MELISSA BLEASE   CHUCK EDDY

JON BREAM   GARY GRAFF

JOHN BUCCIGROSS   DAVE HUNTER

GARTH CARTWRIGHT   GREG KOT

STEPHANIE CHERNIKOWSKI   ROBERT MATHEU

STEPHEN DALTON   JAMES MCNAIR

JIM DEROGATIS   JEFFREY MORGAN

HARRY DOHERTY   DANIEL NESTER

DAVID DUNLAP JR.   SYLVIE SIMMONS

Voyageur Press titles are also available at discounts in bulk quantity for industrial or sales-promotional use. For details write to Special Sales Manager at Quarto Publishing Group USA Inc., 400 First Avenue North, Suite 400, Minneapolis, MN 55401 USA.

To find out more about our books, visit us online at www.voyageurpress.com.

ISBN: 978-0-7603-4947-2

The Library of Congress has cataloged the hardcover edition as follows:

Sutcliffe, Phil.
   Queen : the ultimate illustrated history of the crown kings of rock / Phil Sutcliffe.
      p. cm.
   Includes bibliographical references and index.
   ISBN 978-0-7603-3719-6 (hb w/ jkt)
   1. Queen (Musical group) 2. Rock musicians–England–Biography. I. Title.
   ML421.Q44S87 2009
   782.42166092'2–dc22
   [B]
                              2009007897

Pages 4–5: Band photos, January 1973. © *Michael Putland/Retna Ltd.*; playing cards *Bob Thomas/Popperfoto/Getty Images*
Pages 6–7: *News Of The World* tour, Cobo Hall, Detroit, November 18, 1977. © *Robert Alford*
Page 11: Circa 1975. *Michael Ochs Archives/Getty Images*
Page 12: *News Of The World* tour, Ahoy Hall, Rotterdam, April 1978. *Fin Costello/ Redferns Collection/Getty Images*

Acquisitions and Project Editor: Dennis Pernu
Design Manager: Katie Sonmor
Designer: John Barnett/4 Eyes Design

Printed in China

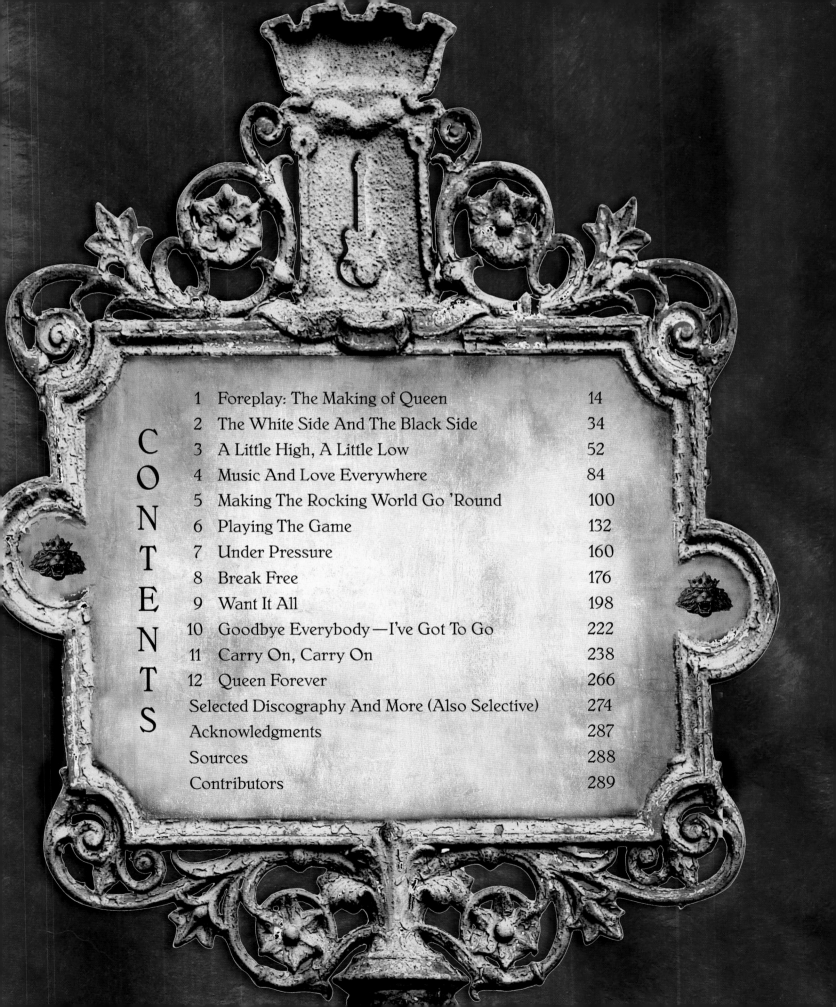

CONTENTS

1 FOREPLAY:
the MAKING of QUEEN

FREDDIE MERCURY, EH? Remember him, imagine him, picture him. From the black, skin-tight bodysuit slashed to the waist, the black nail varnish, and the posturing of the early '70s—a Baryshnikov, a stallion, a satyr, a centaur—to the cropped hair, the gay moustache, the ironic eyebrow raised, the ermine, and the crown of the mid-'80s. Then bow down in unworthy awe, if that's your inclination. Or shake your head and roll your eyes if it's all too much. Or, if what you see somehow hits the spot, just laugh and cry and sing along.

You could never ignore Freddie Mercury. Even when he was a nobody with nothing to declare, this fundamentally shy and secretive man could stride down the King's Road, London, flaunting a red velvet suit with fox-fur trimmings—so like a star that everyone asked, "Hey, who's that?"

Although a reconstructed Queen has gone back out on tour in recent years fronted by master singer Paul Rodgers, Mercury's magnetism is the *sine qua non* of Queen's eccentric rock 'n' roll immortality. The band comprised four remarkably diligent and ambitious musicians—gifted songwriters who each wrote smash hit singles—but they would never have established a place in the cultural memory without the catalyst, the firestarter, the stadium bestrider that was Freddie Mercury.

Not surprising that while May, Taylor, and Deacon grew up in a mundane London suburb and small-town Cornwall and Leicestershire, respectively, winged Mercury blew in from Zanzibar.

First reported flyer for a Queen gig, August 21, 1971, Tregye Country Club, Carnon Downs Festival, Truro, U.K. *Courtesy Ferdinando Frega, Queenmuseum.com*

Early handbill, 1973.

R & B WITH THE
'1984'
at ALL SAINTS CHURCH HALL
CAMPBELL ROAD
(off STAINES ROAD)
ON
SATURDAY 9th JULY 1966
from 8 pm - 11 pm
TICKETS 5/-
REFRESHMENTS AVAILABLE

"1984 was purely an amateur band, formed at school, although perhaps at the end we once got fifteen quid or something. We never really played anything significant in the way of original material."

—Brian May, quoted by Stuart Grundy and John Tobler, *The Guitar Greats*, 1983

Ian Dickson/Redferns Collection/Getty Images

The Guitarist

Brian Harold May lived a noisy life from the cradle. Born on July 19, 1947, and growing up in the outer-London sprawl of Feltham, Middlesex, amid the bedlam of aircraft taking off and landing at London Airport (now Heathrow), the skies always mattered to him. His favorite comic-strip hero was *The Eagle*'s Dan Dare, "pilot of the future." His father, Harold, a World War II fighter-bomber radio operator, became a draftsman for the Ministry of Aviation. Bonding via DIY and a fascination with BBC TV's new astronomy program, *The Sky At Night*, presented by the engagingly hyperenthusiastic Patrick Moore, father and son built a telescope together (May still uses it).

Harold played ukulele too. Brian liked it so much his parents bought him an acoustic guitar for his seventh birthday. Captivated by *The Tommy Steele Story*, a 1957 (auto)biopic starring England's own cheeky Cockney rock 'n' roller, he built his own old-fashioned crystal radio (with his father's help) and started buying 45s: U.K. skiffle king Lonnie Donegan, and Americans Connie Francis, the Everly Brothers, and Buddy Holly. Naturally analytical, in a 1991 interview for *Q* magazine May told this writer that he studied Holly's backing group, the Crickets: "I wanted to know how the harmonies worked, what made one harmony affect you in a certain way."

May contrived a DIY amplifier for his acoustic by hooking it up to his dad's homemade radiogram, a wooden furniture-

1984, circa 1967. From left: Tim Staffell (vocals), Dave Dilloway (bass), Richard Thompson (drums), John Garnham (guitar), and Brian May (guitar).

like console featuring a radio, turntable, and speakers. He loved the sound and asked his father and mother, Ruth, for a proper electric guitar. They said it would cost too much. "We were really close to the breadline. My mother used to secrete sixpences in jars to try and pay the gas bill," May told Ian Fortnam in an unpublished interview later posted to rocksbackpages.com in 1998. So Brian and his father built one.

The rightly renowned "Red Special," which May still plays, was "a matter of being poor. We set about it with files and chisels and penknives"—and a piece of a friend's discarded mahogany mantelpiece, some mother-of-pearl buttons, a knitting needle, and motorbike valve springs. Only the pickups cost money. They finished the job in eighteen months, by fall 1963.

Early the following year, with friends that included guitarist Tim Staffell, May formed a band called 1984. "It mainly came from shyness," said May. "I thought, *If I was up there I wouldn't have to deal with always being rejected by women.*"

The band embarked on four years of going nowhere. While they played covers at minor local gigs, May felt alternately inspired and deflated by the Beat Boom greats who appeared most weekends at clubs within a few miles of Feltham in Eel Pie Island, Richmond, and Twickenham.

"I was supposed to be at college, but we were playing and going out to see people like Pink Floyd, Cream, The Who, Hendrix. You could see all those people in one week. Can you imagine? We never slept."

—Brian May, quoted by Ian Fortnam

Every touring band needs an Isetta. A cagey Brian May and members of 1984.

Foreplay: The Making of Queen   17

U.S. promo copy of the Smile single "Earth" b/w "Step On Me" (1969), which was never released commercially. *Courtesy Ferdinando Frega, Queenmuseum.com*

"We used to see The Rolling Stones, The Yardbirds, and The Who at The Crawdaddy [in Richmond] and that really affected us," he said. "1984 had been into the technicalities and a bit scornful of the blues. But Clapton and The Yardbirds were about raw sex and anger, and with The Who it was total anarchy and destructive power—frightening. Then Hendrix . . . I thought I was pretty damn good, but when I saw him at the Saville Theatre [central London, probably January 29, 1967] I couldn't believe it. Deep jealousy, that was my first emotion. That period felt like the beginning of Creation. Suddenly, amid all the drug culture and peace and love, people were discovering that when you turned a guitar up to max it had a life of its own. It was so new and dangerous, wonderful to be a part of it."

Meanwhile, despite his father's constant worry that he would sacrifice his academic future to rock 'n' roll, May proved an exemplary schoolboy; he left in summer 1965 with such good grades in Advanced-levels maths, applied maths, additional maths, and physics that Imperial College, London, awarded him a scholarship to study physics, which led to him specializing in infrared astronomy (Imperial's staff boasted four Nobel Prize winners in physics at the time).

May and Staffell (by then studying at Ealing College of Art in West London) started growing their hair and writing their own songs, while adding Hendrix's "Stone Free" and Eddie Floyd's "Knock On Wood" to their covers repertoire. But the Summer of Love year ended grimly for 1984. As Staffell told this writer in 2005, a would-be whiz-kid manager "kitted us out with furry Afghan waistcoats, velvet with little mirrors all over them, crushed velvet loons, platform shoes, makeup." He got them on a huge Christmas show at London Olympia, overnight December 22–23—way down the bill to Pink Floyd and Hendrix. May would always remember "plugging into the same stack that Hendrix had plugged into. It sounded like the whole world when he played through it. For me, it sounded like a transistor radio," he told Fortnam. After 1984 performed to the largely unconscious at 5 a.m., they came off to find their wallets stolen from the dressing room and their van towed away by the police.

Discouraged, May left the group early in 1968 to concentrate on his BSc final exams. That summer the Queen Mother presented his degree in a ceremony at Royal Albert Hall. His results were so outstanding that Britain's premier astronomer, Sir Bernard Lovell, offered him a job at Jodrell Bank Observatory near Manchester. But he turned it down, preferring PhD studies at Imperial instead. "I had this burning thing inside me, knowing I wanted to play the guitar," he later explained, and London was the place to do it. That fall he and Staffell began again. With a new name, Smile, and Staffell moving to bass and lead vocals, May pinned an ad to the students' union notice board: "Brilliant Drummer wanted for Heavy Guitar band—must be able to play like Mitch Mitchell, Ginger Baker, Keith Moon." Challenging.

Roger Taylor replied.

THE DRUMMER

He came from way out in the sticks—naturally, given his father Michael's work for the Potato Marketing Board. Roger Meddows Taylor (the middle name a family inheritance) was born on July 26, 1949, in a village, Dersingham, Norfolk, near the East Anglian coast. Oddly enough, he was welcomed into the world by the Queen, who was opening the new maternity wing at West Norfolk and Lynn Hospital (this was Queen Elizabeth, who later became the Queen Mother and, in due course, presented May with his degree). The family first moved ten miles to King's Lynn, then, when Taylor was eight, right across the country to a similarly small town, Truro, in Cornwall, England's most western county.

"I advertised on a notice board at college for a drummer, because by this time, Cream and Jimi Hendrix were around, and I wanted a drummer who could handle that sort of stuff, and Roger was easily capable of it."

—BRIAN MAY, QUOTED BY STUART GRUNDY AND JOHN TOBLER, *The Guitar Greats*, 1983

The Reaction, circa 1966.

He began his musical career that very year, thrashing ukulele in a diminutive skiffle group sweetly named the Bubblingover Boys. "When I was a really young kid, I was inspired by Jerry Lee Lewis and Little Richard," Taylor once recalled.

Always clever in class, if not diligent, in 1960 Taylor won a scholarship to the ancient Truro School. But he already had an instinct for percussion. He told Robert Santelli for *Modern Drummer* in 1985 that his father found him an old snare drum, then a cymbal, then bought him a secondhand and cheap Ajax kit for his Christmas present in 1961. Roger saved up for a high-hat about two years later. The entire ensemble cost about £12—even less than May's "Fireplace" guitar. When he joined local group Cousin Jacks, though, he started on guitar.

Sadly, Taylor's parents separated in 1964. After that, he lived with his mother, Winifred, who told Jacky Gunn and Jim Jenkins, authors of *Queen: As It Began*, that "Roger was so ambitious and his confidence was immense. He just knew that one day he would make a name for himself and be living in London."

He certainly showed a touch of quiet pushiness when, the following year, he started drumming with the top band in Truro, Johnny Quale & The Reaction, purveyors of Elvis, Roy Orbison, and Beatles covers. Within a few months, Taylor replaced Quale as leader and singer. Although he remained on the drum stool, over the next couple of years he urged the Reaction in the general direction of his heroes, "Jimi Hendrix, John Lennon, and Bob Dylan. Archetypal influences I suppose, but why not?" The Reaction covered them all, and Taylor's drumming strove to combine the influences of the Jimi Hendrix Experience's Mitch Mitchell and Keith Moon, who bedazzled him when the Who played Camborne Skating Rink on October 15, 1965. Taylor even experimented, Moon-style, with pouring lighter fuel on a cymbal and setting fire to it.

Taylor finally pulled off his longed-for move to London in September 1967. After scoring useful A-level grades in biology, chemistry, and physics, he accepted a place in the London Hospital medical school's dentistry degree course—not his passion, but he wanted the student grant. His first year proved uneventful, though. Come summer, he was back in Cornwall, co-promoting so-called "happenings" (the Reaction plus psychedelic light show) in a marquee on the rugged, undeveloped beach at Perranporth.

However, the new university year turned the trick. May's ad naming Mitchell and Moon as inspirations caught the eye of Imperial student Les Brown, Taylor's Truro pal and flatmate in Sinclair Road, Shepherd's Bush, West London. He passed it on, and Taylor wrote a letter introducing himself. A musical relationship that's lasted forty years and counting took moments to fall into place.

The audition lodged in May's memory: "I went to the Imperial jazz room, which I'd booked for the evening, and Roger was there already, hitting the skins, fiddling around, turning knobs. I said, 'What're you doing?' He said, 'I'm tuning them.' I'd never seen a drummer do that before! I was impressed. He'd got great energy, but he was very neat too, particularly with the snare drum; he'd do these *ththththrump* things which started and finished very cleanly and precisely on time. Immediately, the sound of my guitar and his drums had that *hugeness*. We hit it off like brothers too. . . ."

Tim Staffell added, "Roger was confident and flamboyant. Funny, too. I said, 'We want to be loud, but we want to be intelligent.' Vocal harmonies *and* the power trio thing. So Roger was it!"

Smile debuted at Imperial that October 26, supporting Pink Floyd (probably the night May met his long-term girlfriend and future wife, Chrissy Mullen). Taylor organized their next couple of gigs back home—hence the billing:

"Smile Featuring The Legendary Drummer Of Cornwall." After the long journey, friends and family would always put them up for the night.

Still studying, though, the band couldn't rehearse and gig regularly, so they remained in a state of flux, which May sometimes found depressing—especially because, just before their own first gig, they'd seen an early Led Zeppelin show, at the Marquee, London, on October 18. "I felt sick because they'd actually done what we were trying to do, only a lot better," said May. "Zeppelin and Jeff Beck defined what everyone else was blindly trying to get to."

Soon they encountered one persuasive reason to be cheerful. Early in 1969, May and Taylor met an Ealing College classmate of Staffell's named Freddie Bulsara. Noting a shared enthusiasm for glam silk scarves and fur coats (though only Bulsara had black-varnished nails), they talked at length. "We came together through Hendrix," Taylor told David Thomas in the August 1999 *Mojo*. "Freddie was a complete Hendrix freak. He once saw him 14 nights in a row in different pubs. . . ."

Before long, the four were flat-sharing in Ferry Road, Barnes, an otherwise posh southwest London suburb where May and Staffell, strumming away in the front room, unwittingly wrote the first Queen song, "Doing All Right."

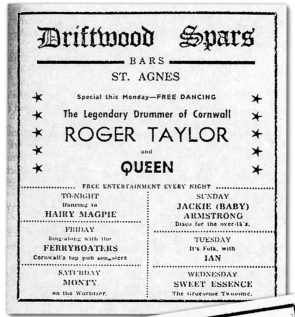

THE SINGER

Farrokh Bulsara came to rock 'n' roll from a different planet. Born to Parsee Indian parents on the East African island of Zanzibar on September 5, 1946, he grew up in the Zoroastrian faith and an old British colonial setting. His father, Bomi, was a cashier at the courthouse; his mother, Jer, ran the household and domestic staff (their daughter, Kashmira, was born in 1952). When Farrokh—the correct spelling, judging by the handwritten birth certificate—was eight they decided to send him to an Indian boarding school, St. Peter's in Panchgani, a hill station about fifty miles from Bombay (now Mumbai). At least it was close to his maternal grandparents and aunt, with whom he'd spend breaks and holidays if he didn't go home to Zanzibar.

The adult Freddie (he was given the nickname by classmates at St. Peter's) reflected to *Melody Maker*'s Caroline Coon in 1974: "My parents thought boarding school would do me good, dear. I look back and think it was marvelous. You learn to look after yourself." You also learn a very English accent, which later helped Freddie keep his origins low-profile. But he did experience the notorious boarding-school hazards; he told *NME*'s Julie Webb, also in 1974, that he'd been regarded as "the pretty boy" or "arch poof" and "had the odd schoolmaster chasing me. . . . I've had my share of schoolboy pranks. I'm not going to elaborate further."

Apart from the pranks, he pitched in: choir, dramatic society, learning piano, sport—he told Queen biographers Gunn and Jenkins, "I could sprint, I was good at hockey and just brilliant in the boxing ring, believe it or not!" (His father wrote to the school to discourage this last activity.) What's more, he and his friends had access to a Dansette record player with a stack of pop 45s. Jer Bulsara told *The Times* in 2006 (she was eighty-three) that after watching Elvis Presley on TV during a vacation he vowed, "'I'm going to be like him one day.' Farrokh always wanted to be a showman."

At twelve, Freddie formed a beat group called the Hectics. At school dances he pounded piano through covers of Elvis, Little Richard, Fats Domino, and British rock 'n' roller Cliff Richard. His return to Zanzibar in 1962, at his own request, interrupted his band life for several years, it turned out.

By then the colonial idyll had waned. Zanzibar gained independence in December 1963. The following month, a revolt by the African population against the Arab-dominated regime saw Indian residents caught between factions. The Bulsaras packed two suitcases and fled. Jer remembered an excited Freddie, full of "swinging London" pop star dreams, exclaiming "England's the place we ought to go, Mum!" But for her—and Bomi, already in his fifties—the enforced migration proved "very hard."

They followed family connections to Feltham where they settled (within a mile of Brian May's home, although he and Freddie never met as teenagers). While Jer became a Marks & Spencer shop assistant, Bomi started as a cashier with catering firm Forte. One blessing of this utter upheaval, Jer insisted, was that in Feltham they encountered no racism at all. Certainly Freddie never mentioned any such experience in interviews, though with his light complexion and barely discernible accent he seems to have never been directly questioned on the subject.

Freddie, who had passed several Ordinary-level exams at St. Peter's, got into nearby Isleworth Polytechnic to study art. In 1966 his A-level grade A saw him accepted to a graphic illustration course at Ealing College of Art ('60s alumni included Pete Townshend and Ronnie Wood), and he moved into the city, sharing a flat in Kensington, near Imperial.

College days. Freddie Balsura, third from right.

At Ealing, he and Tim Staffell became friends. Apart from relating to his Hendrix worship—Freddie covered the walls of his room with posters and his own drawings of his hero—Staffell appreciated his straightforward character: "He was always charming, a nice, reasonable, decent, accepting guy. I think he had to learn to be a diva later, because he wasn't one in the first place." Staffell added that "nobody cared" about sexuality, so Freddie, who acted camp but went out with girls, didn't even rate gossip.

Back then if anybody asked his ambition, Freddie would always declare rock stardom. But he hadn't played in a band since India. While completing his diploma, at twenty-two, he decided, as he put it, to "take the plunge" into music. He bought a guitar. Staffell taught him the rudiments and, at some

Kensington student hangout now forgotten, introduced him to May and Taylor.

Freddie certainly hit May between the eyes. "I remember him already dressed as the kind of rock star you hadn't seen before, flamboyant, androgynous," May said. "I think he was born that way. He was already Freddie Mercury in all but name." (This was probably the Bulsara-to-Mercury transition period; Staffell reckoned he settled on the zodiacal stage name—he was Virgo with Mercury rising—while still a student.) "The first time he invited me 'round to his place," May continued, "he played me Hendrix's *Electric Ladyland* and he said, 'This guy really makes use of the stereo.' So we were going from one speaker to the other, listening to bits of overdub, finding out how Hendrix produced these sounds."

Staffell is sure Mercury reciprocated May's fascination "because Brian was such a seriously musical guitar player and Freddie always recognized that." Others said of Mercury that, when not in May and Staffell's company, Mercury would speak with awe of their ability to write songs, a gift he was still struggling to unlock.

Momentarily a freelance graphic artist after collecting his diploma, from August 1969 to the following spring, Mercury learned a lot about band life by fronting two novice combos, Ibex (August–October) and Wreckage (October–December), and then the more experienced Sour Milk Sea (February–March 1970). Regularly proclaiming, "I'm going to be a legend, dear boy!" he'd earn forgiveness by doing his bit when amps needed humping into venues (despite the white satin trousers and feather boas). Furthermore, Mercury bestrode the stage like a rock god from the outset and asserted his views on songwriting too—dump the blues riffing and adopt an "architectural"

approach. He began to write with his bandmates. Legend avers that at his farewell gig with Wreckage, at Wade Deacon Grammar School for Girls, Widnes, he lucked into his iconic sawn-off mic stand when the base fell off mid-song.

Meanwhile, living with Smile in Barnes, he won favor as a flatmate. In 2005, Taylor told Mark Blake for *Mojo Classic: Queen* that Mercury was "very tidy," *and* his mother used to send a weekly food basket they could all share. Mercury and Taylor found they had such rapport they started a part-time "antique" clothes stall at Kensington Market. May enjoyed the shoddy-glam fashion parade that subsequently passed through the flat: "Sophisticated second-hand velvet jackets, filigree waistcoats from the 1920s . . . and some incredible tat. Freddie would pull a strip of cloth out of a huge bag and say, 'Look at this beautiful garment, this is going to fetch a fortune.' I'd say, 'Fred, that's a piece of rag.' But he could sell it."

It was during this period that Mercury, to no one's surprise, found a steady girlfriend, Mary Austin, who worked at hippy fashion emporium Biba on Kensington Church Street. Mercury later called it "an odd bond," but, whatever became of their romance, their friendship never died.

Sour Milk Sea.

All this time, Smile only stumbled along. Although May and Staffell had written some promising songs, their only hint of a breakout from the London college and Cornish club circuits led to disillusionment. They signed a one-off deal and recorded tracks at Trident Studios, London, yet, strangely, all it led to was an obscure American single release, an equally useless Japanese EP, and nothing in the U.K. at all.

Smile surrendered. In April 1970, Staffell joined a band called Humpy Bong while, May says, "Roger and I gave up completely." He felt fortunate to have his PhD research to turn

to: building observatory equipment at Mount Teide, Tenerife, where he and two professors periodically shared an aluminium hut and studied space dust. ("There's a lot of it around," he explained to Jonh Ingham of *Sounds* in 1975. "I was doing stuff on motion of dust, using a spectrometer to look for Doppler shifts in the light that came from them, and from that you can find out where they're going, and possibly where they came from. It has a lot to do with how the solar system was formed.")

"That summer was when Freddie became the driving force," said May. "He told us we could do it. I can see him saying, yes, Smile had been wonderful, but we weren't presenting a show, we were just standing there. He talked about lights, sounds, clothes, everything. He believed if you've got half an hour on a stage you do everything you can—which was unfashionable at the time."

"Freddie persuaded us," Taylor told *Circus* in 1975. Another new band sprang to life, with Mercury out front. A variant on Smile's "big heavy emotional wave of sound," said May, with even more emphasis on melodies and harmonies. They decided not to call themselves the Grand Dance, or Topfactsnewsandinfo, and adopted instead Mercury's forcible suggestion: Queen. "I thought it up years ago," he once explained. "It's very regal, strong, universal, immediate. Certainly I was aware of the gay connotations. But it sounds splendid!"

By then sharing a flat in Earls Court, the three worked on most of the songs that became their first album, including "Keep Yourself Alive" and "Seven Seas Of Rhye." Debuting live at Truro City Hall on June 27, 1970 (probably, though sources disagree), then gigging wherever they could, they briskly disposed of three bass players until, the following January, a mutual friend asked May and Taylor to a disco at Maria Assumpta Teacher Training College, Kensington, and brought John Deacon along.

"[Freddie] always looked like a star and acted like a star, even though he was penniless."

—BRIAN MAY, QUOTED BY PHIL SUTCLIFFE, Q, 03.1991

Photofest

THE BASSIST

If any member of Queen looked destined for a quiet life, it was John Richard Deacon. His reserved public persona and absence from, or reticence in, interviews have left his aspirations and creative motivations more or less unknown. As a result, he has been called "boring." But "hidden" is a more apt description.

The youngest member of Queen was born in the Midlands city of Leicester on August 19, 1951, and lived there until 1960, when the family moved a few miles to Oadby, a country town, population around twenty thousand. His father, Arthur, worked for an insurance company, Norwich Union.

Even as a small boy, John liked rock 'n' roll on the radio, and when he was seven his parents bought him "a little plastic Tommy Steele guitar" (Steele being the Cockney rocker who also inspired May as a child). But playing didn't come easily at that stage; he told *Music Star* in 1974, "Nothing seemed to click." For a while his other lifelong enthusiasm, electronics, offered more satisfaction. Again echoing May's boyhood, with his father he built various gadgets and set up a ham radio in the garden shed.

However, in 1962 Arthur Deacon died, leaving his widow, Lillian, to bring up John and his sister, Julie (born in 1956). There's no indication the three did anything other than pull together and pull through—probably Deacon's only recorded comment on the experience was to *The Hit* in 1985 when reporter Martin Townsend found he could "still barely talk about it," and all he did say was "It's not easy growing up without a dad."

Passing his eleven-plus that same year, Deacon moved up to grammar school, where he thrived in sciences. But, when he was thirteen, music tugged at his sleeve again. Deacon told *Music Star* that, when "some friends up the road" acquired guitars, "I went along because I had a tape recorder which they could use as an amplifier. But I got interested enough to get my mum to buy me a Spanish guitar and that's when it really started properly."

Soon they had a group of sorts, with the novice Deacon strumming rhythm at first. One of his bandmates' fathers lent him £60 to buy an electric guitar when his mother refused because she thought it would distract him from schoolwork. But Mark Hodkinson's diligent book, *Queen: The Early Years*, quotes old friends portraying him as a boy who, when confronted with any problem, would say "I can do that" and deliver on his promise. His attitude won him the nickname "Easy Deacon."

Calling themselves the Opposition, the band played a school gig, then made their public debut at the Co-Operative Hall in nearby Enderby in December 1965, and went on to about two hundred local gigs over the next four years. In the meantime, Deacon passed through a mod phase, wearing a parka and riding a Vespa motor scooter, and moved to bass. After that, the group shifted from pop to progressive Jethro Tull and Deep Purple influences and changed its name to the Art.

The Opposition.

Still at school, Deacon got results. In summer 1969 he chalked up three A-level grade As, securing a place in an electronics degree course at Chelsea College, London. Purposefully, he left the Art, a clear-cut decision to put away childish things; yet this must have been one of the rare occasions when Deacon misunderstood his own nature and needs. As he said to *Music Star*: "Personally, one of the most important times for me was when I left home to go to college in London. It wasn't so much the event itself, but it steered me in the musical direction."

A year later, after summer vacation, he brought his bass and amp down to London.

That October 16 he saw one of Queen's earliest gigs, at the College of Estate Management, Kensington. His dry recollection appears on official fan club site queenworld.com: "They were dressed in black, and the lights were very dim, so all I could see were four shadowy figures. They didn't make a lasting impression."

Within a month he'd formed an R&B band, but they played only one gig. Now watching the small ads in the music

weeklies, he began a sequence of unproductive auditions—until the Maria Assumpta disco in January 1971. "I'd heard Queen were looking for a bass guitarist," he said. "I chatted to Roger and Brian and they said they couldn't find anybody who seemed to fit."

May says, "Until John, it had been exploding bass player syndrome. If they musically worked they'd look all wrong, and if they felt all right they couldn't play. When I met John I remember shaking hands and saying, 'Great, join the band.' I'd had a couple of drinks. . . ."

But May's woozy instinct proved sound when Deacon tried out with Queen at Imperial. May told David Thomas for *Mojo* in 1999, "This quite shy guy turned up with his immaculate Rickenbacker bass and immaculate amplifier, plugged in, and as soon as he started playing we realized it was right."

"He was great," said Taylor. "We were all so over the top, we thought because he was quiet he would fit in without too much upheaval. And the fact that he was an electronics wizard was definitely a deciding factor!"

MODERN TIMES ROCK 'N' ROLL: THE FIRST ALBUM

Slowed by academic work—Deacon and Taylor for annual exams, May on field trips to Tenerife—the four rehearsed and gigged as best they could. The classic line-up probably debuted on July 2, 1971, at Surrey College, outside London, although some accounts go straight to their summer tour of Cornwall, nine dates scattered over five weeks, starting at The Garden, Penzance, on July 17.

Small time though it was, the Cornish trip meant a lot to new boy Deacon, as he told *Music Star* three years later: "We stuck all the equipment into one van and sailed off. We [rented] a cottage [near Truro] and stayed together. It was good because we got to know each other really well. It settled us as a group. Roger did manage to find us some gigs as well, so we broke even."

While Queen's academics secured their white-collar qualifications and rock 'n' roll marked time, Mercury benefited from the chance to practice—and it wasn't only his "Four-Fingers Freddie" piano playing that needed work. Tim Staffell reckoned that, when Queen began, his friend's voice had been "a bit weak" because, at twenty-three, he'd been singing with bands for less than a year. Taylor, speaking to *Mojo*'s David Thomas, recalled a style issue too: "Freddie had a natural musicality, a real gift, but when we first met he had a very strange vibrato which some people found rather distressing." However, brash Mercury proved he could both criticize himself and listen to others. The drummer watched him "apply himself" and develop his singing craft. Staffell agreed Mercury grew far more "powerful," improved his "timbre," and "just as a little addition, his writing had become idiosyncratic and wonderful."

> *"Brian May remembers Queen's first-ever free gig well. It was in London, five years ago, when the band invited 120 people along to a lecture theatre in Imperial College to hear them play. Orange juice and popcorn were served to the 80 or so who bothered to show their faces and lend an ear."*
>
> —HARRY DOHERTY, *Melody Maker*, 18.09.1976

Still, despite their talents, intelligence, and high ambitions, Queen endearingly remained just as hapless as everyone else. Before one London gig, in a typically nice but vague attempt at showmanship, May cooked up heaps of popcorn that he later handed out to audience members while soliciting comments on the band.

The wheels finally started turning when, in fall 1971, through a friend they secured free demo time by agreeing to

> "When Yes was working on our second or third album, probably around 1970, Freddie used to work in the Kingston Market in the boot store as a shop assistant. [Drummer] Bill Bruford and I used to go there and buy boots from this store, which made really good rock 'n' roll boots at that time. I always remember Freddie bending down on the floor when I was trying on these boots and feeling my toes and how my foot fit in there, and he would say, 'Me and a bunch of guys I know, we're rehearsing. We want to be in a band and do well.' Of course, I was a little patronizing and was like, 'Well, good luck with that,' never thinking that the boot salesman would actually become Freddie Mercury."
>
> —Chris Squire, Yes

test the new De Lane Lea studio. This enabled them to record well-rounded versions of first-album-to-be songs "Liar," "Keep Yourself Alive," "The Night Comes Down," and "Jesus."

But, almost casually, in mid-session, they made a decision that would cause pain and dissension for more than fifteen years. May told the story in *Queen: As It Began*: "'Liar' was one of the first songs we worked on together, the four of us, using some of my own riffs and Freddie's words. We discussed if we should all be credited as songwriters in such cases. Freddie said, 'As far as I'm concerned the person who wrote the words has effectively written the song.'" They all agreed, but it was a very unusual way of allocating publishing royalties. May saw it as the main reason why, until a late-1980s change of heart, they "always argued about money." He said it even hampered them creatively: "The rule almost certainly discouraged us from cooperating on lyrics for a long time and started a trend towards separateness in song-producing in general which was acute from the late '70s onwards when we were recording in Munich."

A friend hawked the demo around every record label he could find. They all said no, bar one: Charisma. Queen had enough nerve to reject that offer as too small. That September, May took a job teaching at Stockwell Manor Comprehensive School, South London, to tide him over.

Then an odd contact started working for them. Producer John Anthony, who in 1969 recorded Smile's few tracks, visited the band at De Lane Lea and suggested fellow Trident staffer Roy Thomas Baker drop by to watch them at work. They played "Keep Yourself Alive"; Baker thought them "fresh, commercial, great" and recommended them to his bosses at Trident, Norman and Barry Sheffield, who wavered, then came up with an offer that cost nothing, not even commitment on either side. The Sheffields said Queen could record at their studio in Soho, central London, during overnight "downtime."

This meant a not unexciting wait until Elton John or David Bowie (the latter then working on *Ziggy Stardust & The Spiders From Mars*) finished their work sometime between midnight and 2 a.m. Then Queen recorded through the small hours until the first paying client arrived in the morning.

A twenty-year-old Trident staffer, David Hentschel, later renowned as a producer for Genesis and Mike Oldfield, engineered Queen's free sessions as a volunteer. "Trident was an oasis in a very seedy Soho," he told me in 2005. "Any night you could watch the hookers plying their trade outside. You'd get a late social drink in The Ship on Wardour Street and breakfast or lunch in The Star Café."

But the temporarily free gift of studio and labor—including co-production by Baker and Anthony—in no way humbled Queen. "From the beginning we were fighting to get reality into the sound," May told *Mojo*'s David Thomas. "I had this huge argument with some studio guy because he wanted to put the guitar amplifier into a box so the sound wouldn't leak into anything else. He said, 'After the event, we can put echo on, make it sound any way you want.' I said, 'No, you can't. It will sound dead.' The drums were close-miked and covered in sticky tape to make them dead too—the exact opposite of what we wanted which was everything sounding like it was in the room, in your face. We had this incredible fight to get the mics out of the drum booth and into the middle of the studio, and to put mics all round the room."

That was just the setup. After that came the performance battles. "I remember Roy Thomas Baker saying the only way to get a good performance was to play a song fifty times over. I said, 'No, the only way is to get the first performance and keep it,'" May recalled. "I'm not putting down Roy at all, but we were fighting to find a place where we had technical perfection *and* the reality of performance and sound."

But at least, as the Queen album sleeve eventually announced, "nobody played synthesizer"—a purist principle of May's.

Although Baker described the experience as "fragmented and tiring," Queen learned a lot about their musical capabilities—such as the nature of their vocal harmonies. "Freddie has this sharp, crystal, incisive tone, Roger is husky and raw, and I have a sort of roundness," May reckoned. "Put them together and it sounds . . . *big*."

Queen didn't know it, but when they finished an album's worth of tracks in January 1972, they were just beginning eighteen months of marking time until its release. Negotiations with Trident wandered along. To Taylor, "It seemed like forever," although, as he told *Circus* in 1975, "We wanted to do it right. So we were really very careful." Offers of a workingman's wage, £20 a week and new equipment all

"Listening to Queen inspired Mötley Crüe to work with Roy Thomas Baker on *Too Fast For Love*. He was just the most eccentric dude you've ever met on the planet. He would come in, 'Hello *dahlings* . . .' and listen for maybe thirty minutes or so and leave. And we're like, 'What?! Where's he going?' But he produced Queen, so, man, we had to have him produce us, too."

—Tommy Lee

A German EMI pressing of "I Can Hear Music" b/w "Goin' Back" (1973), the only release of the single to feature a picture sleeve. Larry Lurex was the name under which Trident Studios engineer Robin Geoffrey Cable was recording the tracks, which had previously been recorded by the Beach Boys and Dusty Springfield, respectively. He enlisted the help of Mercury, Taylor, and May, who were also at Trident recording their debut.

around—except for May's Red Special—eventually won their agreement to contracts for recording, management, and publishing, signed on November 1. The band failed to understand or get expert advice on the inherent conflict of interest created when one company controlled these three areas of their work.

That summer Deacon (a first in electronics) and Taylor (who'd switched from dentistry to biology at East London Polytechnic) concluded their degrees, while May uncharacteristically pulled out of submitting his thesis at the final edit stage, thus missing out on a doctorate (until he returned to it thirty years later) and causing a rift with his father who barely spoke to him for a year.

To Deacon, just earning a wage from music was significant. "It was quite a moment when we decided to turn professional," he told *Music Star*. "Really I didn't think we'd ever do it. . . . Possibly Freddie and Roger were the keenest. Brian was a big career man deeply into studying physics and astronomy and had reservations about it, but the other two are the born stars. Freddie's probably the one who's given us the most push to get on, and is the most insistent with people like managers."

Meanwhile, May fell prey to the demoralizing fear he'd experienced upon seeing Led Zeppelin in 1969: that his band had missed their moment. This time it was Bowie as Ziggy at the Rainbow, London, on December 24, 1972: "I thought, 'He's done it, he's made his mark, and we're still struggling,'" May recalled. It felt the more poignant, no doubt, because, four days earlier at the Marquee, Queen had played a showcase for record company scouts arranged by Trident and blown it with a poor performance. Rosie Horide, who reviewed it for music weekly *Disc*, reckoned their performance had simply outgrown such small venues: "Freddie was hitting his head on the ceiling and bouncing off the walls. Hopeless."

Even so, scouts from the new EMI label began sniffing around. Roy Featherstone, head of artists and repertoire, made enquiries and called the Sheffields' demands "frightening." Eventually, though, on April 9, 1973, he agreed to an advance of around £300,000, enormous for the time. Queen had a deal.

Typically, as they would prove, the band's instinct for total control emerged at once. Uninvited, and without even telling their manager, Trident's Jack Nelson, they designed the album's cover. Graphic artist Mercury devised and drew the Queen crest. He and May worked with Taylor's photographer friend Doug Puddifoot on a heavily tinted live shot for the front of the LP sleeve and a scissors-and-paste collage of informal snaps for the back.

EMI marketing manager Paul Watts took delivery of the *objet d'art*. "The Queen crest was this thin filigree drawing. I wouldn't call it amateurish, but it wasn't pukka," Watts recalled in 2005. "Our old-school creative services manager, Ron Dunton, called it 'crap.' That upset Freddie. He felt his artistry was being questioned. I had to referee the 'discussion' and persuade Ron. But Queen wanted to be involved in everything. To me, they were fantastic to work with, keen to talk business and very marketing aware."

In July, when their first U.K. single, "Keep Yourself Alive," and debut album, *Queen*, barely registered, they were one very disappointed band. ♛

QUEEN
Queen
EMC 3006
on tour with **MOTT THE HOOPLE**

NOVEMBER
12 Leeds Town Hall
13 Blackburn, St. Georges
15 Worcester Gaumont
16 Lancaster University
17 Liverpool Stadium
18 Stoke on Trent, Trentham Gardens
19 Wolverhampton, Civic
20 Oxford, New Theatre
21 Preston, Guildhall
22 Newcastle, City Hall
23 Glasgow, Apollo Centre
25 Edinburgh, Caley Cinema
26 Manchester, Opera House
27 Birmingham Town Hall
28 Swansea, Brangwyn Hall
29 Bristol, Colston Hall
30 Bournemouth Winter Gardens
DECEMBER
1 Southend, Kursaal
2 Chatham Central
14 LONDON, Hammersmith Odeon

IMPERIAL COLLEGE
Nº 404
AT THE UNION
on
Friday, 2nd November
at 8 p.m.
QUEEN
ADMISSION 30p
[Price includes 10% VAT]

Courtesy Martin Skala, QueenConcerts.com

Queen tour, Imperial College, November 1973. © *Mick Rock, 1974, 2009*

With Mott The Hoople. From left: Ian Hunter, Freddie, Overend Watts, Morgan Fisher, and Roger. Oxford, November 1973.
Andre Csillag/Rex USA/Courtesy Everett Collection

b/w "Son And Daughter," Portugal, 1973. *Courtesy Ferdinando Frega, Queenmuseum.com*

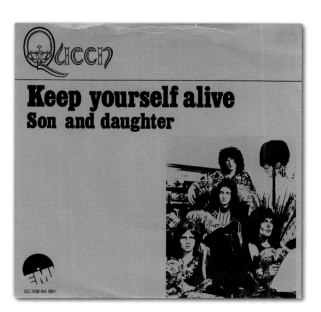

Holland, 1973. *Courtesy Ferdinando Frega, Queenmuseum.com*

"We didn't really want to get into that small club circuit. We all wanted to play big, big concerts, and didn't want to get stuck in that circuit for years and years, which is so easy to do, no matter how good you are."

—ROGER TAYLOR, QUOTED BY HARRY DOHERTY, *Melody Maker*, 18.09.1976

Queen

by John Buccigross

MOST OF US LOOK BACK AT OUR YOUTH and/or early adulthood and we cringe. Inevitably, awkwardness plus inexperience plus a desperate search for acceptance result in an embarrassing, youthful moment involving public nudity, alcohol, and a Garden Weasel.

For most, the lumpy road to mere competence is long and fraught with delusional overconfidence and debilitating underconfidence. The self-retrospective cringe factor multiplies for athletes, musicians, and those who perform in front of a camera. Some performers never survive the negative first impression or even get a second chance. We are either stoned off the stage or drown in our own big pool of I QUIT.

Listening to Freddie Mercury's vocal performance on Queen's debut LP, the cringe factor never surfaces. The first Brian May lyric most of the world ever heard come out of Mercury's mouth is belted out of the park like a first-pitch fastball thrown by an over-the-hill pitcher: "I was told a million times/Of all the troubles in my way/Tried to grow a little wiser/Little better every day."

Going, going, gone. If ever a lyric anticipated the outcome of an event (in this case Freddie Mercury and Queen), well, I haven't heard a better one in rock 'n' roll. The original intent may have been irony, but Mercury's sheer force of personality blew away any hope of literary subtlety.

Despite his admittances to shyness, Mercury was a natural talent never intimidated by a stage or a microphone—an athletic and clutch performer along the lines of Babe Ruth, Marlon Brando, Bobby Orr, Tiger Woods, and Jimi Hendrix. Some of those performers were introverts, some were extroverts, but they knew they were specially gifted at a young age, and whether they were taciturn or bullhorn, they flaunted their skill on the world stage from day one. Their talent was a muscle and their performance was a reflex.

One is born with such greatness. I picture Freddie Mercury exiting the birth canal of his mother, Jer Bulsara, already with crooked teeth, receding hairline, and that porno 'stache, singing with the confidence of Liza Minelli after three highballs. Dude had game from the get-go, born with wings that soared through Brian May's atmosphere of guitar strings. *Queen* was

Freddie Mercury's rookie card, his first work of art, and in many ways his—or should I say your—lost treasure. I promise you there are passionate fans of Queen who haven't heard one note of this 30:36 album. You may be one of them.

Queen's self-titled debut was released in 1973, although it was actually completed in 1972. Mercury was in his mid-twenties. So was guitarist Brian May. Together they would form one of the best singer-guitarist duos of their generation. Like many records of the day this album is best served on headphones.

"Keep Yourself Alive" is a terrific song to begin a discography. I picture a dark theater as Brian May's guitar begins its assault on the open air and another Queen concert begins. (On a side note, Jimmy Iovine, who produced Stevie Nicks' debut album, must have been a Queen fan; I hear a lot of "Keep Yourself Alive" when I accidentally come across Nicks' "Edge Of Seventeen." Also, Nicks' debut album was called *Bella Donna*, as in "I've loved a million women in a belladonic haze"—I'm just sayin'.)

"Doing All Right" begins like a song you would hear in 1973 during a sappy episode of the American TV show *The*

Partridge Family. At the 1:23 mark it shifts to another time, maybe a few years before. Then, at 1:52, it heads to a jazz club and chills with a vodka. At 2:06 the song is performing in a biker bar. At 2:32 we are back on the boring curb of summer suburbia before cable television, sunscreen, and mandatory seatbelts. And back and forth the song goes.

When a hockey player scores three goals in a game it's called a hat trick. When a player scores three consecutive goals, with no other goals scored by either team, it's called a natural hat trick. "Great King Rat," "My Fairy King," and "Liar" are Mercury's natural hat trick—sixteen minutes and nineteen seconds of bombast on full display that, once again, must be experienced through headphones. Brian May's Red Special must have suffered a hernia during "Great King Rat." "My Fairy King" is an early precursor to "Bohemian Rhapsody" with outrageous lyrics, however, Mercury's confident performance makes you believe it is nonfiction. "Liar" is 1970s highway rock twisting through six-plus minutes of complex testosterone. By the end of tracks 3, 4, and 5 the listener is ready to walk outside, find a rabid raccoon, and choke it to death with their bare hands. That, my friends, is the soul of rock 'n' roll.

A few tracks on, "Son And Daughter" finds Freddie belting a Brian May ball-buster. I would have probably done away with "Doing All Right" altogether and put "Son And Daughter" second in the line-up if it meant letting May thrash away for three minutes at the end as intended.

A solid debut and a textbook for life, this *Queen.* The lesson? Don't waste your time worrying about what others think of you and your work. Arrive prepared and competent. Don't hesitate. Don't shirk. Come out, get going, and kick some ass. There may be small moments where you look back and cringe, but by and large you will have your dignity and self-respect for your act of courage. And you will have something to build on. ⚜

Argentina, 1973.

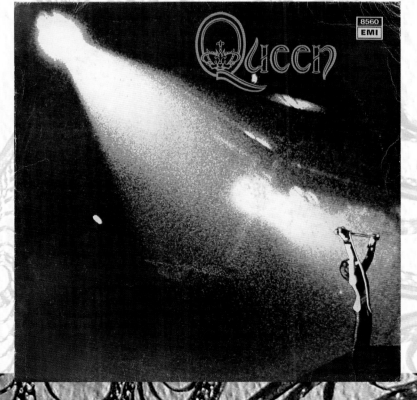

Tour Dates

Early Queen

27.06.1970[1]	City Hall	Truro, GBR
18.07.1970	Imperial College	London, GBR
25.07.1970	PJ's Club	Truro, GBR
23.08.1970	Imperial College	London, GBR
04.09.1970	Swiss Cottage Private School	London, GBR
16.10.1970	College of Estates Management	London, GBR
30.10.1970	College of Technology	St. Helens, GBR
31.10.1970	Cavern Club	Liverpool, GBR
14.11.1970	Balls Park College	Hertford, GBR
05.12.1970	Shoreditch College	Egham, GBR
18.12.1970	College of Technology	St. Helens, GBR
19.12.1970	Congregational Church Hall	St. Helens, GBR
09.01.1971	Technical College	Ewell, GBR
19.02.1971	Hornsey Misto Hall	London, GBR
20.02.1971	Kinston Polytechnic	London, GBR
02.07.1971[2]	College	Surrey, GBR
11.07.1971	Imperial College	London, GBR
17.07.1971	The Garden	Penzance, GBR
19.07.1971	Rugby Club	Hayle, GBR
24.07.1971	Young Farmers Club	Wadebridge, GBR
29.07.1971	The Garden	Penzance, GBR
31.07.1971	City Hall	Truro, GBR
01.08.1971	Marquee Club	London, GBR
02.08.1971	Rugby Club	Hayle, GBR
09.08.1971	Driftwood Spars	St. Agnes, GBR
12.08.1971	Tregye Hotel	Truro, GBR
14.08.1971	NCO's Mess, RAF Culdrose	Culdrose, GBR
17.08.1971	City Hall	Truro, GBR
21.08.1971	Carnon Downs Festival	Truro, GBR
06.10.1971	Imperial College	London, GBR
09.12.1971	Swimming Baths	Epsom, GBR
31.12.1971	Rugby Club	Twickenham, GBR
28.01.1972	College	Bedford, GBR
10.03.1972	King's College Medical School	London, GBR
24.03.1972	Forest Hill Hospital	London, GBR
06.11.1972	Pheasantry Club	London, GBR
20.12.1972	Marquee Club	London, GBR
09.04.1973	Marquee Club	London, GBR
13.07.1973	Mary College	London, GBR
23.07.1973	Marquee Club	London, GBR
03.08.1973	The Mayfair	Newcastle, GBR

LEEDS TOWN HALL
Monday, 12th November 1973
at 7.30 p.m.
MEL BUSH presents
Mott the Hoople
NO PASSOUTS
ORCHESTRA (Unreserved)
90p
254

Tour Dates

Queen I

13.09.1973	Golders Green Hippodrome	London, GBR
13.10.1973	Underground, Bad Godesberg	Bonn, FRG
14.10.1973	Le Blow Up	Luxembourg, LUX
20.10.1973	Paris Theatre	London, GBR
26.10.1973	Imperial College	London, GBR
02.11.1973	Imperial College	London, GBR
12.11.1973	Town Hall	Leeds, GBR
13.11.1973	St. George's	Blackburn, GBR
15.11.1973	Gaumont	Worcester, GBR
16.11.1973	University	Lancaster, GBR
17.11.1973	Stadium	Liverpool, GBR
18.11.1973	Victoria Hall	Hanley, GBR
19.11.1973	Civic	Wolverhampton, GBR
20.11.1973	New Theatre	Oxford, GBR
21.11.1973	Guildhall	Preston, GBR
22.11.1973	City Hall	Newcastle, GBR
23.11.1973	The Apollo	Glasgow, GBR
25.11.1973	Caley Cinema	Edinburgh, GBR
26.11.1973	Opera House	Manchester, GBR
27.11.1973	Town Hall	Birmingham, GBR
28.11.1973	Brangwyn Hall	Swansea, GBR
29.11.1973	Colston Hall	Bristol, GBR
30.11.1973	Winter Gardens	Bournemouth, GBR
01.12.1973	Kursall	Southend, GBR
02.12.1973	Central	Chatham, GBR
06.12.1973	College	Cheltenham, GBR
07.12.1973	Shaftesbury Hall	Cheltenham, GBR
08.12.1973	University	Liverpool, GBR
14.12.1973[3]	Hammersmith Odeon	London, GBR
15.12.1973	University	Leicester, GBR
21.12.1973	County Hall	Taunton, GBR
22.12.1973	Town Hall	Peterborough, GBR
28.12.1973	Top Rank Club	Liverpool, GBR
02.02.1974[4]	Sunbury Pop Festival	Sunbury, AUS

Notes

1. Probably the debut of Mercury, May, and Taylor as Queen (pre-Deacon), though some dispute this date.

2. Seems the probable debut of the classic line-up, though some sources cite the July 17 date at The Garden, Penzance, Cornwall.

3. Two shows.

4. An infected vaccination needle leads to gangrene in May's left arm and the brief threat of amputation.

Tour dates courtesy Martin Skala, QueenConcerts.com

2 THE WHITE SIDE AND THE BLACK SIDE

"I'D LOOK IN THE MUSIC PAPER CHARTS and think, 'Well, where's our record?'" May told me in 1991, recalling the irksome aftermath of Queen's initial releases. "I'd ring Trident and ask, 'Where is it? Why aren't they playing it on the radio?' We'd go to record shops. No sign of it. 'Have you got the Queen record?' 'Queen who?'"

In short, "Keep Yourself Alive" and *Queen* flopped—in America too, despite the *Rolling Stone* review describing Taylor and Deacon as a "sonic volcano," a phrase they quoted at every opportunity.

Still, in that era, record companies expected to develop careers gradually. Trident and EMI offered Queen little chance to fret, sending them straight back to the studio in August 1973. Daytimes now, with a proper budget. The band talked it through with producer Roy Thomas Baker. "We decided *Queen II* [would be] the kitchen-sink album," he said. May confirmed: "We went to town. We said, 'Right, now we're going to paint our pictures.'"

Fired up, Queen conceived the White Side/Black Side juxtaposition of emotions, shades of magic, and May/Mercury compositions—"White Queen (As It Began)" versus "The March Of The Black Queen" (a device undermined when CDs replaced LPs, of course). Drawing the others into his concern for detail, Mercury insisted that the band and Baker accompany him to the Tate Gallery, London, to study *The Fairy Feller's Master-Stroke*, the canvas by Victorian artist Richard Dadd that inspired the song of the same name. Then Mercury told Baker, "Anything you want to try, throw it in."

"*Queen II* was the biggest single step we ever made with our recording craft," May told Roy Wilkinson, writing for *Mojo* in 2004. In a

Queen II tour, eastern United States, May 1974.
www.photosets.net, Brannon Tommey

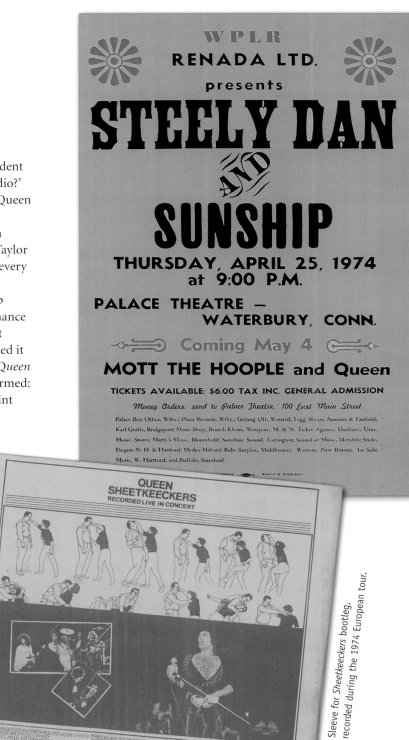

The Fairy Feller's Master-Stroke, 1855–1864, Richard Dadd, oil on canvas, 540×394 mm. © *Tate, London 2009*

1991 interview, he told me he thought it achieved the balance between "reality" and "perfectionism" they'd missed with *Queen*: "*Queen II* was the emotional music we'd always wanted to play. But some of it's pretty complex, so you have to listen harder." Significantly, they took their vocal harmony recording technique to a higher level. May explained the painstaking process: "We sing the line in unison. Then maybe we double-track or triple-track it and then do the same on the next layer." So a six-part harmony passage might include fifty-four voices or more.

But they saw no hard line between ambition and musical ideals; they deliberately framed one track as a hit single. May said, "With 'Keep Yourself Alive' [business] people told us the intro was too long and then it took too long to get to the chorus. With 'Seven Seas Of Rhye' we said, 'Right, everything's going to happen in the first ten seconds.'"

Inertia turned to momentum. With *Queen II*'s release due in spring 1974, Trident bought them on to a hot U.K. tour—twenty-one gigs, November and December, supporting Mott The Hoople (then in the Top 10 with "Roll Away The Stone").

Normal industry practice, it cost £3,000. Well spent, May thought: "It was exactly the kind of audience we were trying to get to. Rock 'n' roll, very dramatic—not glam exactly, we never liked being called glam rock." Mercury agreed, even though he insisted they'd be headlining next time around because he found the support slot "one of the most traumatic experiences of my life" (no blame attached to Mott The Hoople, who became long-term friends).

From the New Year, only May's normally robust health slowed them down. The trouble began with a one-off gig in Australia, when an infected vaccination needle led to gangrene in his left arm and the brief threat of amputation. But the treatment proved effective, and back in the U.K. Queen soon benefited from some smart work by EMI, who got them on BBC TV's *Top Of The Pops*, the weekly chart show, as a last-minute substitute for David Bowie. This despite a Mercury flounce ("I'm not doing *Top Of The Pops*, that rubbish!"), on February 22 they mimed "Seven Seas Of Rhye" to ten

million viewers—one in five of the populace. Extensive radio play followed. EMI rush-released the single a week early, on February 25, and soon it reached No. 10.

Queen took off on that first headlining tour, with Mercury presenting a notable contrast to the embattled national mood. Despite a long coal miners' strike causing frequent power cuts, he strutted about in a black-and-white "winged eagle suit" made for him by top fashion designer Zandra Rhodes. They played twenty-one gigs, from Penzance, Cornwall, to Glasgow, Scotland. Meanwhile, *Queen II*, with Mick Rock's iconic cover shot based on an old portrait of Marlene Dietrich, rose to No. 5 on the U.K. album chart. Reviews were divided between praise and vituperation—"the dregs of glam rock" (*Record Mirror*), "no depth of sound or feeling" (*Melody Maker*)—but Queen had started to win over the popular vote. Deacon remembered the feeling in his 1974 *Music Star* interview: "The most important thing to me was *Queen II* going into the charts. It's nice to see some recognition for your work." The abandonment

Circa 1974. © Michael Putland/Retna UK

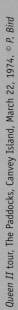

of safety nets followed: Mercury and Taylor gave up the Kensington Market stall and Deacon his masters degree studies.

No slacking, though—"You've got to push yourself, my dears," said Mercury. They pressed on into their first American tour, April to May, again supporting Mott The Hoople (Mercury's horror at the idea evidently bowing to market reality). They completed twenty-five shows and went down erratically. Mott's Ian Hunter remembered Mercury stalking the dressing room, raging, "Why don't these silly bastards get it?" Even so, they reaped some reward when *Queen* belatedly charted at 83 in the States, then *Queen II* rose to 49. But, after a run of nights at the Uris Theatre, New York, they had to quit the tour early because May succumbed to hepatitis.

Again, he'd barely recovered when, in July, as Queen began recording their third album at Rockfield in Wales, then Trident in London, a duodenal ulcer laid him low. It needed surgery. "I was lying in my bed," he recalled, "feeling very sick and sad because I thought, 'Maybe the group will have to go on without me.'" Knowing May's anxieties, Mercury often visited him at the hospital to offer reassurance that he would add the guitar parts later.

Following *Queen II*'s grand aspirations, the band planned *Sheer Heart Attack* as an assault on the singles chart. May told *Mojo*'s David Thomas in 1999, "We simplified so that people would damn well find it accessible . . . which worked!"

> *"I play on the bisexual thing because it's something else, it's fun. . . . the last thing I want to do is give people an idea of exactly who I am. I want people to work out their own interpretation of me and my image."*
> —FREDDIE MERCURY, QUOTED BY CAROLINE COON, *Melody Maker*, 21.12.1974

Simplification? Queen-style, maybe. Without inhibition, the album embraced heavy rock, vaudeville, sweet love songs, harmony operettas, and more. In the same *Mojo* interview, Taylor didn't see the simplicity at all: "'Bring Back That Leroy Brown' is incredibly complex in terms of instrumentation and arrangement. Even the harmonies on 'Killer Queen' took quite a while because we tried all the different inversions of versions and they never sounded quite right."

Gary Langan, then a twenty-one-year-old assistant engineer at Trident, later a producer and member of the Art of Noise, took part in mixing May's late additions, "Now I'm Here" and "Brighton Rock." Talking to this writer in 2005, he described himself as "derailed" by Queen's care and sheer hard labor: "They sweated blood. 'Now I'm Here,' all those delays on the vocal call and response were quarter-inch tape machines, five of them, running at different speeds, the whole room humming. . . . Roy was an eye-opener too. He'd put them down to fire them up. He'd be camp as Freddie and say, 'Darlings, that was truly awful. How could you present such a terrible performance?' It was jocular but . . . he wasn't a put-his-arm-round-you kind of guy."

Queen II tour, eastern United States, May 1974. www.photosets.net, Brannon Tommey

(Once, when Baker wanted another "Killer Queen" vocal and Mercury sat in the studio cafeteria insisting, "I'm not leaving this chair!" the producer got the roadies to pick him up bodily, along with the chair, and place him back in front of the microphone.)

Straightforward or not, May believed the success of "Killer Queen" was "the turning point. We desperately needed it as a mark of something successful happening for us." The Killer Queen's identity, of course, became a matter of curiosity. A fan of Liza Minelli in *Cabaret*, Mercury fluttered, "It's about a high-class call girl—it's one of those bowler-hat, black-suspender numbers." On the other hand, strictly heterosexual EMI plugger Eric Hall claimed that Mercury admitted writing it for *him*, after the singer witnessed Hall amiably reject a pass at the Holiday Inn, Luxembourg.

While the truth is unknowable, for a period in 1974, Mercury, still living with Mary Austin and apparently not yet adventuring with men, did talk about his sexuality with relative openness to female interviewers. To *NME*'s Julie Webb he blurted, "I'm as gay as a daffodil," without it being taken as a coming out, oddly enough. He expounded to *Melody Maker*'s Caroline Coon: "I play on the bisexual thing because it's fun. . . . The man I have as a chauffeur—we've built up such a bond, it's a kind of love, and I don't care what people think about it. But [onstage] the last thing I want to do is

Japan, 1975.

Circa 1974. The photo would later appear in one of *Creem*'s famous "Boy Howdy!" profiles. *Michael Marks photo/Creem Archive*

The White Side and The Black Side   41

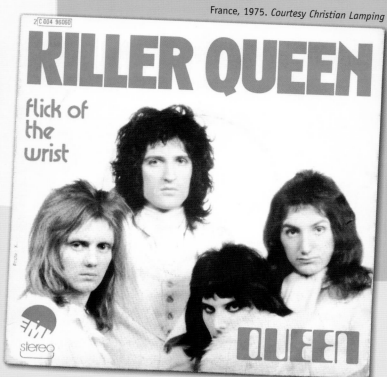

Japan, 1975.

> "We tend to work well under pressure. But do we row? Oh my dear, we're the bitchiest band on earth."
>
> —Freddie Mercury, quoted by Chris Welch, *Melody Maker*, 09.11.1974

give people an idea of exactly who I am. I want people to work out their own interpretation. . . . I don't want to build a frame around myself and say, 'This is what I am' or 'This is all I am.' . . . I'd like people to think there is no falsity in me, because what I do is really my character. But I think mystique, not knowing the truth about someone, is very appealing. There's a lot of freedom today and you can put yourself across anyway you want to. But I haven't *chosen* this image. I'm myself and in fact half the time I let the wind take me." ("Any way the wind blows," as per the last line of "Bohemian Rhapsody"?)

In his candor, Mercury sounded both sincere and contradictory about himself. In 1999, May told *Mojo* the sexuality references in Mercury's lyrics were "heavily cloaked" but added, "A lot of his private thoughts were in there. . . . 'Lily Of The Valley' [*Sheer Heart Attack*] was utterly heartfelt. It's about looking at his girlfriend and realizing that his body needed to be somewhere else."

Nothing enigmatic about *Sheer Heart Attack* commercially, though. Released in November 1974, the album and "Killer Queen" both reached No. 2 in the U.K. and began more gradual ascents in the United States. Their U.K. tour—their set now resplendent with "Big Spender" and "God Save The Queen"—moved them, literally, to champagne class. Roy Thomas Baker recalled the benefits of an innocent product placement in the opening line of "Killer Queen": "Möet et Chandon sent us vats of champagne and passes for Wimbledon and the Grand Prix races."

Now, emotionally, Queen had to adjust from years of frustration to the very different strains of breaking through, whether in their own fraught gig post mortems or in responding to others' demands for instant band decisions. "Do we row? Oh my dear, we're the bitchiest band on earth," Mercury told *Melody Maker*'s Chris Welch in 1974. "We're at each other's *throats*. But if we didn't disagree, we'd just be yes-men." *Disc* writer Rosie Horide, who often traveled with Queen at this time, confirmed that Mercury truly detested flattery he thought unjustified or insincere: "You never went backstage after a gig and said, 'Great gig, guys' when it wasn't. I remember Freddie asking someone what he thought after a show, the guy said 'Fantastic, Freddie' and Freddie said 'Wrong answer' and walked away. 'Perfectionist' doesn't begin to describe it."

Speaking to Caroline Coon after the tour, Mercury revealed how their new life could get under his skin: "Quite often I have vicious nightmares—like the night before the Rainbow [Theatre] concert [November 1974]. I dreamed I went out on to the hotel balcony and the whole thing fell and I was a heap on the pavement. I was petrified when I woke up in the morning. And Roger has this nightmare where he's drinking a bottle of Coke and the bottle smashes and he has broken glass all the way down his system. Ridiculous things like that are caused by the tension which builds up. You have to have confidence in this business. . . . If you start saying to yourself, 'Maybe I'm not good enough, maybe I'd better settle for second place,' it's no good."

Miming "Killer Queen," *Top Pop*, Hilversum, Holland, November 1974. Note Brian is playing a Fender Stratocaster rather than the Red Special. © Peter Mazel/Sunshine/Retna UK

"People think I'm an ogre at times. Some girls hissed at me in the street …'You devil.' They think we're really nasty. But that's only on stage. Off stage, well I'm certainly not an ogre."

—FREDDIE MERCURY, QUOTED BY CHRIS WELCH, *Melody Maker*, 09.11.1974

Rainbow Theatre, London, 1974. © *Mick Rock/Retna Ltd.*

Further disorientation arose from everyone they met presuming they were rich already. "Suddenly we had this image of driving around in Rolls-Royces," May told me. "But really we were all sitting in London bedsits like any struggling rock 'n' roll band." They were. Since the Barnes "commune" gradually broke up, May had moved to a tiny South Kensington flat that had to be entered via the boiler room, and the Holland Park place Mercury shared with Mary Austin had rising damp. As to Rollers, car fan Deacon had just bought his first motor, a £40 secondhand Mini.

But they had begun to wonder about money. After *Sheer Heart Attack*, Trident put Queen's wages up from £20 to £60. But when Mercury asked for a grand piano, and when Deacon asked for a loan to put a deposit down on a house because he and his girlfriend Veronica Tetzlaff were marrying,

Trident refused. The band's belief that intelligent caution had secured them a good deal began to wane. After their U.K. and European tours ended in December 1974, Queen engaged music business lawyer (and part-time jazz musician) Jim Beach to investigate. Trident told him the band *owed them* £190,000.

With show business an ambiguous thrill, even stolid John Deacon wasn't entirely sure how to conduct himself. Before Christmas 1974, he went home to Oadby and asked his old Opposition bandmate Nigel Bullen out for a drink. Deacon insisted on driving out to a country pub to avoid attention. Nonetheless, he was soon spotted and, Bullen told this writer in 2005, seemed very uncomfortable with the looks and the autograph requests. Then again, he *was* wearing a road crew bomber jacket emblazoned with the Queen logo. ♕

Queen II
by Andrew Earles

THE LPs

IT COMES AS NO SURPRISE that 1974's *Queen II* elicited the same response in the United States as the band's self-titled debut from the previous year: deafening silence. Less friendly toward the whims and hairpin turns of prog rock and the blunt-force trauma of proto–heavy metal, the American hard-rock audience at large greeted *Queen II* as yet another in a long string of head-scratchers from across the pond. But is *Queen II* the great proto-metal missing link between Black Sabbath's *Volume 4* and Led Zeppelin's *Houses of the Holy/ Physical Graffiti* heyday?

Absolutely. But similar to the powerful early albums by Rush, *Queen II* has never garnered the respect awarded to the first five albums by Sabbath or Zeppelin, not to mention early Deep Purple, Blue Cheer's *Vincebus Eruptum*, or the first few Alice Cooper band albums. *Queen II* deserves to be mentioned in the same breath as these examples—and one member in particular is responsible.

On *Queen II* (and to a lesser degree, the debut), Brian May was a single pair of hands introducing a guitar technique subsequently appropriated by a succession of now-famous heavy metal/hard rock guitar duos. May's trademark tone can be heard in the work of Thin Lizzy's Scott Gorham and Brian Robertson and in Iron Maiden's Dave Murray and Adrian Smith. With copious overdubbing, May created the sound of one guitar tuned an octave lower or higher than another; soloing sounds like power chords, and power chords have the extra melodic punch of soloing. Front to back, *Queen II* provided a prescient playground anticipating the adroit fretwork and melodic attributes of heavy metal up to this day.

Written entirely by Freddie Mercury, the second half of *Queen II* (the "black" side) explores a dark fantastical netherworld worthy of '80s prog-metal monsters Queensrÿche, Dream Theater, or Fates Warning. The opening blast, "Ogre Battle," is a tale about, well, ogres embroiled in battle. Mercury leads the rest of the band in operatic falsettos, there's no discernable repetition of chorus, and the tempo fluctuation puts the most restless of prog-rock bands to shame . . . this cluster of sonic elements spells disaster on paper. Then

Queen II LP featuring iconic Mick Rock photo. Argentina, 1974.

the song comes out of the speakers and everything blows by in such a seamless manner—the disparate parts put together like an engine. Elsewhere on the "black" side, both "The March Of The Black Queen" and "The Seven Seas Of Rhye" exude a timeless bombast that challenges the heaviest 1974 had to offer. Oddly, the latter emerged as the band's first hit by entering the U.K. charts at No. 10 and steering *Queen II* to No. 5 on the album charts.

Excluding "The Loser In The End"—drummer Roger Taylor's sole credit on *Queen II*—the opposing "white" selection is composed by May and rocks with a little more variety. After one minute of May's guitar tones (the opening "Procession"), "Father To Son" proves that someone made a mistake in choosing the album's single. Creatively, it's the first superlative statement of the band's 1974–1979 heyday. Written in the voice of a father addressing his son, the song clearly shares the allergy to metaphor that "Ogre Battle" exhibits, though Mercury could be singing about mowing his lawn or the nautical history of Greenland when those Olympic-sized hooks take over. Imagine a top-shelf Elton John composition played by a time-traveling hybrid of The Sweet, T. Rex, *Sin After Sin*–era Judas Priest, early Van Halen, and Yes at their mid-'70s pompous best; then imagine it sung by a choir of four guys making mockery of the octave scale. May's two remaining tracks, "White Queen (As It Began)" and "Some Day One Day" are all over the map—flirtations with heavy metal notwithstanding—and the latter features three simultaneous May solos.

If used at all in the mid '70s, "heavy metal" was a negative term for a style that weathered widespread ear-covering and upturned noses until the late-'70s when bands like Judas Priest used the term with reverence and pride. Mercury, May, Taylor, and John Deacon never set out to make one of the heaviest albums of the early '70s, much less a "heavy metal" album; it just happened that way. As such, they did something else for the growing heavy rock genre: years before Van Halen would take a similar (though simpler) agenda to the bank, May's warm riffs and Mercury's untouchable vocal prowess spoke an emotional musical language, one with heart and the feel of triumph. Call it "optimist metal," but *Queen II* was the first album to plaster a celebratory smile across the face of the seedling heavy metal movement otherwise rendered malevolent by the menacing overtones of Sabbath, Alice Cooper, Budgie, and Atomic Rooster (and overtly sexual by Zeppelin). Surviving the years unscathed, packing the strongest long-term influence of any Queen album, *Queen II* made a lasting mark on innumerable sub genres of heavy metal and the alternative hard rock explosion of the early 1990s. ⚜

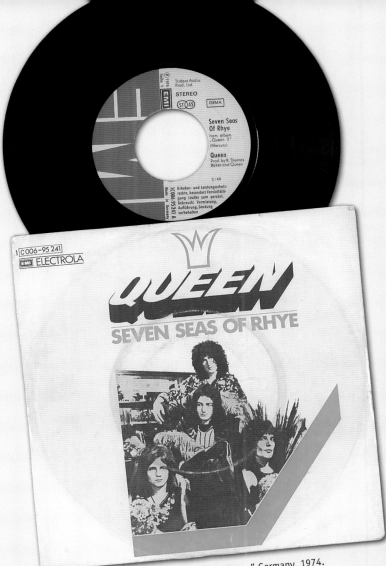

b/w "See What A Fool I've Been," Germany, 1974.

"*Queen II* was a point where all the adventurous ideas came out. There are seeds in *Queen II* of almost everything we've done since, but it was so compressed that all of it didn't come out unless you'd listened very closely."

—Brian May, quoted by Harry Doherty, *Melody Maker*, 18.09.1976

Sheer Heart Attack

by Greg Kot

THE LPs

ON ITS THIRD ALBUM, and second of 1974, Queen's crown finally fit.

On its previous releases, the quartet was still rummaging around for an identity, rifling through a mismatched wardrobe of influences. Their songs were dressed in the drag of progressive rock, the outrageousness of glam, the cold steel of metal, the velvet of cabaret balladry. On *Sheer Heart Attack*, those elements finally jelled into a one-of-a-kind sound.

Taste? Restraint? Subtlety? How boring. Queen delighted in upending stereotypes, perhaps the first band to prompt comparisons to both Black Sabbath (for their heavy-metal flourishes) and 10cc (for their buoyant, tongue-in-cheek finesse). Unlike other boundary-jumping contemporaries like Yes or King Crimson, they had a wicked sense of humor. They were into fey frills as well as anvil-hard stomp, and topped it with a dash of theatricality, complete with top hats, canes, and the occasional ironic codpiece. Above all, however, there was an intense and effervescent musicality abetted by producer Roy Thomas Baker, a flood of excess that presaged the Queen stadium-rock bombast on the albums for which the band is best known, *A Night At The Opera* and *News Of The World*.

Sheer Heart Attack captures the moment before all that restless creativity turned into commercial formula. It is a transitional album, a template for a sound that would expand, then harden, on future releases. But in the fall of 1974, Queen was still in flux, a more fluid band, chasing the intoxicating sounds in its head with a what-have-we-got-to-lose boldness. They were still relative unknowns who had yet to make a significant commercial impact.

Their new album would change all that. Its first single, "Killer Queen," shot the band into the upper reaches of the pop charts for the first time. With a bicycle bell punctuating Roger Taylor's drum rolls, and harmony vocals coming every which way at the listener, the song is a pop frolic. Freddie Mercury camps it up, name-dropping Kennedy, Kruschev, Marie Antoinette, and a particularly snooty brand of French champagne within the first few lines. Even before he was a rock star, Mercury was posing like one.

Sheer Heart Attack LP featuring another Mick Rock classic on the sleeve. Argentina, 1974.

Sheer Heart Attack brims with look-at-us primping. It opens with what is literally a carnival of sound: the pomp of a circus organ, the crack of a lion tamer's whip, the swirl of a jam-packed big tent awaiting the arrival of a three-ring extravaganza. Queen delivers, with Mercury easily flipping genders in a dialogue between flirting teen lovers "'neath the gay illuminations along the promenade." This side of Oscar Wilde, who ever wrote rock lyrics like that? Then there's Brian

May's guitar. To call his mid-song excursion a "solo" really doesn't do it justice. Layering parts in echo-laden splendor, he piles on harmonics and contrapuntal melodies with the glee of someone who has little use for the amped-up blues tropes that were all the rage among U.K. guitarists.

May also pummels the thrash-metal prototype "Stone Cold Crazy," later covered by Metallica. Along with the tales of tour excess on "Now I'm Here" and Taylor's thumping ode to rawkish high-jinks, "Tenement Funster," Queen never made a harder-edged album, a celebration of rock for rock's sake. And yet it also contains "Flick Of The Wrist," which peels back the tales of coke-and-hookers debauchery to reveal a far more jaded view of Rock Inc. as just another form of feudal servitude.

The crunch of these tracks gave Queen the latitude to explore less conventional terrain on the rest of the album. There is the florid balladry of "Lily Of The Valley," with Mercury trilling like a diva while cushioned by succulent harmonies. "Dear Friends" is barely a minute of lovely Mercury-May solitude, just voice and piano. John Deacon's "Misfire" flirts openly with a Caribbean groove, the Queen equivalent of a pink umbrella cocktail at a tiki bar. Mercury revisits the dance-hall shtick of his grandparents' era with "Bring Back That Leroy Brown," with May madly strumming a ukulele-banjo. On "She Makes Me (Stormtrooper In Stilettoes)," the guitarist settles into the narcotized bliss of one of his strangest love songs, complete with the sound of a wailing police siren.

Queen provides a glimpse of its mega future on the two side closers. "In The Lap Of The Gods" opens with a falsetto scream from Taylor, ushering in a three-minute rock opera of tympani-style drums, choir upon choir of harmony vocals phasing in and out of the mix, ripples of piano, and May's humming, liquid-toned guitar. It's a blueprint for Queen's crowning achievement, "Bohemian Rhapsody," which would be released the next year.

"In The Lap of the Gods . . . Revisited" hints at the genesis of another Queen anthem, "We Are The Champions," with its overdriven guitar and soccer-stadium chorus. It ends with—what else?—an explosion, a fanfare for Queen's arrival on the world stage. As if there was ever any doubt. ⚜

Korea, 1974.

 "The album [*Sheer Heart Attack*] is very varied, we took it to extreme I suppose, but we are very interested in studio techniques and wanted to use what was available."

—Freddie Mercury, quoted by Chris Welch, *Melody Maker*, 09.11.1974

Tour Dates

Queen II

01.03.1974	Winter Gardens	Blackpool, GBR
02.03.1974	Friars	Aylesbury, GBR
03.03.1974	Guildhall	Plymouth, GBR
04.03.1974	Festival Hall	Paignton, GBR
08.03.1974	Locarno	Sunderland, GBR
09.03.1974	Corn Exchange	Cambridge, GBR
10.03.1974	Greyhound	Croydon, GBR
12.03.1974	Dagenham Roundhouse	Dagenham, GBR
14.03.1974	Misto Hall	Cheltenham, GBR
15.03.1974	University of Glasgow	Glasgow, GBR
16.03.1974	University	Stirling, GBR
19.03.1974	Winter Gardens	Cleethorpes, GBR
20.03.1974	University	Manchester, GBR
22.03.1974	The Paddocks	Canvey Island, GBR
23.03.1974	Links Pavilion	Cromer, GBR
24.03.1974	Woods Leisure Centre	Colchester, GBR
26.03.1974	Douglas Palace Lido	Isle of Man, GBR
28.03.1974	University	Aberystwyth, GBR
29.03.1974	The Garden	Penzance, GBR
30.03.1974[1]	Century Ballroom	Taunton, GBR
31.03.1974	Rainbow Theatre	London, GBR
02.04.1974	Barbarellas	Birmingham, GBR
16.04.1974[2]	Regis College	Denver, CO
17.04.1974	Memorial Hall	Kansas City, MO
18.04.1974	Kiel Auditorium	St. Louis, MO
19.04.1974	Fairgrounds Appliance Building	Oklahoma City, OK
20.04.1974	Mid-South Coliseum	Memphis, TN
21.04.1974	St. Bernard Parish Civic Auditorium	New Orleans, LA
26.04.1974	Orpheum Theatre	Boston, MA
27.04.1974	Palace Theatre	Providence, RI
28.04.1974	Exposition Hall	Portland, ME
01.05.1974	Farm Arena	Harrisburg, PA
02.05.1974	Agricultural Hall	Allentown, PA
03.05.1974	Kings College	Wilkes-Barre, PA
04.05.1974	Palace Theater	Waterbury, CT
07–11.05.1974[3]	Uris Theatre	New York, NY

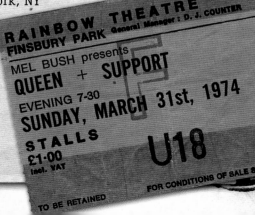

Tour Dates

Sheer Heart Attack

30.10.1974	Palace Theatre	Manchester, GBR
31.10.1974	Victoria Hall	Hanley, GBR
01.11.1974	Empire Theatre	Liverpool, GBR
02.11.1974	University	Leeds, GBR
03.11.1974	Theatre	Coventry, GBR
05.11.1974	City Hall	Sheffield, GBR
06.11.1974	St. George's Hall	Bradford, GBR
07.11.1974	City Hall	Newcastle, GBR
08.11.1974	The Apollo	Glasgow, GBR
09.11.1974	University	Lancaster, GBR
10.11.1974	Guildhall	Preston, GBR
12.11.1974	Colston Hall	Bristol, GBR
13.11.1974	Winter Gardens	Bournemouth, GBR
14.11.1974	Gaumont	Southhampton, GBR
15.11.1974	Brangwyn Hall	Swansea, GBR
16.11.1974	Town Hall	Birmingham, GBR
18.11.1974	New Theatre	Oxford, GBR
19–20.11.1974	Rainbow Theatre	London, GBR
23.11.1974	Koncerthus	Gothenburg, SWE
25.11.1974	Helsingin Kulttuuritalo	Helsinki, FIN
27.11.1974	Olympen	Lund, SWE
02.12.1974	Brienner Theater	Munich, FRG
04.12.1974	Jahrhunderthalle	Frankfurt, FRG
05.12.1974	Musikhalle	Hamburg, FRG
06.12.1974	Sartory Saal	Cologne, FRG
07.12.1974	Unknown	Singen, FRG
08.12.1974	Congres Gebouw	Hague, NLD
10.12.1974	Ancienne Belgique	Brussels, BEL
13.12.1974	Palacio Municipal de Deportivo	Barcelona, ESP

Notes

1. Two shows.
2. U.S. debut.
3. Two shows on May 10.

Tour dates and tickets courtesy Martin Skala, QueenConcerts.com

3 A LITTLE HIGH, A LITTLE LOW

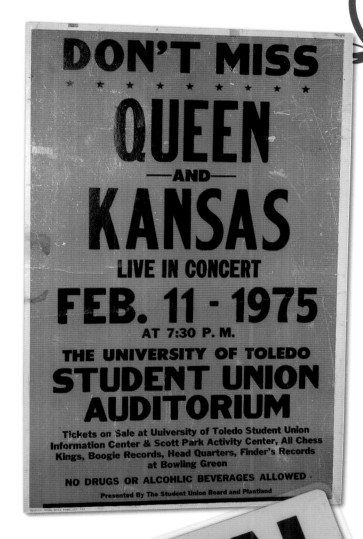

DON'T MISS
QUEEN
—AND—
KANSAS
LIVE IN CONCERT
FEB. 11 - 1975
AT 7:30 P. M.
THE UNIVERSITY OF TOLEDO
STUDENT UNION
AUDITORIUM

Tickets on Sale at University of Toledo Student Union
Information Center & Scott Park Activity Center, All Chess
Kings, Boogie Records, Head Quarters, Finder's Records
at Bowling Green

NO DRUGS OR ALCOHLIC BEVERAGES ALLOWED

Presented By The Student Union Board and Plantland

"THE SITUATION IS AN EXACT REPLICA of Led Zeppelin back in 1969," Freddie Mercury told Ron Ross of *Circus* as Queen contemplated their second North American tour in January 1975. He meant Queen was about to conquer the U.S.A. But if his hubris remained rampant, his vocal cords couldn't take the strain of thirty-odd shows and began to flare up three weeks in. Despite his declaration that he would "sing until my throat is like a vulture's crotch!" intermittent cancellations ensued. Even so, the disrupted tour belatedly boosted both *Sheer Heart Attack* and "Killer Queen" to No. 12 on the U.S. charts.

After their closing U.S. date, in Seattle on April 6, the band took a break on Kauai, Hawaii, en route to Japan where, phenomenally and unexplained, their records had ousted Deep Purple as top international band. The tour proved a startling experience.

The moment they reached the arrivals hall at Haneda Airport, Tokyo, as May recalled to this writer in 1991, "The whole place was seething with little girls screaming. A bunch of bodyguards met us, and they had to heave us over the top of these people, bits of hair being pulled out, and I lost a clog. I was half-scared, half-amused." The girls followed them everywhere, forming an orderly line astern when they went out shopping. At the gigs they screamed, rushing wildly to the front and forcing Mercury to plead for calm lest hysteria lead to tragedy.

Yet Queen also felt overwhelmed by their fans' delicate kindness. "They gave us masses of presents, it made you feel bad by comparison," said May. "Someone even sent back my clog with a note, 'So sorry we gave you a hard time at the airport.' It got to us. We were in tears, leaving. It wasn't a rock band thing. This was being a teen idol—which didn't sit very easily with us because we were *musicians*. But we had to admit it was fun."

A Night At The Opera tour, Hammersmith Odeon, London, November 29, 1975. © *Martyn Goddard/Corbis*

Crew and staff luggage tag, *A Night At The Opera* U.S., Japan, and Australian tour, 1976. Courtesy Peter Hince

Courtesy Ferdinando Frega, Queenmuseum.com

"In Japan something clicked. When we went through customs into the airport lounge in Tokyo there were 3,000 little girls screaming at us. Suddenly we were the Beatles. We literally had to be carried over the heads of these kids."

—BRIAN MAY, QUOTED BY PHIL SUTCLIFFE, Q, 03.1991

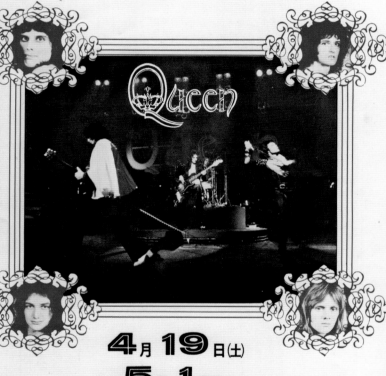

4月 19日(土)
5月 1日(木)
日本武道館大ホール　P.M.6:30開演

ロックの貴公子
クイーン
日本公演

●¥3,500	
S ●¥3,000	
A ●¥2,700	
B ●¥2,300	
C ●¥1,600	

●主催／(株)ワールドレジャー・(株)渡辺プロダクション
●後援／フジテレビ・文化放送・週刊平凡／パンチ
●協賛／ミュージックライフ・ワーナーパイオニア株式会社・アポロン音楽工業株式会社
☆お問合せは渡辺プロダクション友の会　Tel(460)2811／(株)ワールドレジャー　Tel(504)2786－7
☆都内各プレイガイドにて絶賛前売中！

Ticket stub, Budokan, Tokyo, April 19, 1975.
Courtesy Martin Skala, QueenConcerts.com

QUEEN

54

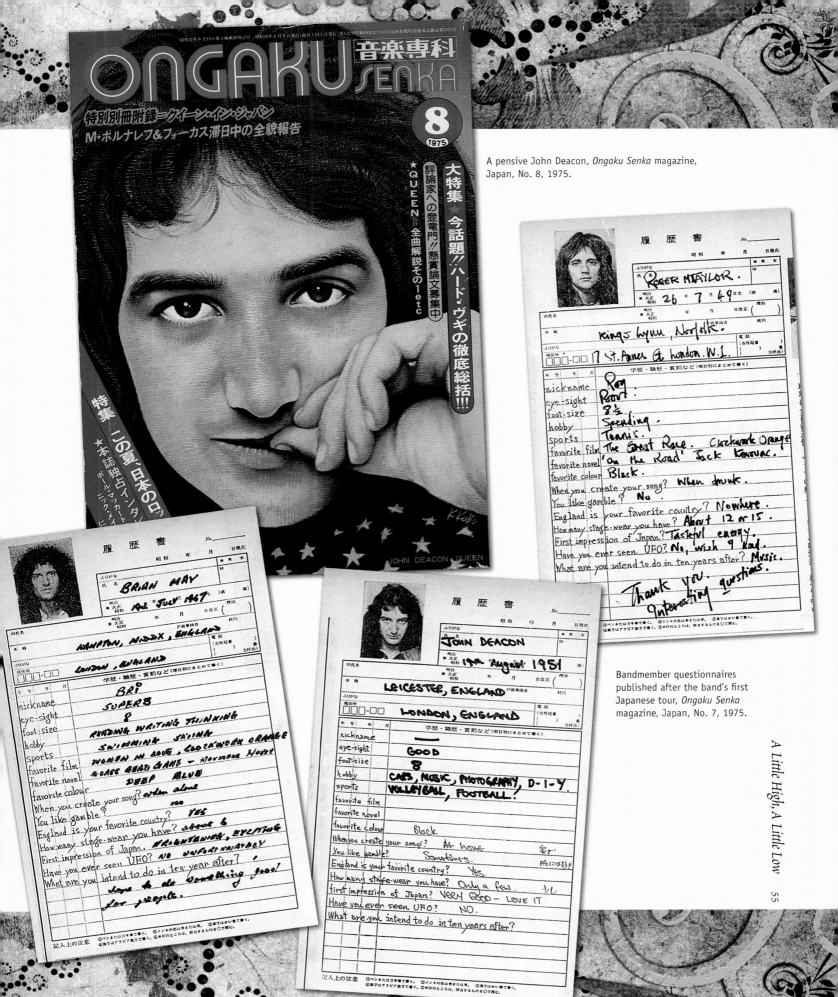

ONGAKU 音楽専科 SENKA

特別別冊附録＝クイーン・イン・ジャパン
M・ポルナレフ＆フォーカス滞日中の全貌報告

8
1975

大特集★今話題!!ハード・ヴギの徹底総括!!!

★QUEEN全曲解説その1etc
評論家への登竜門!!
懸賞論文募集中

特集＝この夏、日本のロ

JOHN DEACON QUEEN

K.KUBO

A pensive John Deacon, *Ongaku Senka* magazine,
Japan, No. 8, 1975.

履歴書 No.

ROGER M TAYLOR.
26 年 7 月 49 日生

Kings Lynn, Norfolk.
17 St. Annes St. London. W.1.

nickname   Roy.
eye-sight   Poor.
foot-size   8½
hobby   Spending.
sports   Tennis.
favorite film The Great Race. Clockwork Orange
favorite novel 'On the Road' Jack Kerouac.
favorite colour Black.
When you create your song? When drunk.
You like gamble? No.
England is your favorite country? Nowhere.
How many stage-wear you have? About 12 or 15.
First impression of Japan? Tasteful energy.
Have you ever seen UFO? No, wish I had.
What are you intend to do in ten years after? Music.

Thank you.
Interesting questions.

Bandmember questionnaires
published after the band's first
Japanese tour, *Ongaku Senka*
magazine, Japan, No. 7, 1975.

履歴書 No.

BRIAN MAY
July 1947

HAMPTON, MIDDX, ENGLAND
LONDON, ENGLAND

nickname   BRI
eye-sight   SUPERB
foot-size   8
hobby   READING WRITING THINKING
sports   SWIMMING SKIING
favorite film WOMEN IN LOVE, CLOCKWORK ORANGE
favorite novel GLASS BEAD GAME - Hermann Hesse
favorite colour DEEP BLUE
When you create your song? often alone
You like gamble? no
England is your favorite country? YES
How many stage-wear you have? about 6
First impression of Japan. FRIGHTENING, EXCITING
Have you ever seen UFO? NO UNFORTUNATELY
What are you intend to do in ten year after?
Love to do something good
for people.

履歴書 No.

JOHN DEACON
19th August 1951

LEICESTER, ENGLAND
LONDON, ENGLAND

nickname   —
eye-sight   GOOD
foot-size   8
hobby   CARS, MUSIC, PHOTOGRAPHY, D-I-Y.
sports   VOLLEYBALL, FOOTBALL!
favorite film
favorite novel
favorite colour Black
When you create your song? At home   家で
You like gamble? Sometimes.   時にはある?
England is your favorite country? Yes.
How many stage-wear you have? Only a few. 少し
First impression of Japan? VERY GOOD - LOVE IT
Have you ever seen UFO? NO.
What are you intend to do in ten years after?

Back home that May, multiple awards from teen weekly *Disc* and a prestigious Ivor Novello songwriting prize for "Killer Queen" confirmed their new standing. However, they found themselves right back in the mire of their management dispute. It felt all the more acute, said Taylor, returning from Beatlemania-like scenes and Mercury shopping sprees in Japan to sixty quid a week in London. The practical matter of John Deacon's wish to buy a house had also grown more pressing because he and Veronica Tetzlaff had married on January 18, and she was pregnant (their son Robert was born on July 18).

An initial attempt to break the Trident contracts by Electric Light Orchestra's notoriously "heavy" manager Don Arden (Sharon Osbourne's father) had come to nothing. The struggle began to grind Queen down. "The debt side of it was becoming a pressure," said May. "If you don't pay people like sound companies, lighting companies, they don't want to do it any more. Our careers were actually threatened. It was awful." Later in 1975, he told Jonh Ingham of *Sounds* that business worries crippled the band's creativity too: "It affects your morale. It dries you up completely. . . . We couldn't write at all that summer."

With lawyer Jim Beach they drew up a weighty shortlist of possible new managers: Led Zeppelin's Peter Grant wanted them to join his Swan Song label, they couldn't find The Rolling Stones' Peter Rudge, and Elton John's John Reid said yes immediately. (Mercury agreed he was "the right person for the job the moment he fluttered his eyelashes at me.")

Bandmember questionnaires, *Ongaku Senka* magazine, Japan, No. 9, 1975.

It was actually Elton John manager John Reid who took over Queen's affairs (Jim Beach was the band's lawyer). Still, this page from the American comic book *Hard Rock* provides a good glimpse of Queen's early management woes. *Hard Rock* No. 9, Revolutionary Comics, December 1992. *Courtesy Jay Allen Sanford*

Reid and Beach talked turkey with the Sheffields. Queen had to pay up: £100,000 plus one percent of Queen's royalties on their next six albums. Queen raised the cash by shifting their song publishing to EMI and securing an advance against future royalties. Severance from Trident concluded in August 1975.

Freed in every sense, May told Ingham that "all the emotions came out in a big flood," and they immersed themselves in their fourth album. Its grand operatic tendencies led them to name it after a Marx Brothers movie they all loved: *A Night At The Opera*.

Taylor described the writing process to *Circus*: "Everybody goes off to their separate homes. [To me] it's a very soul-destroying time. I get something written and then I listen to it the next day and I throw it away. The others usually never get to hear them. Anyway, then we all get together for about two weeks and pool the material we have—play around with it, pull it to pieces, change bits, throw some out." Mercury told *Melody Maker*'s Harry Doherty, "We go through so many traumas, and we're so meticulous. We're probably the fussiest band in the world. We feel so much about what we put across."

Amid the mutual testing and rejections, May suffered the ache of creative isolation. "I'd like to see us work together more on songs," he said to Doherty. "Making *A Night At The Opera*, it was impossible because we hadn't got enough time and a couple of us were in one studio and the others in another—you lose a bit of the group feeling. The relationship gets strained sometimes." For example, recording his '30s pastiche "Good Company," May got wrapped up in assembling an "orchestra" with all instruments impersonated by his Red Special guitar: "I spent days trying to get into the character of trumpets and trombones. The others would pop in and say, 'Well, you haven't done much since we last saw you.' I got offended and worried that I was doing something the rest of the band didn't really approve of."

"It's more extreme. It's varied, but it goes further in its various directions. It has a couple of the heaviest things we've ever done and probably some of the lightest things as well."

—Brian May, on *A Night At The Opera*, quoted by Jonh Ingham, *Sounds*, 27.09.1975

Onstage, 1975. *Ian Dickson/Redferns Collection/Getty Images*

Onstage, 1975. *Howard Barlow/Redferns Collection/Getty Images*

GEN. ADM.

SEC	ROW	SEAT
		2094

ADMIT ONE   THIS DATE

MAR 6 1975

DAYDREAM
PRODUCTIONS
PRESENTS
R.E.O.
SPEEDWAGON
& QUEEN

BALCONY

SEC	ROW	SEAT
RGT	J	26

ADMIT ONE   THIS DATE

FEB 23 1975

ELECTRIC
FACTORY
CONCERTS
PRESENT
* * *
* Q U E E N *
* * *
ERLANGER THTR
FEB 23 1975
SUN 7 00 PM

NO REFUNDS PRICE NO EXCHANGES
$4.50

SEC	ROW	SEAT
RGT	J	26

BALCONY

QUEEN
2-23-75 $4.50

"It's just what came out. They're offshoots of our main direction. There's plenty of time for the rock."

—BRIAN MAY, ON *A Night At The Opera,*
QUOTED BY JON TIVEN, *Circus,* 04.1975

"Critical response to the band is now almost unanimously favorable in both Great Britain and the United States, which is quite phenomenal when you stop and think of how anxious many critics were to pan them two years ago."

—JON TIVEN, *Circus,* 04.1975

It pained him that "we wouldn't open our hearts to each other" at a time when he was realizing how his own deepest emotions broke through in his writing. He came to see his acoustic folk song "'39"—ostensibly about a sea voyage—as a "subconscious" reflection of himself "going out in search of an artistic career and being afraid of leaving everything behind. This business destroys your family life quicker than anything else I think. . . . The pressures are to become a stereotyped rock star. . . . I definitely try not to be and I succeed partly. The only way I can do that is by continually taking stock, asking myself what it all means and how worthwhile it is."

Similarly, "The Prophet's Song" developed from a dream he'd had years earlier about the aftermath of an unspecified disaster and ended up symbolizing a personal preoccupation: "In the dream, people walked the streets trying to touch each other's hands, desperate to make some sign that they cared about other people. And this is one of my obsessions: that people don't make enough contact with each other. I worry about not doing anything about it."

Conversely, no such public revelations from Mercury about his greatest composition and Queen's greatest recording, "Bohemian Rhapsody"—nothing, that is, beyond his delight in the "outrageous opera bit" demonstrating that "vocally we can outdo any band." Roy Thomas Baker, again producing, told *Mojo*'s David Thomas in 1999 how he first heard it at Mercury's apartment: "He said, 'I've got this idea for a song' and started playing it on the piano—with some words and bits of melody missing. Then he stopped and said, 'Now dears, this is where the opera section comes in.' I went, 'Oh my God.'"

By the time he brought it to the studio—they started in Rockfield, Wales, then moved on to Scorpio, Sarm, and others in London—as Taylor told Roy Wilkinson of *Mojo* in 2004: "Freddie had a complete map of the thing in his head. He also had notes in these books his dad would have used for accounting at work. Freddie at the piano conducted us through it." Nobody resented taking orders. In 1975, May told Harry Doherty at *Melody Maker,* "Freddie's got a knack of using me to my best advantage. Usually, he has everything sorted out to the last note and tells me what he wants. There's never any friction."

The track just grew and grew—Mercury periodically trilling, "I've just added a few more 'Galileos,' dear"—while hard labor evolved into a technical drama about the evanescence of creativity as, pre-digitally, they "bounced" the ever-expanding music from one tape to another. "We ended up with about 180 voices on 'Bohemian Rhapsody,' and the guitar orchestra too," May told me. "The tape went through so many times it wore out. We got in a panic once because we held the tape up to the light, and we could see straight through it.

Disco 45 magazine, U.K., 1975.

The music had practically gone. We had to transfer it—which meant losing quality. You're holding on to this elusive sound signal which is gradually disappearing because every time you add something you lose something too. Strange business. . . ."

Queen wore themselves out. By the end, despite the glorious outcome, May reckoned they were "a bit down and depressed," and even Mercury allowed, to Ingham of *Sounds*, that the studio was "the most strenuous part of my career. It's so exhausting, mentally and physically."

Summing up *A Night At The Opera* to Jon Tiven of *Circus* in 1976, a still diffident May did find vindication in the album's musical variety: "At least, it negates the Led Zeppelin comparisons we've been living with for the past three years. While we were recording we were thinking, 'Yeah, it's getting a bit light,' but instead of trying to heavy it up we pressed on." He dismissed complaints that the recording cost—£40,000–45,000, allegedly the most expensive album ever to that date—breached some notion of artistic morality: "We wouldn't have spent so much if the studios weren't so bloody expensive! We weren't mucking about, it was four months of solid work."

That October 1975, Queen presented the 5:59 "Bohemian Rhapsody" to John Reid as their new single. Stunned, he argued that no radio station would playlist such a long track. EMI plugger Eric Hall, whose job was pushing singles to radio producers, recalled to me in 2005, "I never understood that record. 'Scolahoosh, scolamoosh,' what's all that about? I said to Freddie, 'There's two minutes that can go. Get rid of all that *mamma mia!*'"

But Reid finally acquiesced and gave his full support. Release date looming, Taylor admitted "We're not nervous, we're just nervous wrecks." But Mercury told Ingham in 1976, "I felt if it was successful it would earn a lot of respect." He saw no harm in giving "Bohemian Rhapsody" a pre-release shove by presenting a copy of the single to his influential Capital Radio DJ friend Kenny Everett (they'd met the year before and found common ground as closeted gay men living with women). Everett loved it, disregarded the record company embargo, and lit the fuse by playing it fourteen times in two days. He reported the switchboard ablaze with requests to hear it yet again.

On October 31, EMI released "Bohemian Rhapsody" in the U.K., and it charted immediately. A striking promo video sustained and propelled it. "The starting point [of the video] was the *Queen II* cover, the shadowed images," May later told me. "The multi-track visuals went with the multi-track sound. I laughed when I first saw it. It is crude, almost cartoonish, but it worked." The cost of £4,500 when such promos averaged £600 caused conniptions at EMI, but Queen used it as a substitute for their presence on chart show *Top Of The Pops*—they were touring the U.K. from November 14 to December 24; besides, they couldn't credibly mime the track anyway. *TOTP* broadcast the video first on November 20 and then again each of the nine weeks it remained at No. 1.

In the meantime, on November 22 at the Roundhouse studio, *A Night At The Opera* previewed to an audience of around fifty friends, businesspeople, and journalists. Mercury fidgeted around, demanding attention only when the final track, May's Hendrix-referencing version of "God Save The Queen," the British national anthem, followed "Bohemian Rhapsody"—then he yelled, "Stand up, you cunts!"

That night did have one peculiar consequence: a final joust with Trident. Somebody told Norman Sheffield about the opening song, Mercury's "Death On Two Legs" (subtitle, "Dedicated to . . ."). It snarled, "You suck my blood like a leech" and "Was the fin on your back/Part of the deal?(shark!)." Sheffield claimed people might think it referred to him. He threatened to sue Mercury, Queen, and EMI and block the release of the album. While, naturally, nobody ever admitted anything, another substantial sum—a second advance against publishing, according to May—finally placated the Trident bosses.

Carefully pointing no fingers, Mercury did talk about the song to *Sounds*' Jonh Ingham: "I wanted to make the vocal as coarse as possible. My throat was bleeding, the whole bit. I was changing lyrics every day trying to get it as vicious as possible. When the others first heard it they were in a state of shock. Frightened. But I was completely engrossed in it, swimming in it. Wow! I was a demon for a few days." 🖒

"A lot of my songs are fantasy. I can dream up all kinds of things. That's the kind of world I live in. It's very sort of flamboyant, and that's the kind of way I write. I love it."

—Freddie Mercury, quoted by Caroline Coon, *Melody Maker*, 21.12.1974

QUEEN

The genesis of "Bohemian Rhapsody." *Hard Rock* No. 9, Revolutionary Comics, December 1992. *Courtesy Jay Allen Sanford*

DJ Kenny Everett, liking what he hears. *Evening Standard/Getty Images*

Capital Radio DJ Kenny Everett falls in love with "Bohemian Rhapsody." *Hard Rock* No. 9,
Revolutionary Comics, December 1992. *Courtesy Jay Allen Sanford*

Portugal, 1976.

France, 1975.

Blue vinyl limited edition
of 200, U.K., 1975.

Turkey, 1975.

Italy, 1975.

Denmark, 1975.

66 QUEEN

U.K., 1975.

Germany, 1975.

Japan, 1975.

"We ran the tape through so many times it kept wearing out. Once we held the tape up to the light and we could see straight through it, the music had practically vanished. . . . Every time Fred decided to add a few more 'Galileos' we lost something too."

—Brian May, quoted by Phil Sutcliffe, *Q*, 03.1991

Test pressing label.
Courtesy Ferdinando Frega, Queenmuseum.com

Belgium, 1975. *Courtesy Ferdinando Frega,*
Queenmuseum.com

Yugoslavia, 1975.

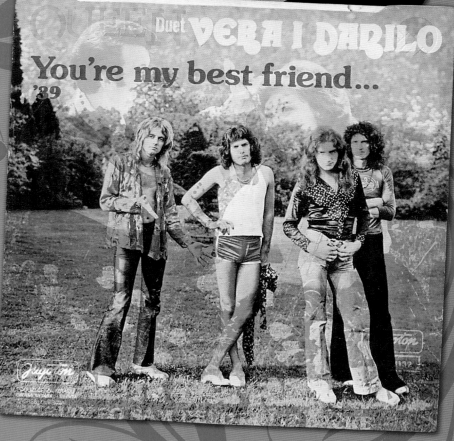

Leads and amps not required. *Top Of The Pops*, London, 1975.
David Redferns/Redferns Collection/Getty Images

As It Began

Longtime Rock Journo Recalls Meeting Queen In Their Salad Days

by Harry Doherty

I vividly recall my first "Freddie experience." In 1974, as a young reporter fresh off the boat from Ireland, I was dispatched to the Kensington offices of Queen's PR man, Tony Brainsby, to interview the flamboyant frontman of a fairly new band that had been making waves. *Sheer Heart Attack* was about to be released, and the band was gearing up. Brian May was supposed to be there too, but . . . "Dahling, he's *far* too busy in the studio playing guitar. He *shouldn't* have got ill on that American tour. Now he has a lot of work to do to catch up . . . and it better be good."

This was Freddie Mercury introducing himself. I would have to wait to meet May; he'd contracted hepatitis on the U.S. tour supporting Mott The Hoople and ended up writing songs for the album in hospital. Now he was ensconced in the studio.

It was the start of a relationship with Queen that has gone on, much to my surprise, to this day.

All the world was a stage for Freddie, Brian, Roger, and John. With their fey dress and aerie-faerie nonsense songs (on *Queen* and *Queen II*), they were looked (down) upon by critics as a passing fad. When the second album hadn't yielded any hit singles, that suspicion seemed confirmed. But behind the scenes, it was obvious to me that Queen was deadly serious about setting the record straight.

In 1976, as much as its glam image might have disputed the fact, Queen was a band fighting off bankruptcy. As Roger Taylor told me recently when asked about the band's drug intake: "Our only highs then were from cigarettes and cheap wine. We were going through a bit of a crisis."

I found Queen, then, to be no fools—except in business.

As the band's solvency increased creatively with the release of *Sheer Heart Attack*, financially it was diminishing fast as a brick when the career-defining *A Night At The Opera* came along. The band's management also owned Trident Recording Studios, in Soho, and that's where they did most of their recording—being charged handsomely for the privilege.

In fact, once the management charges were totaled up, there wasn't much left—a state of flux immortalized with much bitterness by Freddie on "Death On Two Legs," the album opener.

"Our backs were right to the wall financially," said Taylor. "We had sold a lot of records and not been paid a lot of money—the old, *old* story really. So that album was our big shot. Had it failed, we probably wouldn't have been around much longer."

But, as usual, the public persona belied the backroom crisis, as I found when hanging out with the band at John Reid's Rocket Records office in Soho before the *A Night At The Opera* playback. By then, Trident had been replaced by Elton John's manager, John Reid, in the business seat; and Queen had spent a fortune recording said album.

They were, I recall, in various stages of slump, as media interviews were being conducted by telephone with various journalists in various parts of the world. While Queen loved being loved by the media, they weren't exactly in love with the process of earning it.

"I'm pissed off listening to the bloody album," a weary Roger Taylor was saying to no one in particular. They had come straight to Reid's office from the studio after completing it.

In another corner, Mercury was slamming the phone down after a particularly difficult interview

"The Mick Rock photo sessions from 1973 to 1975 were a coup. By hiring the photographer who had captured Bowie in his exotic prime, Queen made a statement of sorts. In fact, Rock's pictures of Queen at what is considered their breakthrough gig at Imperial College, London, in 1973, are among rock music's most iconic.

"Queen, in turn, loved working with Rock. The two parties were made for each other. I recall Mercury fawning at one session—what to wear, what not to wear—as Thin Lizzy's *Vagabonds Of The Western World* (a favorite that put Queen in the mood for prancing) played in the background. And then there was that sweaty, feverish cover of *Sheer Heart Attack* itself, an image that many have tried (and failed) to emulate ."

—Harry Doherty

London, 1975. © *Mick Rock/Retna Ltd.*

in which he could not understand a word his Spanish interrogator was asking. "I'll never forget this album, dear," he suddenly proclaimed. "NEVER. But we've got to have this playback. Just to let friends hear what we've been up to." He turned his attention to me. "The thing is that they'll never understand it with one listen. Later on, we'll all go out, get pissed, and forget all about the damned album."

Over there, John Deacon was fingering his way through the itinerary for a forthcoming U.K. tour and picking holes here, there, and everywhere. Little wonder he's not touring with the band these days. Even then he wasn't one of rock 'n' roll's great troubadours. (Later, as we arrive at the Roundhouse studio for the playback, he'll comment, "Welcome to *A Night At The Opera.* Hope Joe Public's not going to be here.")

With the playback imminent and just a car drive away, the band decided that I should be the first critic subjected to a new six-minute opus from the new album. It's called "Bohemian Rhapsody," and I am suitably gobsmacked, much to the satisfaction of Mercury, Taylor, and Deacon (Brian May is absent again—is he trying to tell me something?).

As with Queen parties then and since, the *Opera* playback was suitably raucous for everyone but the bandmembers, who went out of their way to make sure that everyone had a good time. Freddie and I made an early exit. We had a dinner date—just the two of us, I thought. "Thank goodness that's over," he sighs in the relative tranquility of the car. "Some of those people really bore me."

The people who didn't bore Fred were his train of colorful and mostly gay friends, who were to greet us at the exclusive Elephant on the River restaurant. So much for an intimate chat, I thought as we were pumped into the throng. "There are my friends," he announced with uninhibited glee. One of them was the late, outrageous English DJ Kenny Everett, who would endear himself to Freddie for all time by playing "Bohemian Rhapsody" fourteen times over the next weekend on his popular Capital Radio show.

We weren't the quietest group in the restaurant, and I was sure that the management was glad to see the back of us but grateful for the amount of champagne we'd quaffed and the EMI person Freddie had purloined to settle the bill!

But before we left, I did have time to talk one-to-one with Mercury. Although his public persona was one of the extravagant, flamboyant showman, he also had a great ability to switch to being down-to-earth and personable, and could make you feel as if you were the most important person in a packed room.

He talked freely about his ambitions for Queen: "After the third album [*Sheer Heart Attack*] we thought 'Now we've established ourselves and we can do certain things.' Like, vocally we can outdo any band. We just thought that we would go out, not restrict ourselves with any barriers, and just do exactly what we want to do. It just so happened that I had this operatic thing and thought, 'Why can't we do it?' We outdo anybody. And that's because we've taken it on our musical terms.

"We've always done that. We've always put our necks on the line. We did it with *Queen II*. On that album we did so many things that people started to say, 'Self-indulgent crap, too many vocals, too many everything.' But that is Queen. After that they seemed to realize that that was what Queen are all about. We always have. That *is* what Queen are all about."

It also struck me that Mercury and Queen shared no affinity with the press. Bitten badly early on by rabid critics for their image, Queen suffered the press and the necessity to speak to them in order to communicate with fans and record buyers. Mercury would have loved these days of YouTube when the press can effectively be bypassed.

They seemed to be happy enough with my presence, though, having probably sussed that I was a fan as well. I got on particularly well with Brian May when I eventually caught up with him at a sound check on the U.K. *Opera* tour. He was as different to Mercury as chalk to cheese but no less passionate about his music and band. Roger Taylor had forewarned me about May's erratic ways with a story of how they went through a song at a soundcheck once, and it wasn't until midway through it that May realized he didn't have his guitar on. He was so immersed, he was playing air guitar!

May, of course, has a brain the size of China, so it was surprising to find that he was (still is, in fact) a very insecure man. At the point of release of *A Night At The Opera*, he was fretting about his parts, how good they were, and if his work stood up to examination.

"Generally," he explained, "the working relationship with the band is that we tend to leave each other alone musically, unless asked. That would be my interpretation. If someone has an idea, you assume that they want to be left alone to get on with it and put it across the best way. Sometimes, they'll come and talk about it, which I do a lot. Maybe I can't make a decision so I'll come to the others and say, 'How does this strike you?' and they'll suggest something and usually I'll agree.

"The relationship gets strained sometimes. I got very worried once that I was going out on a limb and that the rest of the band didn't really approve of what I was doing. It happened on a track of *A Night At The Opera*, 'Good Company.' I spent days and days doing these trumpet and trombone things and trying to get into the character of those instruments.

"The others were doing other things and they'd pop in from time to time and say, 'Well, you haven't done much since we last saw you.' They probably wouldn't mean it in a dire sense, but I got very offended and very worried that I was doing something which their heart wasn't in but, in the end, it turned out well."

(In 2008, I spoke with Brian as they were about to release *The Cosmos Rocks*, the first album with Paul Rodgers, and was shocked to find that he was still confronting the same crises of confidence. I guess it's what keeps him in the creative frame.)

In early 1977, I found myself accompanying the band on the historic Queen/Thin Lizzy tour of America, by which stage they were well on their way to becoming one of the biggest bands in the world. It was to their credit that they had taken a band as good as Lizzy as their support act, for Phil Lynott and company were truly "dangerous" on stage then.

This was the tour on which Queen had all the trimmings that went with arena-rock status, including residence at the Plaza Hotel on Fifth Avenue in New York City, where I enjoyed an afternoon of Scalextric slot-car racing through Roger Taylor's rooms.

Mercury was now playing the star card to the max. At airports, it was strange to see that he didn't mingle with the rest of the band, who mingled with Lizzy. Freddie would sit in another part of the lounge, accompanied by his friendly neighborhood masseur and other friends. And, true to his adorable camp nature, he'd decided not to do interviews. At one after-show party, eyeing me from the other side of the room, he sauntered over, gave my bum a gentle pat and whispered, "Harry, dahling, I'm so sorry about the interview. But I'm just not giving them anymore . . . no exceptions." And that was that.

Or so I thought. Having forged a close relationship with Queen, it seemed my report on the Queen/Thin Lizzy tour was about to dismantle it. I was realistic enough to know that it's always dodgy covering your favorite bands, especially when you innocently offer a flavor of criticism. I found this out a couple of weeks after my on-the-road piece appeared in *Melody Maker*. I'd been to the Rainbow Theatre to see Elton John and spotted Brian and Roger in the audience. Up I went to say hello. Roger was his usual affable self. Brian, on the other hand, had seen my piece and wasn't best pleased. "Nobody blows us off in Boston," came the opening salvo. "Boston is our town. Nobody blows us off and Thin Lizzy didn't. You weren't even there. You left with Lizzy before we came on." Which, I hadn't, but what can you do? May apologized for the outburst later, but at least he was passionate in defense of his band. Still is.

Brian and I maintained a relationship throughout the years. Some years later, when I was editor of *Metal Hammer*, I had a phone call from the careers master at his alma mater, Teddington School, in West London. Brian had advised him to call me because he wanted to place a pupil for work experience. Brian, he told me, felt I was a person who could be trusted. If he was appealing to my ego, it certainly worked. No problem, I said, welcoming this young man into the bosom of a culture that embraced a love of hard rock, not to mention alcohol and a life of luxury!

Then, a few years back, I sent a CD of an Irish band called Relish to Brian, asking what he thought of it. A week later, a four-page handwritten letter arrived, raving about their music, providing a critique of each track, and tantalizingly ending, "The singer is great . . . would he like a part in a West End musical?"

I took this as some sort of flippant goodbye. Little was I to know that he was offering the singer a lead part in the forthcoming musical *We Will Rock You*. Of course, Brian May was serious, as usual. It was a lesson learned again . . . never underestimate Queen! ⚜

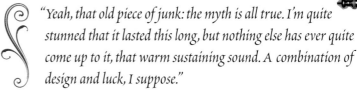

The Sound & Amplification, Listen!

The Gear of Brian May

By Dave Hunter

A flurry of attention is drawn to the equipment used by all true guitar heroes, but fans seeking to divine the secret of Brian May's distinctive tone have undertaken a more intensive analysis than most. Rising to prominence in an era when the Marshall stack and a Gibson Les Paul formed the cornerstone of the heavy-rock sound, May's unique tone—hot, rich, searing, and cutting in equal proportions—sliced through the sonic mélange of the day to leave its mark on the collective consciousness of music fans like few signature sounds heard before it, or since. While May's playing clearly has a lot to do with this, his selection of gear, which ranges from the classic to the quirky to the downright odd, plays an enormous part in forming his unmistakable sound. A tech-minded tinkerer with a pioneering DIY mentality, May has tweaked and perfected every link in his sound chain throughout his career, rather than relying on the off-the-shelf guitars, amps, and effects to which so many other players have turned. From hot-rodded amps to modified effects to homemade guitars, this constant striving for the sound in his head, rather than the sound everyone else was and is making, has helped to set him far apart from the rock guitar crowd.

> *"Yeah, that old piece of junk: the myth is all true. I'm quite stunned that it lasted this long, but nothing else has ever quite come up to it, that warm sustaining sound. A combination of design and luck, I suppose."*
>
> —BRIAN MAY, QUOTED BY PHIL SUTCLIFFE, Q, 03.1991

Electric Guitars

Brian May has played other guitars on occasion, but his famous homebrewed "Red Special" is far and away the electric at the center of his sound. With help from his father, Harold, May designed and built the guitar almost completely from scratch between 1962 and 1964, using many found items to fashion its hardware and components. The bulk of the wood for the body came from an eighteenth-century oak mantelpiece that a neighbor was disposing of, and the thick, wide neck was carved from a mahogany support post. This large, club-like neck is also considered a major component of this unique guitar's resonant tone, while its dimensions provide the kind of playability that the large-handed May demands. Although it appears to be solid, the Red Special's body is actually what is referred to today as a chambered or semi-solid construction: block-board "wings" were carved to form the outer bouts of the guitar and glued to the oak core, then the entirety was covered with mahogany veneer front and back to hide the hollow chambers (one of which is still visible when the large scratch plate is removed). The twenty-four-fret fingerboard was also cut from oak, and the neck, body, and fingerboard were finished in Rustin's Plastic Coating.

May's ingenious vibrato tailpiece is made from a hardened-steel knife-edge fulcrum tensioned by two motorcycle engine valve springs, and the bridge is handmade from six individual blocks of aluminum, each of which carries an adjustable roller saddle. The only significant pre-manufactured components are the tuners and the pickups, the latter a trio of Burns Tri-Sonics. May rewound the middle pickup to be reverse-wound/reverse-polarity and potted all three himself with Araldite epoxy (a thick glue available in Britain) to reduce microphony and squealing feedback.

> *"It was a matter of being poor. We were very scientific about it, lots of tests as we went along. My dad was wonderful like that, an electronics wizard. It's a good memory. It was really a great compromise for him to help me—he wanted me to concentrate on my studies...."*
>
> —BRIAN MAY, QUOTED BY PHIL SUTCLIFFE, Q, 03.1991

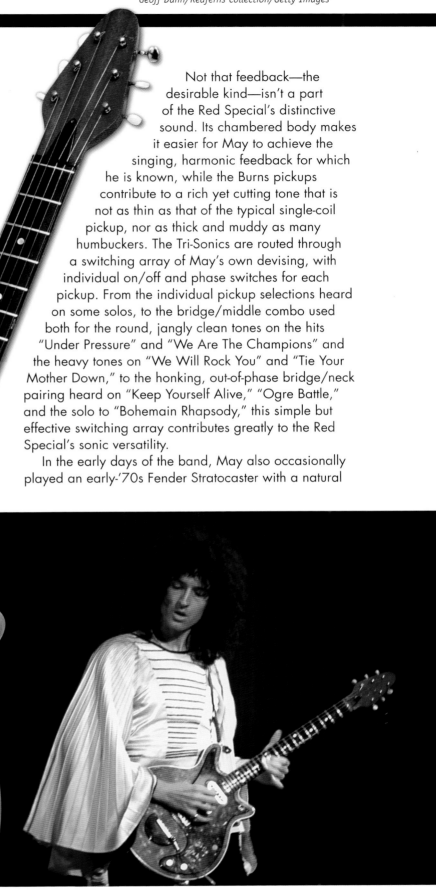

Not that feedback—the desirable kind—isn't a part of the Red Special's distinctive sound. Its chambered body makes it easier for May to achieve the singing, harmonic feedback for which he is known, while the Burns pickups contribute to a rich yet cutting tone that is not as thin as that of the typical single-coil pickup, nor as thick and muddy as many humbuckers. The Tri-Sonics are routed through a switching array of May's own devising, with individual on/off and phase switches for each pickup. From the individual pickup selections heard on some solos, to the bridge/middle combo used both for the round, jangly clean tones on the hits "Under Pressure" and "We Are The Champions" and the heavy tones on "We Will Rock You" and "Tie Your Mother Down," to the honking, out-of-phase bridge/neck pairing heard on "Keep Yourself Alive," "Ogre Battle," and the solo to "Bohemain Rhapsody," this simple but effective switching array contributes greatly to the Red Special's sonic versatility.

In the early days of the band, May also occasionally played an early-'70s Fender Stratocaster with a natural

Sheer Heart Attack tour, Ford Auditorium, Detroit, February 10, 1975. © Robert Matheu

finish, maple neck, and large headstock with "bullet" truss-rod adjustor, and he used drummer Roger Taylor's vintage Telecaster to record the solo on "Crazy Little Thing Called Love." He has picked up other electrics now and then over the years, including a mid-'70s Gibson Les Paul Deluxe, a Gibson Flying V, and copies of the Red Special made by both Guild and Fryer, all taken on tour as backups. In Queen lore, however, none of these is of any comparable consequence to the original Red Special.

> *"I use coins because they're not flexible—I think you get more control if all the flexing is due to the movement in your fingers."*
>
> —BRIAN MAY, QUOTED BY STUART GRUNDY
> AND JOHN TOBLER, *The Guitar Greats*, 1983

acoustic guitars

Queen is undoubtedly an electric rock band first and foremost, but May has made effective use of acoustic textures on many occasions. One of the best known of these is undoubtedly his part on "'39" (*A Night At The Opera*), played on an Ovation twelve-string, a guitar he also used on "Love Of My Life" from the same album. Rather than stringing this guitar in the manner traditional to twelve-strings, with the thinner octave strings above their thicker partners, May strung his Ovation with the thin strings under the low-octave strings, making it easier to pick individual standard strings and to hit higher tones more prominently on the upstrokes.

May has also used a Martin D-18 six-string acoustic guitar on several recordings and has swapped the Ovation for a Guild twelve-string on recent live performances.

amplifiers

Just as much the Red Special is *the* Queen guitar, May's beloved Vox AC30 amplifiers have long been at the center of the Queen tone. May first stumbled upon the AC30 in the mid-'60s, and it has been his amp of choice ever since. Known particularly for its associations with early British rock 'n' roll at the hands of bands who pushed it from clean to mildly gritty at the most, the Vox AC30 is turned into a different kind of tone machine by Brian May. Using four EL84 output tubes in a configuration nominally referred to as "class A" (meaning cathode biased, with no negative feedback), the AC30 offers chiming clean tones at lower volumes but segues smoothly into a rich, creamy, harmonically saturated overdrive tone when pushed hard. The result is a lead guitar sound that's sweeter and more soaring than the big, beefy crunch and roar put out by Marshall or Hiwatt stacks.

Although the AC30 is best known for its "top boost" channel, which incorporates a highly interactive two-knob tone stage, May has always preferred the rounder, warmer-sounding "normal" channel, which he runs at full volume with no tone control in the circuit. Live, May generally uses three AC30s at a time, with spares on stage in case any of these go down. The amp in the center receives his guitar signal unaffected by anything other than his treble booster (more of which below), while those to its left and right receive the stereo feed from his effects.

In addition to the AC30s, May has frequently recorded with a small, one-watt, solid-state amplifier built by Queen bassist John Deacon and referred to as "the Deaky." When cranked up, this little amp elicits the raw, sizzling distortion tone famously heard in the solos to "Bohemian Rhapsody" and "Procession," where it was double-tracked (as is often the case) with other tracks recorded through an AC30.

effects and accessories

Even before discovering his lifelong amp of choice, May had locked in on the Dallas Rangemaster treble booster as one of the secrets to his tone. More than simply a device to boost treble, as the name might imply, the Rangemaster is a semi-clean, full-range booster that smoothes out treble frequencies somewhat and adds some thickness to the overall tone. Unlike an overdrive or distortion pedal, which generates a degree of clipping in itself, a booster like the Rangemaster is used to push the amplifier into distortion. After using a genuine Rangemaster initially, May moved on to modified copies of the pedal and in recent years has used a strap-mounted treble booster built by Greg Fryer.

May has also used a wah-wah pedal from the start, originally a Vox wah but more recently a rack-mounted CryBaby system. Having used a number of other effects in the earlier years (although usually sparsely), including a Foxx phaser and a Maestro Echoplex, along with a range of chorus pedals a bit later on, the remainder of his effects requirements are now covered by a series of rack-mounted multi-FX devices, including multiple units of the T.C. Electronics G-Force and the Rocktron Intellifex XL.

The smallest of all of May's accessories, but no less significant than any of them, are the British sixpence coins he has used as guitar picks for

nearly four decades. This small coin was minted in Great Britain before decimalization was introduced in 1971 but remained legal tender until 1980 and had the value of around two and a half new British pence. Made from a soft metal with a serrated edge, the coin gives May a firmer, more direct attack against the string than a semi-flexible synthetic plectrum provides.

 "Brian May is my guitar hero. He has the best sound in rock, and he's such a nice guy on top of it all. It's my goal to get up on stage with six AC30s stacked—that is such an amazing tone."

—DAVE GROHL, FOO FIGHTERS, QUOTED BY DAVE HUNTER, *The Guitar Magazine*, 01.2000

News Of The World tour, Maple Leaf Gardens, Toronto, November 21, 1977.
www.photosets.net, Brannon Tommey

A Night At The Opera
by Jon Bream

SORRY, ELTON. Queen's *A Night At The Opera* was the gayest mainstream rock album of the 1970s—we straights just didn't know it at the time.

We'd figured out Lou Reed's walk on the wild side on *Transformer*, and with *Goodbye Yellow Brick Road*, we understood Elton John's affection for Marilyn Monroe and louder-than-Liberace outfits. But Freddie Mercury trumped them on *A Night At The Opera* by waving his freak flag with excursions into mock opera, dancehall, ukulele balladry, vaudevillian jazz, and choral harmonies gone wild. We always thought Freddie was the king of queen. But he almost outed himself on this fanciful fandango.

Queen's fourth album was as boldly ambitious as Led Zeppelin's fourth LP. Like Zep in 1971, this quartet outdid themselves in '75 with a combination of hard and soft, grand and bizarre, the unabashedly commercial and the unorthodox radio opus. *A Night At The Opera* was unquestionably Queen's crowning moment.

While many theories exist about the (un)title of Zep's fourth album, the source of the title of Queen's fourth LP is obvious: *A Night At The Opera* was a popular Marx Brothers movie that Freddie, Brian, Roger, and John happened to watch while recording their album. (Their appreciation for the Marx Brothers continued as they named their ensuing LP *A Day At The Races*, after a similarly titled comedy starring Groucho, Chico, and Harpo.)

Like a spectacular opera, Queen's album was a grand production, costing a king's ransom to record at several different studios with longtime producer Roy Thomas Baker. At the time, *A Night At The Opera* was considered the most expensive rock album ever made. ("Bohemian Rhapsody" alone used 180 vocal overdubs and five separate studios.) But its preposterous price tag would later be eclipsed by the soap opera that was Fleetwood Mac (*Tusk*) and, more recently, Axl Rose (*Chinese Democracy*).

Queen commences its opera with aggressive drama, "Death On Two Legs (Dedicated To . . .)." Rolling piano gives way to majestic Spanish-flavored electric guitar, big drums, big layered vocals, and eventually the payoff line, delivered a

Mexico, 1976.

cappella with vitriolic vigor by Mercury: "But now you can kiss my ass good bye." This uncompromising lambasting/purge was presumed by many to be directed at Queen's recently deposed manager, Norman Sheffield, who threatened to sue for defamation. In concert, Mercury would often rededicate "Death On Two Legs" to—well, let's just say he would use an ungentlemanly expletive as an adjective to describe the "gentleman." (By the by, after Queen canned Sheffield in 1975, they signed on with John Reid, Elton John's manager.)

With nary a pause to catch his breath, Mercury segues from the angry to the sublime on "Lazing On A Sunday Afternoon." On this dancehall piano stroll, he's happy as a lark, going to work, bicycling around London, checking out the Louvre, proposing to his love on Saturday, and lazing on Sunday afternoon. In the vaudeville tradition, Mercury sounds like he's

singing through a megaphone, but in reality he was vocalizing into a tin bucket for full echo effect.

With nary a pause, Queen moves from the sublime to the ridiculous with "I'm In Love With My Car," written and sung by drummer Roger Taylor. This dark, sludgy rocker sounds un-Queen-like, save for the Mercury-May-Taylor vocal harmonies on the second chorus. Taylor dedicates the tune to roadie "Johnathan Harris, boy racer to the end," whose love of his Triumph TR4 apparently inspired the song. Taylor gives it a bit of his own personal touch by ending the number with a rev of the engine in his own Alfa Romeo.

Faster than Taylor can shift into overdrive, Queen juxtaposes love of a car with love for one's lady. "You're My Best Friend" is not only bassist John Deacon's lone composition here, but it's the first song he'd ever written on piano. In fact, his bouncy Wurlitzer electric drives this pure, unabashed pop love song (written for his wife, Veronica), featuring overdubbed vocal choruses, booming drums, and May's chiming guitar.

May steps into the spotlight with "'39," a twelve-string acoustic guitar piece that merges skiffle with sea shanty. He has described it as a science fiction story about someone who leaves his family and returns one hundred years later. However, the protagonist has aged only one year and comes back to his daughter, in whom he can see his wife. Got that? May's voice is so soft that it's hard to tell if he's unassertive or merely singing in the corner of another room. The guitarist also wrote the ensuing "Sweet Lady," but Mercury sings this generic 1970s pop-metal workout with its ringing Doobie Brothers–like guitars, fragments of lyrics, and bluesy boogie ending.

After that not fully realized rocker, Mercury can't wait to escape to "Seaside Rendezvous," a lovably old-fashioned olio with some whistling, scatted wind and brass, French phrases, group harmonies on merely one word at a time, and the très charmant ten-dollar lyric "jollification."

To start side two, May takes off on another flight of fantasy on "The Prophet's Song," an eight-minute, seventeen-second epic with several movements and musical styles (prog rock, Broadway, Biblical lyrics, and even a la-la chorus) that sounds like the work of the Madman he asks us to laugh about in the last line.

Mercury brings "Opera" back from the future with "Love Of My Life," an unadorned piano piece featuring Freddie's feathery voice and theatrical phrasing. His simple classical piano lines and May's harp add unobtrusive sophistication to this pretty, romantic declaration. However, Queen can't be conventional for too long—May picks up his "genuine aloha" ukulele for "Good Company," his commentary on the pros and cons of marriage. The song is noteworthy for two reasons: Queen never performed it live, and May, utilizing only a special guitar, created the sound of an entire Dixieland jazz backup band.

If *A Night At The Opera* seems a bit like a competition between songwriters Mercury and May, then Freddie wins hands down, if only for the iconic "Bohemian Rhapsody." In short, it's his "Tommy," done in a mere five minutes and fifty-five seconds. It's a masterwork of mock opera, taking a story line through different movements and dynamics, musical styles and textures, with magnificent choruses that sound like one-hundred-voice choirs, not three guys spliced together through eight generations of recordings.

A Night At The Opera could easily have ended right there. Instead, May picks up his electric guitar for an instrumental version of "God Save The Queen," the British anthem with its traditional pomp and rumbling timpani exclamation point. It's the perfect Queenly underture, a fitting finale for this gay old time at the opera.

 "At the moment, we've made an album which, let's face it, is too much to take for most people. But it was what we wanted to do."

—FREDDIE MERCURY, QUOTED BY
JONH INGHAM, *Sounds,* 27.09.1975

A Little High, A Little Low

81

Tour Dates

Sheer Heart Attack

05.02.1975	Agora	Columbus, OH
07.02.1975	Palace Theater	Dayton, OH
08.02.1975[1]	Music Hall	Cleveland, OH
09.02.1975	Morris Civic Auditorium	South Bend, IN
10.02.1975	Ford Auditorium	Detroit, MI
11.02.1975	Student Union Auditorium	Toledo, OH
14.02.1975	Palace Theater	Waterbury, CT
15.02.1975[2]	Orpheum Theatre	Boston, MA
16.02.1975[3]	Avery Fisher Hall	New York, NY
17.02.1975	War Memorial	Trenton, NJ
19.02.1975	Armory	Lewiston, ME
21.02.1975	Capital Theater	Passaic, NJ
22.02.1975	Farm Arena	Harrisburg, PA
23.02.1975[4]	Erlanger Theatre	Philadelphia, PA
24.02.1975	Kennedy Center	Washington, DC
05.03.1975	Mary E. Sawyer Auditorium	La Crosse, WI
06.03.1975	Dane County Coliseum	Madison, WI
07.03.1975	Uptown Theater	Milwaukee, WI
08.03.1975	Aragon Ballroom	Chicago, IL
09.03.1975	Kiel Auditorium	St. Louis, MO
10.03.1975	Coliseum	Fort Wayne, IN
12.03.1975	Municipal Auditorium	Atlanta, GA
13.03.1975	Civic Auditorium	Charleston, SC
14.03.1975	Sunshine Speedway	St. Petersburg, FL
15.03.1975	Marine Stadium	Miami, FL
18.03.1975	St. Bernard Parish Civic Auditorium	New Orleans, LA
20.03.1975	Municipal Hall	San Antonio, TX
23.03.1975	McFarlin Auditorium	Dallas, TX
25.03.1975	Municipal Theater	Tulsa, OK
29.03.1975[5]	Civic Auditorium	Santa Monica, CA
30.03.1975	Winterland	San Francisco, CA
02.04.1975	Kinsmen Sports Centre	Edmonton, CAN
03.04.1975	Corral	Calgary, CAN
06.04.1975	Paramount Northwest Theater	Seattle, WA
19.04.1975[6]	Nippon Budokan	Tokyo, JPN
22.04.1975	Aichi Taikukan	Nagoya, JPN
23.04.1975	Kokusai Kaikan	Kobe, JPN
25.04.1975	Kyuden Kinen Taikukan	Fukuoka, JPN
28.04.1975	Okayama Kenritsu Taikukan	Okayama, JPN
29.04.1975	Yamaha Tsumagoi Hall	Shizuoka, JPN
30.04.1975	Yokohama Bunka Taikukan	Yokohama, JPN
01.05.1975	Nippon Budokan	Tokyo, JPN

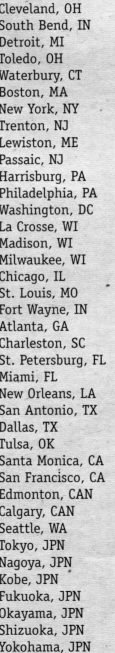

QUEEN
***
PALACE THTR
WATERBURY, CT
FEB 14 1975
FRI 8 00 PM
5.91 + .59 TAX
NO REFUNDS PRICE NO EXCHANGES
$6.50
SEC   ROW   SEAT
309

Tour Dates

A Night At The Opera

14–15.11.1975	Empire Theatre	Liverpool, GBR
16.11.1975	Theatre	Coventry, GBR
17–18.11.1975	Colston Hall	Bristol, GBR
19.11.1975	Capitol	Cardiff, GBR
21.11.1975	Odeon	Taunton, GBR
23.11.1975	Winter Gardens	Bournemouth, GBR
24.11.1975	Gaumont	Southhampton, GBR
26.11.1975[7]	Free Trade Hall	Manchester, GBR
29–30.11.1975	Hammersmith Odeon	London, GBR
01–03.12.1975	Hammersmith Odeon	London, GBR
07.12.1975	Civic Hall	Walverhampton, GBR
08.12.1975	Guildhall	Preston, GBR
09.12.1975	Odeon	Birmingham, GBR
10.12.1975	Odeon	Birmingham, GBR
11.12.1975	City Hall	Newcastle, GBR
13.12.1975	Caird Hall	Dundee, GBR
14.12.1975	Capitol	Aberdeen, GBR
15–16.12.1975	The Apollo	Glasgow, GBR
24.12.1975[8]	Hammersmith Odeon	London, GBR

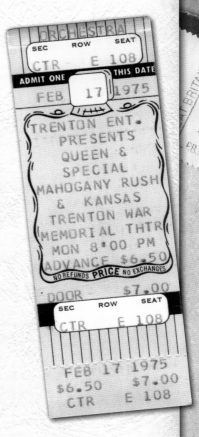

Notes

1–5. Two shows.

6. Japanese debut.

7. Two shows.

8. Show broadcast simultaneously on BBC2.

Tour dates and tickets courtesy Martin Skala, QueenConcerts.com

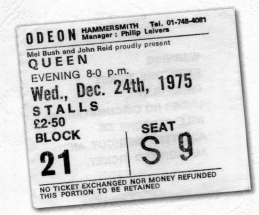

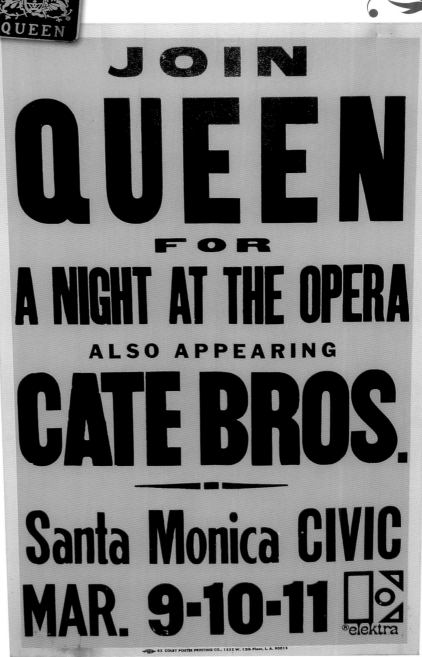

SUDDENLY, EVERYONE LOOKED AT FREDDIE. Writing a live review late in 1975, Jonh Ingham of *Sounds* identified one reason why: "Everything north of the waist is tighter than skin-tight—with a zip-up front open to AA rating. But further south, definitely in X territory, lurks a bulge not unlike the *Sunday Telegraph* . . . never has a man's weaponry been so flagrantly showcased. . . . Oh to be that hot costume, writhing across the mighty Fred!"

But Mercury's one-off post-colonial/Asian-Anglo/public-school/art-studenty/rag-trading/camp-rock 'n' rolling character attracted as much talk as his anatomy. Like when police stopped Queen's tour bus en route from Newcastle to Scotland; a constable asked, "Do you take drugs, Mr. Mercury?" and he replied, "Don't be impertinent, you stupid little man!" Or the *A Night At The Opera* gold disc presentation at EMI, where he broke the record out of its frame and played it to confirm it was the real thing, not just any old LP dipped in gold paint—then turned to the onlooking (and vindicated) board member, Sir Joseph Lockwood, and said, "Sorry, it accidentally broke itself, Sir Joseph, may we have another one?"

In late January 1976, with a million "Bohemian Rhapsody" singles and five hundred thousand albums sold at home, and their three earlier albums also charting simultaneously in the U.K. Top 25, Queen set off on a three-month tour of the United States, Japan, and Australia.

Acutely aware that America had yet to succumb following his premature prediction of Led Zeppelin status, Mercury nevertheless defied the working-man, jeans-and-T-shirt stereotype of American rock 'n' roll. Prancing and posturing, he toasted audiences with champagne and

Courtesy Ferdinando Frega, Queenmuseum.com

A Night At The Opera tour, Masonic Temple, Detroit, February 1976.
© Robert Alford

Queen Invites you to
A Night At The Opera
World Tour '76

Jan 27 Palace Theatre, Waterbury, Conn. Jan 29 & 30 Music Hall, Boston, Mass. Jan 31 Tower Theatre, Philadelphia, Pa. Feb 1 & 2 Tower Theatre, Philadelphia, Pa. Feb 5-8 Beacon Theatre, New York City Feb 11 & 12 Masonic Temple, Detroit, Mich. Feb 13 Riverfront Coliseum, Cinn., Ohio Feb 14 Public Hall, Cleveland, Ohio Feb 15 Sports Arena, Toledo, Ohio Feb 18 Civic Center, Saginaw, Mich. Feb 19 Veterans Mem. Aud., Columbus, Ohio Feb 20 Stanley Theatre, Pittsburgh, Pa. Feb 22 & 23 Auditorium Theatre, Chicago, Ill. Feb 26 Kiel Aud., St. Louis, Mo. Feb 27 Indiana Convention Ctr., Indianapolis, Ind. Feb 28 Dane County Col., Madison, Wisc. Feb 29 Coliseum, Fort Wayne, Ind. Mar 2 Auditorium, Milwaukee, Wisc. Mar 3 St. Paul Aud., Minn./St. Paul, Mn. Mar 7 Berkeley Comm., Berkeley, Ca. Mar 9-11 Civic Aud., Santa Monica, Ca. Mar 12 Sports Arena, San Diego, Ca.

elektra

threw roses (carefully de-thorned by tour manager Pete Brown to avoid lawsuits)—and Mercury tantrums.

It must have worked this time. "Bohemian Rhapsody" rose to U.S. No. 9 while they toured (conducting *A Night At The Opera* to No. 4). Unrepeatable live, the single challenged their militant opposition to the use of backing tapes in concert. Taylor once railed at *Melody Maker*'s Harry Doherty: "Why the hell go on stage with backing tapes behind you and pretend you can do it like the record?" Initially, they left their signature hit out of the set, but audience demand compelled a degree of compromise; they decided to start the song live but roll the tape and leave the stage for the opera section, no pretence. May called it "a kind of interval. Change the frocks, have a pee."

They cheerfully endured an arduous thirty-plus dates in America, without mishap this time, except that Mercury stomped out of a few "meet and greets" with local record company reps and DJs. Then they moved on to a second scream-laden tour of Japan and a better experience of Australia. The previous trip, in February 1974, had been

ruined both by May's serious illness and noisily macho Aussie contempt for Queen's airy-fairy manner. But by April 1976, the records had won through, "Bohemian Rhapsody" and *A Night At The Opera* topping the charts before they arrived.

Nonetheless, Mercury is reported to have committed one terrible display of incipient stardom's worst, partly provoked by rowdy Aussies. Talking to Laura Jackson for her book, *Brian May: The Definitive Biography*, Pete Brown said Mercury could be "very tough, he often made me cry during the years I worked for him." Then he described what happened before a gig at Sydney Hordern Pavilion on April 17. Driving the band to the venue, Brown found the route led through a crowded fairground and suggested they'd have to get out and walk. Mercury said, "My dear, I can't possibly walk anywhere!" So Brown drove very slowly through the throng. Irate pedestrians banged on the windows, flipped V-signs, and yelled "Pommy pussies!" "When we got inside," said Brown, "Freddie was in such a cold rage that he picked up a big mirror and literally smashed it over my head. Then he ordered me to find a brush

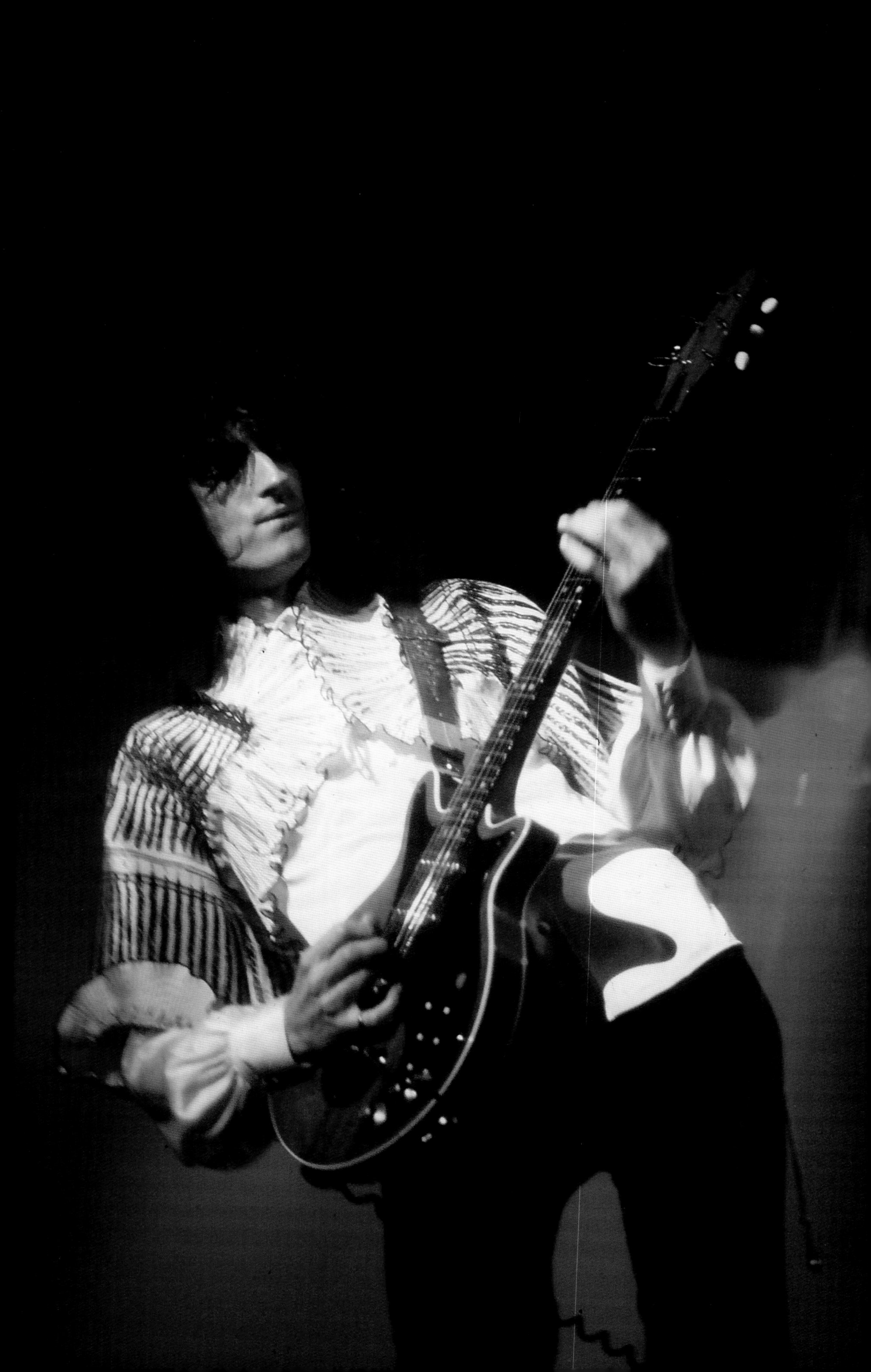

BOTH: *A Night At The Opera* tour, Masonic Temple, Detroit, February 1976. © *Robert Alford*

BOTH: *A Night At The Opera* tour, Masonic Temple, Detroit, February 1976. © Robert Alford

Music Life, Japan, November, 1976.

Ongaku Senka magazine, Japan, No. 11, 1976.

ロジャー・テイラー物語　文／星加ルミ子

ROGER TAYLOR STORY

金髪のドラマー、ロジャー・テイラーの青春

スポット・ライトを浴びて無心にドラムをたたき続けるロジャー、ステイックが振りおろされるたびに、その美しい金髪が宙に舞う。最高のクイーンのドラマーとして観客の熱い視線を集める彼の青春は、一体どのように流れてきたのだろうか？その青い瞳は、なにを追い求めてきたのだろうか？1968年、ブライアン・メイとの運命的な出会いによって、ロジャーにもたらされたものは何だったのだろうか？当時19才だった医学生がたどった、熱い青春の軌跡をたどってみよう。

Music Life, Japan, July 1976.

"I think maybe people are just being pushed into the limelight too soon, and there is a tendency to get swept along by image to the exclusion of musical direction…. We never had that trouble because we were just totally ignored for so long, then completely slagged off and slated by everyone."

—BRIAN MAY, QUOTED BY MICK HOUGHTON, *Sounds*, 22.01.1977

and shovel to sweep up the glass at once." Oddly enough, Brown forgave him: "You see it was the humiliation he had suffered. He just had to take it out on someone. I understood."

Back home, May married Chrissy Mullen, his girlfriend of eight years, on May 29 at St. Osmund's Roman Catholic Church in Barnes. Three weeks later Queen had a hit with a song written by John Deacon, "You're My Best Friend," U.K. No. 7. As the "Bohemian Rhapsody" royalties began to flow, the inequity of rewards resulting from the strange song publishing agreement they'd struck between themselves was about to become a source of bitterness. Nobody disputed Mercury's authorship of the hit. It was the B-side that got them snarling.

"So 'Bohemian Rhapsody' sells a million," May explained in 1991. "The B-side is 'I'm In Love With My Car' which Roger wrote and he's paid the same as Freddie for the A-side. He made a disproportionate amount of money out of 'Bohemian Rhapsody.'" Taylor may not have helped matters when, that year, he became the first member of Queen to acquire a country mansion, in Surrey's "stockbroker belt" (while married men May and Deacon bought more modest suburban homes in Barnes and Putney, respectively). This source of conflict had more than ten years to run, during which, May said, they "always argued about money."

Still, as friends in poverty before wealth, they did find ways to work out such resentments between flare-ups. That July when they started recording their next album (at Virgin Records boss Richard Branson's home, The Manor, Oxfordshire—after rehearsals at another residential studio, Ridge Farm, near Dorking, Surrey), May explained to Mick Houghton of *Sounds* that the bandmembers' "contributions have become more complementary." With Deacon writing very occasionally and Taylor ruthlessly culling of his own prolific output before going to the band, May and Mercury's compositional dominance seemed natural. May thought they'd come to "realize how to use each other . . . not only on the music side where we work on all the arrangements, but . . . in the psychological side where you're holding each other together on tour."

Proving May's point to a degree, Queen decided to produce *A Day At The Races* themselves with the help of former Trident

Japan, 1976.

Promo copy, Eddie Howell, "Man From Manhattan" b/w "Waiting In The Wings,"
featuring Freddie and Brian, Japan, 1976

Belgium, 1976. *Courtesy Christian Lamping*

Holland, 1976. *Courtesy Christian Lamping*

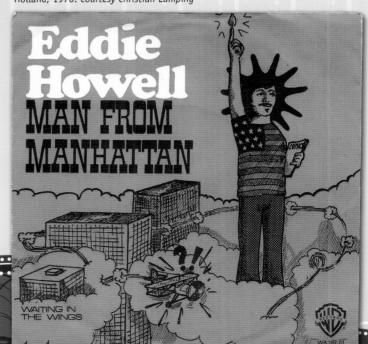

Paris, September 1976. *Keystone Features/Hulton Archive/Getty Images*

engineer Mike Stone—without Roy Thomas Baker for the first time. Mercury told Wesley Strick of *Circus* in 1977, "We were quite confident in doing it ourselves. . . . Taking more responsibility has been good for us."

However, mid-recording, a big idea took hold: a huge, free "thank you" concert in Hyde Park, London. May said it appealed to him because he remembered the atmosphere of the first rock event there, Pink Floyd and Jethro Tull in 1968: "We wondered whether we had the status, but John Reid was sure we should take the risk and do it." May thought the original proposal came from Reid, although Richard Branson has claimed it and certainly took a persuasive hand in briskly securing official permissions for September 18. (Via his involvement, Taylor fell for Branson's French personal assistant, Dominique Beyrand, soon to be sharing his Surrey mansion and Fulham townhouse.)

Queen rehearsed at Shepperton film studios and played warm-ups in Edinburgh, Scotland, and Cardiff, Wales.

Come the day of the show, with 150,000 to 200,000 reportedly watching the support acts, the band piled into a laundry van outside Reid's house in nearby Montpellier Square, Knightsbridge, and entered the backstage area incognito. May admitted to this writer, "It was one of the few times I can remember being really nervous. You get a lot of stick off the press, and you tend to believe it after a while—I had the feeling that everyone in Britain thought we were idiots." Even Mercury seemed rattled. When he got out of the van to find himself surrounded by gawping "liggers," he yelled, "You fucking load of wankers! Go out and watch it with the rest of them!" Later, talking to *Circus'* Wesley Strick, he described the prospect of "You Take My Breath Away," his solo at the piano, as "nerve-wracking—I didn't think my voice would come through."

But Queen proved the boys for the big occasion. From the moment Mercury swaggered on in a white leotard and uttered a lightly mocking, "Welcome to our picnic by the

Serpentine!" (Hyde Park's main lake), every note and every pyro hit the spot—until the very last when, as the crowd roared for an encore and the band turned to go back on, the police intervened. Half an hour past the agreed curfew, they said. Queen raged, so the police switched off the power, plunging the crowd into darkness too, just to make sure.

Although Branson called Hyde Park a "turning point in their career," May came away feeling wounded, as he explained to *Sounds*' Mick Houghton: "It sounds trivial I know, but . . . to be denied the encore, that sense of release, having worked up to such a pitch, was very hard to take. I was very depressed after Hyde Park."

They returned to the studio for another few weeks, fashioning the trademark eclecticism of, arguably, the first "typical" Queen album: a combination of hard-rocking vocal and guitar harmony extravaganzas, swoony romance, pop, and old-time vaudeville (though that leaves out a couple of oddities in May's swamp-bluesy lament for American Indians, "White Man," and Taylor's personal manifesto cum acrid satire, "Drowse").

Then and later, the band always expressed particular pride in "The Millionaire Waltz," which was about John Reid, as Mercury told Kenny Everett on Capital Radio. Taylor told Strick from *Circus* it was "comparable to 'Bohemian Rhapsody,'" and Mercury praised the guitar "tubas and piccolos and cellos," which had "taken weeks." From the Marx Brothers–referencing title onward, Queen acknowledged *A Day At The Races* as the "twin of *A Night At The Opera*." The negative take on that came from Roy Thomas Baker, who told Martin Aston for the *Mojo Classic* edition on Queen, "I thought it reeked of sequel."

Reid launched the album with a Queen Day at Kempton Park racecourse, where EMI sponsored the Day At The Races Hurdle. He may also have had something to do with the arrival of a telegram from Groucho Marx, who wrote, "I know that you are very successful recording artists. Could it, by any chance, be your sage choice of album titles?" Still not above a strenuous promotion campaign around the U.K. talk show and children's TV circuit, Queen inadvertently triggered a symbolic moment in pop history when, on December 1, because Mercury was suffering after some dental work, they pulled out of an ITV early-evening magazine program called *Today*; their last-minute replacements, punk firestarters the Sex Pistols, sneered and swore—and a new era hit the tabloids the next morning.

But after all the plugging, with *A Day At The Races* topping the U.K. chart and "Somebody To Love" No. 2, by January 1977, May had concluded their fifth album was "as far as we could go in that direction." Mercury extemporized around his

frustrations by telling *Circus*' Wesley Strick, "We've done as much as we can with guitars—I think Brian concurs!" With a twinkle, he proposed they employ a full orchestra next time.

In truth, for Mercury 1976 had been a year of change more significant than the minutiae of musical development. In late 1975, he had met David Minns, an artist manager working for Paul McCartney's company, and begun his first serious gay relationship. In the oral history Minns co-edited, *More Of The Real Life . . . Freddie Mercury*, he wrote that Mercury told him one song on *A Day At The Races* was about him: "I remember feeling shattered for days that anyone was prepared to write a song like that for me." Minns didn't specify, but surely it must have been "You Take My Breath Away" (choral voices by Mercury alone).

Some months later, Mercury told Mary Austin about the relationship. "I don't think he enjoyed hiding those things and lying to me," she said in a TV documentary, *When Freddie Mercury Met Kenny Everett*. He moved out of their flat in Holland Road, Kensington, to nearby Stafford Terrace to make a new home with Minns ("I want to lead the Victorian life, surrounded by exquisite clutter," he once said). But he and Austin remained devoted friends for the rest of his life. Soon after they separated, he bought a large apartment for her to live in not far from his own. ♛

A Day At The Races
by James McNair

IN MARCH 1977, actor and venerable comedic great Groucho Marx invited Queen to visit him at his Los Angeles home. The group's latest album and its predecessor, *A Night At The Opera*, had titles borrowed from the Marx Brothers' movies, and now came the chance to say thank you in person. Freddie and company presented Groucho with an engraved gold disc, their gift a signifier of Queen's ascendancy. Orders for *A Day At The Races* ahead of its December 1976 release had exceeded half a million units. Better yet, it soon followed *A Night At The Opera* to the U.K. No. 1 slot before reaching a very respectable No. 5 in the U.S. charts.

A Day At The Races powered from the starting line, but *A Night At The Opera*, featuring the magnum opus that was "Bohemian Rhapsody," had been a tough act to follow. How, after all, was Queen to trump a three-section rock opera that multitracked 180 voices? When the group began work on *A Day At The Races* at The Manor, Oxfordshire, during a summer heat wave, they decided they'd do well to pick up where *A Night At The Opera* had left off, retaining something of its opulence. That the cover design for *Races* was ostensibly a white-on-black inversion of that for *Opera* underlined matters: Queen saw the albums as twins.

One clear difference, though, was that Mercury, May, Deacon, and Taylor were now without their long-term producer Roy Thomas Baker. The terms of his four-album contract had been met upon delivery of *A Night At The Opera*, so he and the band parted amicably, Queen opting to self-produce while retaining the services of Baker's engineer, Mike Stone.

The group thought Stone's expertise in recording vocals indispensable, and he would certainly earn his fee on "Somebody To Love." A yearning, masterfully arranged vocal extravaganza that Mercury had penned in a gospel style after listening to Aretha Franklin records, the song was the big-hitter that Queen needed—a bona fide classic that charted at No. 4 in 2005 when *Q* magazine polled the band's fans to establish the "30 Greatest Queen Songs Of All Time."

Sessions for Queen's fifth album ran from July to November 1976. No expense was spared, the group running up a then-profligate £40,000 on production costs. Given the quality of the resulting material, it seems a tad unfair that *A Day At The Races* has been somewhat overshadowed by its twin. Though "White Man," Brian May's sledgehammer-heavy song about the plight of the Native American Indians lacks the lyrical deftness required of its emotive subject matter, the rest of the record stands up nicely.

Once again, it's Freddie Mercury's imagination that runs riot, his melodic flair formidable and his songs packing arrangements that are constantly in flux. No matter that "Good Old-Fashioned Lover Boy" is a feel-good music hall and vaudeville–informed nugget à la earlier Queen songs like "Seaside Rendezvous"; Mercury's camped-up, fully lived-in performance is riveting, as are May's horn section–impersonating lead guitars.

Much sparer, by contrast, is Mercury's classy piano ballad "You Take My Breath Away," a song whose airy vocal harmonies he multitracked without the help of his bandmates. Owing more to the operatic *lieder* tradition than it does to anything in rock's back pages, it's deliberately sequenced alongside May's ace, if straight-ahead rocker, "Tie Your Mother

SOMEBODY TO LOVE

b/w "White Man," U.K. 1976.

"Somebody To Love" video shoot, Wessex Studios, London, autumn 1976. © *Peter Hince*

Down." Queen knew that such clever use of dynamics would crank up the drama.

Elsewhere, Taylor's woozy acoustic strummer "Drowse" finds Queen's drummer reflecting upon his childhood; John Deacon's propulsive, piano-led love song "You And I" is a true group effort; and "Long Away" finds keen astronomer May looking skyward. (Tantalizingly, history also records that Rod Stewart dropped in to record a song called "Another Piece Of My Heart" with Queen during sessions for *A Day At The Races*. Alas, it never saw the light of day, but it was eventually reinvented without Stewart's vocal for Queen's 1995 album *Made In Heaven*, though by then it had been renamed "Let Me Live.")

Debut albums by U.K. punk acts The Clash and The Damned were just months away as Queen unveiled *A Day At The Races* in December 1976. British music weekly *Sounds* called the album "the most definitive justification of punk ever recorded," but the public voted with their wallets, many still finding Queen's pomp and the preening regal toff that Mercury played tongue-in-cheek far more absorbing than punk's squalid, no-frills riffage.

"Make me feel like a millionaire," implored Freddie on "The Millionaire Waltz," and the lavish release party for Queen's fifth album that EMI Records hosted at Kempton Park racecourse, Middlesex, only served to crank up the ostentation. Out of touch the group may have been, but ultimately it mattered not a jot. *A Day At The Races* was another thoroughbred, and punk's attempts to depose Queen would prove fruitless. ⚜

The American publication *Rock 'N' Roll Comics* re-imagines tour high jinks, Hyde Park, the release of *A Day At The Races*, and the arrival of punk rock. *Rock 'N' Roll Comics* No. 4, Revolutionary Comics, June 1992. *Courtesy Jay Allen Sanford*

Tour Dates

Sheer Heart Attack

27.01.1976	Palace Theater	Waterbury, CT
29–30.01.1976	Music Hall	Boston, MA
31.01.1976	Tower Theatre	Philadelphia, PA
01–02.02.1976	Tower Theatre	Philadelphia, PA
05–08.02.1976	Beacon Theatre	New York, NY
11–12.02.1976	Masonic Temple	Detroit, MI
13.02.1976	Riverfront Coliseum	Cincinnati, OH
14.02.1976	Public Hall	Cleveland, OH
15.02.1976	Sports Arena	Toledo, OH
18.02.1976	Civic Center	Saginaw, MI
19.02.1976	Veterans Memorial Auditorium	Columbus, OH
20.02.1976[1]	New Stanley Theater	Pittsburgh, PA
23–24.02.1976	Auditorium Theatre	Chicago, IL
26.02.1976	Kiel Auditorium	St. Louis, MO
27.02.1976	Convention Center	Indianapolis, IN
28.02.1976	Dane County Coliseum	Madison, WI
29.02.1976	Coliseum	Fort Wayne, IN
01.03.1976	Auditorium	Milwaukee, WI
03.03.1976	Auditorium	St. Paul, MN
07.03.1976	Berkeley Community Theatre	Berkeley, CA
09.03.1976[2]	Civic Auditorium	Santa Monica, CA
10–12.03.1976	Civic Auditorium	Santa Monica, CA
13.03.1976	Sports Arena	San Diego, CA
22.03.1976	Nippon Budokan	Tokyo, JPN
23.03.1976	Aichi Taikukan	Nagoya, JPN
24.03.1976	Kosei Kaikan	Himeji, JPN
26.03.1976[3]	Kyuden Kinen Taikukan	Fukuoka, JPN
11.04.1976	Entertainments Centre	Perth, AUS
14–15.04.1976	Apollo Stadium	Adelaide, AUS
17–18.04.1976	Horden Pavilion	Sydney, AUS
19–20.04.1976	Festival Hall	Melbourne, AUS
22.04.1976	Festival Hall	Brisbane, AUS

"What we want to do as soon as we start our set is to create an immediate atmosphere, if possible, of excitement, expectation and, ultimately, enjoyment."

—ROGER TAYLOR, QUOTED BY HARRY DOHERTY,
Melody Maker, 18.09.1976

Tour Dates

Summer 1976

01–02.09.1976	Playhouse Theatre	Edinburgh, GBR
10.09.1976	Castle	Cardiff, GBR
18.09.1976[4]	Hyde Park	London, GBR

Note

1. Some sources cite the Syria Mosque as the location of this show, but reliable band personnel confirm that the Stanley was the venue.

2–3. Two shows.

4. The show that was cut short by police and that Richard Branson, who secured permission for the event, dubbed the "turning point" in Queen's career.

Tour dates and tickets courtesy Martin Skala, QueenConcerts.com

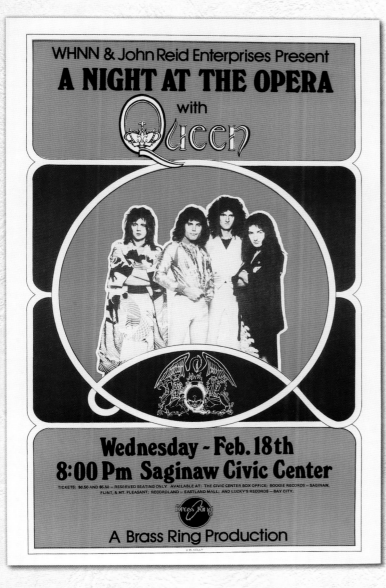

5 MAKING THE ROCKING WORLD GO 'ROUND

BY 1977, QUEEN could whimsically enjoy the fruits of considerable wealth and eminence. Freddie Mercury's Rolls-Royce Silver Ghost crawling alongside him as he strolled from EMI to his favorite restaurant, lest fans ambush him. Roger Taylor transporting a giant Scalextric toy slot-car layout on tour so that he could set it up in his hotel suite if a back-to-boyhood mood took him. The whole band visiting Groucho Marx for afternoon tea when they played Los Angeles.

Yet many who knew them attested that they still understood the value of an acquaintance with reality. In *More Of The Real Life . . . Freddie Mercury*, the singer's partner David Minns described how Mercury sought out reactions to his songwriting: "He was very keen on hearing the opinions of others and would endlessly ask me what I thought of this or that lyric. . . . It was fascinating to watch how he would soak up every atom of life, every particle of every person and situation he encountered, to assist in the creative process."

Again, when Queen embarked on a forty-one-date North American tour that January, bandmembers chose Thin Lizzy as support band. Brian May called them "a real challenge," but where headliners often undermine the second on the bill's chances by careless or hostile treatment, Queen refrained from abusing its power. Thin Lizzy guitarist Scott Gorham told Laura Jackson, author of *Brian May: The Definitive Biography*, "They said, 'Now, you'll need soundchecks and lights—and what else?'"

Jazz tour, Cobo Hall, Detroit, January 18, 1977. © Robert Matheu

"[I]n contrast to most hard rock bands that have an overpowering singer raving in front of a thick, monotonous background, Queen relies a great deal on multi-layered harmonies and complicated song structure that frees their stage act from the Tyranny of the Chord."

—Mitchell Cohen, *Phonograph Record*, 03.1976

BOTH: *A Day At The Races* tour, Sports Arena, Toledo, January 30, 1977. © *Robert Alford*

Rare, limited-edition T-shirt given by promoter to Queen and personal crew for concert at Cobo Hall, Detroit, January 18, 1977. *Courtesy Peter Hince*

Brass Ring Productions Presents

Queen

With Special Guest **THIN LIZZY**

January 18th · Cobo Arena Detroit

COBO ARENA
JEFFERSON AVE.
FOOT OF WASHINGTON BLVD.
DETROIT. MICH.

SEC. B23G ROW 5 SEAT 5

Queen

WABX presents

TUE. EVE. 8:00 P. M.
TIER B

Admission **$7.50**
NO REFUNDS

JAN. **18** 1977

Courtesy Martin Skala, QueenConcerts.com

BRIMSTONE PRODUCTIONS

Queen EDM. CAL.

STAGE PASS

Stick-on promoter's pass for Canadian shows, A Day At The Races tour, 1977. Courtesy Peter Hince

Afternoon sound check, *A Day At The Races* tour, Civic Centre, Ottawa, January 25, 1977. © *Peter Hince*

104

ROW (1)   SEAT
A   25
F
L
O
O
R

Retain Stub — Good Only
No Exchange — No Refund
TUE.   FEB. 1
8:00 P.M.   1977
Davis Printing Limited
"QUEEN"
PRICE—7.00+RST .70—$7.70
ADMIT ONE. Entrance by Main
Door or by Church Street Door.
Maple Leaf Gardens
LIMITED
CONDITION OF SALE
Upon refunding the purchase
price the management may
remove from the premises

"Bring Back That Leroy Brown." Brian pulls out the "George Formby
ukulele-banjo," *A Day At The Races* tour, Maple Leaf Gardens, Toronto,
February 1, 1977. *www.photosets.net, Brannon Tommey*

A Day At The Races tour, Nassau Coliseum, Uniondale,
February 6, 1977. © *Stephanie Chernikowski*

BOTH: *A Day At The Races* tour, Nassau Coliseum, Uniondale,
February 6, 1977. © *Stephanie Chernikowski*

Concerts West promoter pass, *A Day at The Races* U.S. tour, 1977. *Courtesy Peter Hince*

BOTH: *A Day At The Races* tour, Sam Houston Coliseum, Houston, February 26, 1977. *www.photosets.net, Brannon Tommey*

Courtesy Martin Skala, QueenConcerts.com

> "I'm always affected by criticism. . . . It doesn't matter how far you get, if someone says you're a load of shit it hurts."
>
> —Brian May, quoted by Mick Houghton, *Sounds*, 22.01.1977

Courtesy Jason Cullen

> *"Queen is a band people either love or hate with a vengeance—that's okay."*
>
> —ROGER TAYLOR, QUOTED BY PENNY VALENTINE, *Creem*, 04.1978

Yet, as punk took hold of rock 'n' roll, especially in the U.K., Queen found the media accusing them of elitist arrogance and isolation. Interviewers relentlessly implied that publicists and pluggers had manipulated their chart/fame breakthrough. The band hated it but wearied of invoking the true story of their privations, failures, and rejections. On that U.S. tour, a pained Mercury told Don Rush of *Circus*: "It destroys the soul to hear that you're all hype, that you have no talent, and that your whole career has been contrived."

Some live reviewers would dismiss their stage performance as artificial too. On the early 1977 tour, Taylor railed to a Boston radio DJ that U.K. music papers had called Queen "too slick" and "too good." He fumed, "I just don't understand that kind of criticism. . . . I don't like to see sloppy musicians or even sloppy shows, they don't entertain me." Likewise, Mercury couldn't see why these writers refused to accept a rock concert as "flamboyant . . . a spectacle . . . a theatrical event . . . a fashion show."

Back playing Britain in May and June after gigs in five European countries, Queen gave its capacity audiences the full

Courtesy Peter Hince

treatment: Scottish pipers; leotards; dry ice; thunderflashes; five thousand red, white, and blue balloons tumbling from the rafters; and the unveiling of "The Crown" to eighteen thousand fans at Earls Court on June 6–7. This £50,000 lighting rig rose from the stage at the start of the set like the *Close Encounters* spacecraft. And it resembled the royal headgear enough to symbolize the conflicting spirits of the time. Queen and its "Crown" dedicated the gig to Queen Elizabeth II's jubilee (twenty-five years since her coronation),

A Day At The Races tour, Broendby Hall, Copenhagen, May 12, 1977.
David Redferns/Redferns Collection/Getty Images

EARLS COURT, LONDON
(Opposite Warwick Road Exit, Earls Court Tube Station)

Harvey Goldsmith and John Reid
cordially invite you to a night with

Queen

BLOCK

72

MONDAY, 6th JUNE, 1977
at 8.00 p.m.

2nd Floor Gallery £2.00

For Conditions of Sale see over

H 7

To be retained

A Day At The Races tour, Earls Court, London, June 1977. *Mirrorpix/Courtesy Everett Collection*

closed it with May's version of "God Save The Queen," and donated all proceeds to the monarch's charity fund; meanwhile, a week earlier, the Sex Pistols had released a second single, "God Save The Queen" ("Her fascist regime/It made you a moron, a potential H-bomb").

After Earls Court, *NME* published a denunciatory review by Tony Stewart, who then asked for an interview with Mercury. Surprisingly, the singer agreed and, Stewart reported in the June 18 edition, opened on the attack. "You're too narrow-minded," sneered Mercury. "You're the bloody arrogant sods that just don't want to learn. . . . You feel you know it all." Stewart's response read: "Mercury needs putting straight. . . . A rock gig is no longer the ceremonial idolisation of Star by Fans. That whole illusion, still perpetrated by Queen, is quickly being destroyed."

Mercury continued with naïve sincerity by talking about his recent introduction of a Nijinsky-inspired stage costume: "I'm into this ballet thing . . . and trying to put across our music in a more artistic manner than before. [It] may not be quite right for rock 'n' roll . . . [but] if you don't try these bloody things out, you'll never know."

 "I remember speaking to you three or four years ago. That right? So you're still working for *NME?* . . . Life is not treating you very well, is it?"

—Freddie Mercury to journalist Tony Stewart, *NME,* 18.06.1977

The article appeared under the notorious headline "Is This Man A Prat?"

However, the supposed (see Peter Hince's sidebar, "When Fred Met Sid") culturo-philosophical confrontation between Queen and the Sex Pistols reached a fine comic conclusion a couple of weeks later. When Queen began its sixth album, they discovered the Pistols occupied an adjoining studio at Wessex, London. "We looked at each other with real distrust," Taylor recalled to *Mojo*'s David Thomas in 1999. But then the ice broke. Clearly, Pistols bassist Sid Vicious had read the *NME* interview because, as May tells it, he walked into their studio and asked, "'Oo are you then? You that Freddie Platinum that's supposed to be bringing ballet to the masses?' Fred was completely unphased and said 'Ah, Mr Ferocious! Well, we're trying our best, dear.'"

A Day At The Races tour, Earls Court, London, June 6, 1977, dedicated to Queen Elizabeth's silver jubilee. *Gus Stewart/Redferns Collection/Getty Images*

Stick-on guest pass, *A Day At The Races* U.K. tour, 1977.
Courtesy Peter Hince

Making The Rocking World Go 'Round

WHEN FRED MET SID
SETTING THE RECORD STRAIGHT ON A QUEEN LEGEND
BY PETER HINCE

Wessex Studios, a converted church in Highbury, North London, is where, in autumn 1976 during the recording of *A Day At The Races*, Queen first witnessed punk. The Sex Pistols, freshly signed by EMI, were also booked into Wessex for some early sessions. Soon the world would know about the Sex Pistols. When EMI replaced Queen with the punk upstarts on the *Today* TV program, their infamous interview with host Bill Grundy became a seminal moment in the Pistols' short but explosive careers.

I first spotted Johnny Rotten upstairs in the lounge area of Wessex, on a brown corduroy seating unit of the sort that was fashionable in the '70s. He was wearing a lime green, mohair jumper and ripped jeans; safety pins were inserted in any available space, and his hair was dyed the color of a red hamster, spiked, and lacquered. Despite all this, he seemed a quiet, pleasant sort of bloke who was relaxing and watching the telly—what was all the fuss about?

He didn't even mind when I asked to change the channel. There was no surly

snarl, just an indifferent shrug. As roadies, we *were* scruffy; the Pistols were "statement scruffy," a form of sociopolitico scruff.

The following year Queen was back at Wessex recording *News Of The World*. The Sex Pistols were back as well, compiling their *Never Mind The Bollocks* LP. The Pistols had a new bass player, and one afternoon when Queen were working in the control room, that new bass guitarist, Sid Vicious, stumbled in through the door, very worse for wear, and addressed Fred: "Have you succeeded in bringing ballet to the masses yet?" (a reference to a quote Fred had made in the music press when he started wearing leotards on stage).

Fred casually stood up, walked over to him, and quipped: "Aren't you Stanley Ferocious or something?" took him by the collar, and threw him out.

So much for the mean edge of punk.

Fred did not care for this new, limited-chord musical movement. He cared even less for its wardrobe.

Sid Vicious, wishing he was back at Wessex Studios with Freddie. *Michael Ochs Archives/Getty Images*

The sixth album, *News Of The World*, named after a sex-and-scandal British Sunday newspaper, lacked the orchestras Mercury advocated six months earlier. Taylor, who had even talked about how harmonies could be "dangerous," summed up the band's feeling to *Mojo*'s Mark Blake in 2008: "We wanted something raw and basic and we found it."

Although this new album fell short of Queen's usual variety and consistent strength, two tracks met the Taylor brief: "We Are The Champions" by Mercury and "We Will Rock You" by May. Mercury explained his improbable inspiration to *Record Mirror*'s Rosie Horide: "I was thinking about football. It was aimed at the masses. I wanted a participation song. It worked a treat. . . ." Coincidentally, May had drawn on the same source for "We Will Rock You" when, between numbers at New Bingley Hall, Stafford, on May 29, 1977, the audience started singing "You'll Never Walk Alone," Liverpool FC's signature tune. "We thought, 'God, it's like a football match except with everyone on the same side,'" said May.

New Musical Express, October 29, 1977.

BOTH: *News Of The World* tour, Maple Leaf Gardens, Toronto, November 21, 1977.
www.photosets.net, Brannon Tommey

QUEEN
U.S. WINTER TOUR 1977
14
PETE HINCE
ACCESS
ALL AREAS

Crew and staff luggage tag and pass, *News Of The World* U.S. tour. *Courtesy Peter Hince*

As a double A-side single in November, the two songs hit No. 2 in the U.K. and the U.S. and did well worldwide. That fall's World Series winners, the New York Yankees, adopted "We Are The Champions" as their team anthem, and sports crowds generally took to the bleacher foot stomp of "We Will Rock You" (the beat really is all feet, no drums). Even the undemonstrative May allowed that, "We sort of owned [America] around the time of *News Of The World*."

Yet this more straight-ahead Queen still couldn't please the critics. The apparently self-regarding bombast of "We Are The Champions" raised hackles. "I can understand that," said May

equably to this writer in 1991. "The first time I heard that 'No time for losers' line I said, 'You can't do this, Fred. You'll get killed.' But it wasn't saying that Queen are the champions, it was saying, 'We, *everybody*, are the champions.' It is schmaltzy and it does slightly make you shudder, but Freddie can pull that sort of thing off where most people would just make you feel sick attempting it."

The year closed with another larger-scale American tour during which the band "commuted" in their own private jet. Given a night off, Mercury would explore local gay scenes and cocaine supplies. "When I'm in New York, I just slut

Turkey, 1977. *Courtesy Ferdinando Frega, Queenmuseum.com*

"Spread Your Wings" b/w "Sheer Heart Attack," U.K., 1977.

Japan, 1977

"Darling, I'm simply dripping with money! It may be vulgar, but it's wonderful."

—FREDDIE MERCURY

116 QUEEN

myself. It is Sin City with a capital S," he once said. The others had their own pleasures to pursue, but Queen proved they could still be troupers; they defied a blizzard to play Dayton, Ohio (December 4), and Taylor refused to cancel Oakland, California (December 17), despite nineteen stitches in his right arm after a drunken encounter with a plate-glass window the previous night.

But for May, Madison Square Garden in New York City (December 1) proved *the* special occasion. He flew his parents over on the Concorde—a plane Harold May had spent much

of his working life helping to design. The gig, with May, as ever, playing the guitar he and his father had fashioned out of bric-a-brac, at last evoked paternal approval for his career choice. "At Madison Square Garden I suppose it was undeniable," said May. "That's where he actually admitted he was proud—until then it had been, 'OK, but you'll have to get a proper job later. . . .'"

When they flew home on Christmas Eve, it was Mercury's turn to revisit parental hang-ups. He told Horide, "My mother would have killed me if I wasn't home for Christmas."

Big in Japan. *Ongaku Senka* magazine, Nos. 1 and 3, 1977; official Japanese fan club publication, Vol. 11; and *Young Rock*, No. 8, 1978.

New Year 1978 began with Taylor meeting Dominique Beyrand's parents near Paris, Veronica Deacon giving birth to a second son, Michael, and Queen's second and last major business upheaval. With John Reid's time divided between them and Elton John, May said, "We got that powerless feeling again." They decided they had to split with Reid, even though they knew they would have to pay heavily for it.

Bundling into the back of Mercury's Rolls-Royce parked in the snow outside Taylor's mansion, band and manager agreed severance. Queen paid a lump sum and fifteen percent of the royalties on its first six albums in perpetuity. Shifting to self-management, they hired their lawyer, Jim Beach, to run the business. On Deacon's prudent recommendation—"The rest of the group won't do anything unless John says it's all right," Mercury told Horide—they also switched accountants (offloading Keith Moore, the man jailed in 1995 for stealing £6 million from another client, Sting) and set up a group of "tax efficient" companies to handle their earnings from different media and territories.

A spring tour of Europe saw Taylor and May pass through Checkpoint Charlie for a look at East Berlin where the drummer spotted graffiti he adapted for the next album's geometric sleeve design. Mercury, in another unguarded interview, handed Tim Lott of the *Daily Mail* a quote that has been rehashed ever since: "I'm like a mad dog about town. . . . I'll go to bed with anything. My sex drive is enormous."

By July, after the Mays' first child, James, arrived on June 15, Queen began recording abroad for the first time, at Mountain Studios, Montreux, Switzerland, then at brand-new Super Bear Studios in the Alps above Nice, France (their accountant had advised them to take twelve months out of the U.K. to create a tax-free year domestically).

Courtesy Ferdinando Frega, Queenmuseum.com

"Good Old-Fashioned Lover Boy" and "Death On Two Legs (Dedicated To. . .)" b/w "Tenement Funster" and "White Queen (As It Began)," U.K., 1977.

Freddie with Mary Austin at a reception in the gardens of Eden Au Lac Hotel, Montreux, during recording of the *Jazz* album, July 1978. © *Peter Hince*

With favorite engineer Mike Stone unavailable, they returned to co-production with Roy Thomas Baker, fresh from the Cars' hit debut album. He soon restored his working relationships, especially with Mercury who, when singing, had earlier come to like watching Baker's face to determine whether he'd nailed it. At Montreux, discovering the control-room window was hidden from the vocal booth, they had CCTV installed so that Mercury could see Baker's reactions.

However, Queen's musical output had begun to reflect a sour unease as their initial, relatively innocent joy in their success faded. The perversely named *Jazz* fielded only one durable Queen classic, "Don't Stop Me Now," and a rather crude gimmick double A-side single, "Bicycle Race"/"Fat Bottomed Girls." Of itself, the accompanying video of sixty-five naked women, all professional models, cycling around Wimbledon's greyhound stadium would hardly be remembered. But the whole idea seemed of a piece with the sleazy event that followed.

Touring America, they launched the album with the biggest, most exotic party they'd ever thrown—in New Orleans after their show on Halloween, the £200,000 cost divided between EMI and Elektra. Mark Mehler of *Circus*, one of four hundred guests (including international press) invited to the Fairmont Hotel on Canal Street, witnessed Queen's midnight entrance amid the Olympia Marching Band: "Suddenly . . . a legion of

ideo for "We Will Rock You" video shoot in the snow-covered gardens of Roger Taylor's country house, early 1978. © *Peter Hince*

Jazz tour, Ahoy Hall, Rotterdam, April 1978.
© Peter Mazel/Sunshine/Retna Ltd.

French ads for *Jazz*.

All Thailand. *Courtesy Ferdinando Frega, Queenmuseum.com*

strippers, vulgar fat-bottomed dancers, snake charmers, drag queens, and bizarrely festooned revellers, begin to strut their stuff. . . . Three obese black women in g-strings do a pathetic bump and grind, and another female participant amuses a small gaggle of onlookers by putting a cigarette in an unlikely place." He missed the dwarves with trays of cocaine strapped to their heads, a legendary detail clarified (sort of) by Taylor talking to *Mojo*'s Mark Blake in 2008: "[It's] not true. Or if it was, I never saw it. . . . Actually it could have been true." Jacky Gunn and Jim Jenkins, in their authorized book *Queen: As It Began*, blandly note, "An endless stream of executives from both record companies were shown . . . into a back room, where one of the groupies spent the whole evening on her knees making them extremely happy."

For years, Queen dismissed all criticism of the event. May told this writer he enjoyed surreal performers like the man whose speciality was to "dress up as a piece of liver, hide on a table in a pile of real offal and squirm around." He said he felt Queen had been "excessive . . . in a fairly harmless way. I don't think we ever did anyone a great disservice." But in that same interview, in 1991, this renowned straight arrow remarked, "I missed a lot because I was chasing someone else at the time. I was deeply in love and she wasn't there so I went off."

Talking to *Mojo* in 2008 May revealed more of the road romance that haunted and partly unglued him thirty years earlier, as a young husband and new father: "I remember thinking all is not quite right. I went out looking for Peaches [as in "Now I'm Here" from *Sheer Heart Attack*: "Down in the dungeon just Peaches 'n' me/Don't I love her so"]. I didn't find her, but she found me later on." Band life and family life, he said, had been "incredibly difficult to reconcile."

A quote attributed to May further suggested, "The excess leaked out from the music and into life and became a need. We were always trying to get into a place that has never been reached before and excess is part of that." Taylor summed up succinctly to Blake: "Trouble is we got better and better at having a good time." 👑

"When I was a little kid in the '70s, I'd watch stuff like *Don Kirshner's Rock Concert* on TV and everything was insane. I was into Kiss, Alice Cooper, Elton John—and Queen. I didn't realize how unusual they were. I thought everything was like that; if you have a band, it's this giant, crazy thing. It warped my mind into thinking that's the way it's supposed to be. It's hard to erase that once it's in your mind."

—Rob Zombie

Jazz tour, Cobo Hall, Detroit, November 1978. © *Robert Alford*

Crew and staff laminate, *Jazz U.S. tour, 1978. Courtesy Peter Hince*

U.S. TOUR 1978 QUEEN

9130CB27
14BALC
212 ADULT
sec
E $6.50
row price
tax
28NOV

OAKLAND COLISEUM ARENA
NIMITZ & HEGENBERGER RD.
BILL GRAHAM/KFRC PRESENT
Q U E E N
* * *
SAT DEC 16 1978 8:00 PM
BALCONY
212 E 5
sec row seat
ADULT $6.50

OCB270
212
sec
E
row
A28NOV
5
seat

W 183844
BASS
NO REFUNDS NO EXCHANGES

ARENA LEVEL
SEC ROW SEAT
101 CC 1
DEC. 8, 1978
197
8
ADMIT ONE THIS DATE ONLY
CHRIS FRITZ And CONTEMPORARY PROD.
In Cooperation With KY-102
Present
QUEEN
KEMPER ARENA
KANSAS CITY, MISSOURI
DEC 8 FRIDAY - 8:30 P.M.
Net $7.71
Tax(Local) 34
User Fee 45
TOTAL $8.50
NO PRICE NO EXCHANGE
$8.50
SEC ROW SEAT
101 CC 1
ARENA LEVEL

Jazz tour, Cobo Hall, Detroit, November 1978. © Robert Alford

News of the World

by Chuck Eddy

WHEN IT FIRST CHARTED IN THE STATES, on November 26, 1977, exactly one year after the Sex Pistols released "Anarchy In The U.K."—Queen's sixth album, *News Of The World* was widely touted as a back-to-basics reining in of the band's more brazenly ornate and rhapsodic multi-part-epic tendencies. Some people even called it a response to punk rock (a genre the band reportedly wasn't too fond of), which is kind of a weird theory—if Queen hated punk's simplicity so much, wouldn't they have made the music *more* ornate? Either way, the album's pinnacle, "Sheer Heart Attack," complete with insane proto-no-wave guitar solo and proto-Devo lyrics blaming teenage angst on DNA (i.e., nature not nurture), plus a toppling-over-itself tempo that (also royally named) Prince may have ripped off outright in his own punkiest song, "Sister," three years later, is easily the most punk-sounding track Queen ever recorded (doubly interesting since 1974's *Sheer Heart Attack*, which in the tradition of Led Zeppelin's *Houses of the Holy* did not contain its own title track, easily has the most punk-rock-looking cover of any Queen LP).

Thing is, when you actually listen to the record, it's hard to deny that *News Of The World* more often sounds like a response to *funk*. Three years later on *The Game*, Queen would go all minimal and hip-hoppy with "Another One Bites The Dust," but "We Will Rock You" was obviously their initial venture into rhythmic-vocals-over-phat-beat proto-rap sparseness, as its eventual sampling and/or retooling by Grandmaster Flash, Kool Moe Dee, Eminem, 2 Live Crew, and Ice Cube demonstrates. But even more obvious funk-metal moves are the remarkably big-bottomed (talk about mudflaps, it's got 'em) "Fight From The Inside"—which contains in its tight genes the prototype DNA for "Dragon Attack" (also off *The Game*) and therefore Billy Squier—and "Get Down, Make Love," which though perhaps a little sluggish at first, is even more blatant in its funktionality, not to mention in the proto-industrial-music perviness that eventually inspired Nine Inch Nails to cover it ("You say you're hungry/I give you meat/I suck your mind/You blow my head"), and which eventually opens up into sex-moaning psychedelic spaces that are even more inadvertently dub-metal than those in Zep's "Whole Lotta Love."

(By the way, this seems like a good place to interject that, growing up in the Midwest in the mid-'70s, I'm pretty sure it never occurred to my classmates or me to question Freddie Mercury's gender preferences. I mean, it's not like he had a girl's name, like Alice Cooper. Then again, I'm pretty sure lots of kids I grew up with also assumed the Village People were genuine macho men.)

News Of The World also features a dainty piano eulogy to Freddie's pet cat ("All Dead, All Dead"); some working-class show bizness about a kid who hates his job sweeping up an Irish bar ("Spread Your Wings"); a not-back-to-basics-at-all 6:27 opus that exists primarily to support its kick-ass guitar solo ("It's Late"); a tentative reggae homage (every '70s British rock band had to have one!), albeit with Spanish rather than Jamaican guitars ("Who Needs You"); some off-the-cuff blues strut aimed at ingrates who don't give a damn about any trumpet-playing band 'cause it ain't what they call rock 'n' roll ("Sleeping On The Sidewalk"); and a cabaret-torch finale that has less to do with blues than the previous song despite having "blues" in its title ("My Melancholy Blues").

Featuring three songs each by Freddie, Brian May, and Roger Taylor, and two by John Deacon, *News Of The World* has gone quadruple-and-a-half platinum in the United States, triple platinum in Canada, and double platinum in the U.K. Its Frank Kelly Freas cover painting updates his October 1953 cover of *Astounding Science Fiction* magazine, and it is the third consecutive Queen LP whose title can be diagrammed: [Noun] [Preposition] The [Different Noun]. (Okay, the previous two actually had articles at the beginning, but no need to get technical.)

Mainly, though, as years have passed, *News Of The World* has come to be best known as *The Album With "We Will Rock You" And "We Are The Champions" On It*. Which is clearly a triumph to get triumphant about, even though those two classics appeared on a 45 that went to No. 2 in the U.K. and No. 4 in the United States long before they were sports anthems. "We Will Rock You" was just a ditty with lyrics about a muddy-faced, can-kicking disgrace of a boy aging into a bloody-faced, banner-waving, shouting-in-the-street hard young man and finally into a muddy-faced old codger who deserves to be put back into his place. Admit it, you've heard it a million times, and you never even noticed all that, did you? Neither, probably, did Def Leppard, whose "Pour Some Sugar On Me" seemingly inherited the song's bleacher beat. As one fan writes online, "This song reminds me of when i was a kid and in the school yard in brooklyn we used to sing this to kids when we thought we were all tough and crap :) [sic]." Somebody else insists the facial mud is a slap at Kiss, but who knows where that wacky idea came from? And speaking of schoolyards, yet another fan observes that "We Are The Champions" resembles a cross between "Send In The Clowns" and the classic playground taunt "naa-naa na-NAA-naa!"

By now, of course, it's impossible to imagine a world in which these two Queen numbers didn't exist. And they will be inextricably linked until the end of time, both by the eternally melodic Brian May guitar climax of "We Will Rock You" and by the fact that both titles employ journalism's revered "editorial we," forever enabling clever headline writers to construct puns like "Wii Will Rock You" and "Oui Are The Champions." Not to mention forever inspiring athletes to run faster and jump higher, and fans to order more beer.

No time for losers, indeed!

"[Metallica's] Kirk Hammett has a guitar tech who used to work with Brian May. We were sitting in a bar one night talking about old stuff and telling stories, and I woke up the next day and had the 'We Are The Champions' solo stuck in my head."

—Rex Brown, Down and Pantera

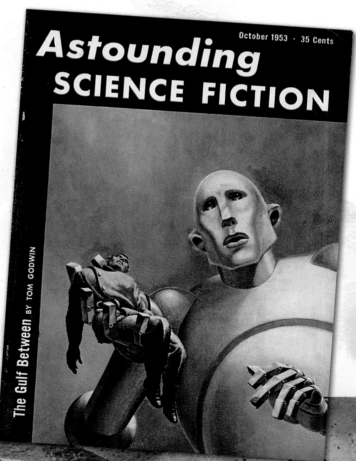

The Frank Kelly Freas cover of *Astounding Science Fiction*, October 1953, that inspired the *News Of The World* album art.

Jazz

by Jim DeRogatis

To be sure, the music on Queen's seventh studio album is as extraordinary as anything the band created during its now legendary career. If none of the thirteen tracks on the original release are as absurdly ambitious as "Bohemian Rhapsody," as perfectly anthemic as "We Are The Champions" and "We Will Rock You," or as cut-to-the-chase, lean, mean, and ultimately irresistible as "Sheer Heart Attack" and "Killer Queen," they are nonetheless wildly diverse in their stylistic experimentation (from the Middle Eastern tonalities and snippets of Arabic lyrics in "Mustapha," to the Elvis Presley–in-a-1920s-dancehall approximation of "Dreamer's Ball," to the convincing and prophetic funk-disco of "Fun It"), fist-thumpingly inspirational (with "Fat Bottomed Girls" and "Bicycle Race" more than matching the rousing quality of those two stadium-raising mega-hits from *News Of The World*), and plenty powerful but very tuneful ("If You Can't Beat Them," "Let Me Entertain You," "Dead On Time," and "Don't Stop Me Now").

Jazz rocks, plain and simple, and the critics that panned it upon its release in November 1978 were dead wrong, utterly joyless, and possibly stone-cold deaf. ("Queen hasn't the imagination to play jazz; Queen hasn't the imagination, for that matter, to play rock & roll"—Dave Marsh, *Rolling Stone*; "Their music is so absurdly dull on *Jazz*, so filled with dumb ideas and imitative posturing"—Mitchell Cohen, *Creem*.) It was mind-blowing then, and it's still mind-blowing now, three decades later—though to be honest, here I must confess that when I first discovered and fell in love with this album as a freshman at Hudson Catholic Regional High School for Boys, courtesy of my lockermate, Queen superfan, and best friend Lou DePinto, well . . . it was all about the poster.

You see, kids, back in the days before CDs, much less digital downloads or free-flowing Internet porn, rock music came encoded on twelve-inch slabs of sleek black vinyl, which in turn were packaged in big square sleeves of glossy cardboard, sometimes—especially in the case of chart-topping if critically reviled bands like Queen and Led Zeppelin—with elaborate gatefold designs, and occasionally bearing the bonus of a full-color, fold-out poster. And the one that came with *Jazz*—before retailers, parents, and prudes forced the band to

remove it from the second pressing—was really something special: three panels that, when unfolded, formed a thirty-six-inch-long, twelve-inch-high panoramic vision of paradise, with no fewer than forty-nine women (Lou and I counted), all naked save for their bike helmets, and all but one sitting astride their seats at the starting line of a race for which any red-blooded fourteen-year-old American boy would happily wave the flag, if you know what I mean.

That photo was taken on September 17, 1978, at Wimbledon Stadium in London, when the band staged this fleshy gathering to hype the release of the double A-side single "Bicycle Race"/"Fat Bottomed Girls." (Legend holds that its managers rented the vehicles from Halfords, the U.K.'s primary bicycle retailer, but upon returning them were informed that they had to purchase all of the seats, since they'd been used with blatant disregard for sanitary considerations—i.e., without pants.) A few weeks later, to trumpet the actual album release, the band went even further over the top, holding a now infamous Halloween-night press party—more of a bacchanal, really—in that capital of American decadence, New Orleans, complete with, as *Circus* reported, "a deranged ringmaster, a legion of strippers, vulgar fat-bottomed dancers, snake charmers, drag queens, and bizarrely festooned revellers."

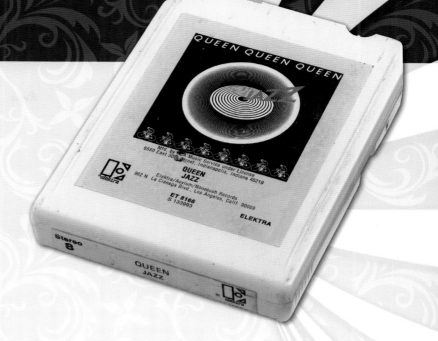

At the time, all of this was cited as more evidence of Queen being woefully out of step with, if not downright contemptuous of, the prevailing punk aesthetic—and never mind that it all sounds like a jolly good time, and funny as heck to boot. "People think we take ourselves a lot more seriously than we actually do," Roger Taylor said at the press conference the following day, while Freddie Mercury, quizzed about the poster controversy, shrugged and replied, "It's cheeky—naughty, but not lewd. Certain stores, you know, won't run our poster. I guess some people don't like to look at nude ladies."

Far from being sexist, the poster was a celebration of female diversity, with women of every size, shape, and color represented, and none of them *Playboy*-perfect supermodels. "Fat Bottomed Girls" wasn't mocking unconventional beauty; it was celebrating it! The members of Queen never thought they were better than their fans; after the phenomenal success of *News Of The World*, they were simply giving us "more of that jazz," hoping we'd enjoy it because their goal truly was to entertain us, and they'd pull out all of the stops to do it. You wanna talk punk contrarianism? Their idea of a good-time spectacle was far from the prevailing blockbusters ("*Jaws* was never my scene/And I don't like *Star Wars*"). They just wanted to . . . ride their bicycles, and they invited us to do the same—though the bicycle race was really just a metaphor, if you haven't gathered that by now.

"We lost some of our audience with *Jazz*: 'How could you do it? It doesn't go with your spiritual side,'" Brian May has said. "But my answer to that is the physical side is as much a part of a person as the spiritual or intellectual side. It's fun, and I'll make no apologies. All music skirts around sex, sometimes very directly. Ours doesn't. In our music, sex is either implied or referred to semi-jokingly, but it's always there."

And here, in the end, we get to the heart of this album's enduring appeal. *Jazz* isn't Queen's bestselling, most popular, or most groundbreaking album. But in addition to all its musical rewards—and I haven't even mentioned how "Jealousy" is one of the group's finest ballads, or why "Leaving Home Ain't Easy" is the song The Beatles should have written in "She's Leaving Home," or that this was the last fruitful flowering of the band's partnership with its ideal producer, Roy Thomas Baker—*Jazz* is both the band's *funniest* and *sexiest* release. And with Queen, that says it all. ⚜

"One of the greatest rock 'n' roll bands to ever grace the fine earth. I was just singing 'Fat Bottomed Girls' the other day and thinking how amazingly great that song is."
—Darius Rucker, Hootie & the Blowfish

Bolivia, 1978. *Courtesy Ferdinando Frega, Queenmuseum.com*

b/w "Fat Bottomed Girls," U.K., 1978.

Tour Dates

A Day At The Races

13.01.1977	Auditorium	Milwaukee, WI
14.01.1977	Dane County Coliseum	Madison, WI
15.01.1977	St. John Arena	Columbus, OH
16.01.1977	Convention Center	Indianapolis, IN
18.01.1977	Cobo Hall	Detroit, MI
20.01.1977	Civic Center	Saginaw, MI
21.01.1977	The Gardens	Louisville, KY
22.01.1977	Wings Stadium	Kalamazoo, MI
23.01.1977	Coliseum	Richfield, OH
25.01.1977	Civic Centre	Ottawa, CAN
26.01.1977	Forum	Montreal, CAN
28.01.1977	Stadium	Chicago, IL
30.01.1977	Sports Arena	Toledo, OH
01.02.1977	Maple Leaf Gardens	Toronto, CAN
03.02.1977	Civic Center	Springfield, MA
04.02.1977	University of Maryland	College Park, MD
05.02.1977	Madison Square Garden	New York, NY
06.02.1977	Nassau Coliseum	Uniondale, NY
08.02.1977	War Memorial Auditorium	Syracuse, NY
09.02.1977	Garden	Boston, MA
10.02.1977	Civic Center	Providence, RI
11.02.1977	Civic Center	Philadelphia, PA
19.02.1977	Sportatorium	Hollywood, FL
20.02.1977	Civic Center	Lakeland, FL
21.02.1977	Omni	Atlanta, GA
22.02.1977	Auditorium	Birmingham, AL
23.02.1977	Kiel Auditorium	St. Louis, MO
25.02.1977	Moody Coliseum	Dallas, TX
26.02.1977	Sam Houston Coliseum	Houston, TX
01.03.1977	Coliseum	Phoenix, AZ
02–03.03.1977	Forum	Inglewood, CA
05.03.1977	Sports Arena	San Diego, CA
06.03.1977	Winterland	San Francisco, CA
11.03.1977	PNE Coliseum	Vancouver, CAN
12.03.1977	Paramount	Portland, OR
13.03.1977	Arena	Seattle, WA
16–17.03.1977	Jubilee Auditorium	Calgary, CAN
18.03.1977	Northlands Arena	Edmonton, CAN
08.05.1977	Ice Stadium	Stockholm, SWE
10.05.1977	Scandinavium	Gothenburg, SWE
12.05.1977	Broendby Hall	Copenhagen, DNK
13.05.1977	Congresscentrum	Hamburg, FRG
14.05.1977	Festhalle	Frankfurt, FRG

16.05.1977	Phillipshalle	Dusseldorf, FRG
17.05.1977	Ahoy Hall	Rotterdam, NLD
19.05.1977	Sporthalle	Basel, CHE
23–24.05.1977	Hippodrome	Bristol, GBR
26–27.05.1977	Gaumont	Southhampton, GBR
29.05.1977	New Bingley Hall	Stafford, GBR
30–31.05.1977	The Apollo	Glasgow, GBR
02–03.06.1977	Empire Theatre	Liverpool, GBR
06–07.06.1977	Earls Court	London, GBR

News Of The World

11.11.1977	Civic Center	Portland, ME
12.11.1977	Garden	Boston, MA
13.11.1977	Civic Center	Springfield, MA
15.11.1977	Civic Center	Providence, RI
16.11.1977	Memorial Coliseum	New Haven, CT
18–19.11.1977	Cobo Hall	Detroit, MI
21.11.1977	Maple Leaf Gardens	Toronto, CAN
23–24.11.1977	The Spectrum	Philadelphia, PA
25.11.1977	Scope Arena	Norfolk, VA
27.11.1977	Coliseum	Richfield, OH
29.11.1977	Capital Centre	Washington, DC
01–02.12.1977	Madison Square Garden	New York, NY
04.12.1977	University Arena	Dayton, OH
05.12.1977	Stadium	Chicago, IL
08.12.1977	Omni	Atlanta, GA
10.12.1977	Tarrant County Convention Center	Fort Worth, TX
11.12.1977	Summit	Houston, TX
15.12.1977	Aladdin Center	Las Vegas, NV
16.12.1977	Sports Arena	San Diego, CA
17.12.1977	County Coliseum	Oakland, CA
20–21.12.1977	Long Beach Arena	Long Beach, CA
22.12.1977	Forum	Inglewood, CA
12.04.1978	Ice Stadium	Stockholm, SWE
13.04.1978	Falkoner Theatre	Copenhagen, DNK
14.04.1978	Ernst-Merck Halle	Hamburg, FRG
16–17.04.1978	Forest National	Brussels, BEL
19–20.04.1978	Ahoy Hall	Rotterdam, NLD
21.04.1978	Forest National	Brussels, BEL
23–24.04.1978	Pavillon	Paris, FRA
26.04.1978	Westfallenhalle	Dortmund, FRG
28.04.1978	Deutschlandhalle	Berlin, FRG
30.04.1978	Hallenstadion	Zurich, CHE
02.05.1978	Stadthalle	Vienna, AUT
03.05.1978	Olympiahalle	Munich, FRG
06–07.05.1978	New Bingley Hall	Stafford, GBR
11–13.05.1978	Empire Pool	London, GBR

Promoter's laminate pass, Montreal (December 1) and Toronto (December 3–4),
Jazz tour, 1978. *Courtesy Peter Hince*

Tour Dates

Jazz

28.10.1978	Convention Center	Dallas, TX
29.10.1978	Mid-South Coliseum	Memphis, TN
31.10.1978	Municipal Auditorium	New Orleans, LA
03.11.1978	Sportatorium	Hollywood, FL
04.11.1978	Civic Center	Lakeland, FL
06.11.1978	Capital Centre	Washington, DC
07.11.1978	Coliseum	New Haven, CT
09–10.11.1978	Cobo Hall	Detroit, MI
11.11.1978	Wings Stadium	Kalamazoo, MI
13.11.1978	Garden	Boston, MA
14.11.1978	Civic Center	Providence, RI
16–17.11.1978	Madison Square Garden	New York, NY
19.11.1978	Nassau Coliseum	Uniondale, NY
20.11.1978	The Spectrum	Philadelphia, PA
22.11.1978	Auditorium	Nashville, TN
23.11.1978	Checkerdome	St. Louis, MO
25.11.1978	Coliseum	Richfield, OH
26.11.1978	Riverfront Coliseum	Cincinnati, OH
28.11.1978	War Memorial Auditorium	Buffalo, NY
30.11.1978	Civic Centre	Ottawa, CAN
01.12.1978	Forum	Montreal, CAN
03–04.12.1978	Maple Leaf Gardens	Toronto, CAN
06.12.1978	Dane County Coliseum	Madison, WI
07.12.1978	Stadium	Chicago, IL
08.12.1978	Kemper Arena	Kansas City, MO
12.12.1978	Coliseum	Seattle, WA
13.12.1978	Coliseum	Portland, ME
14.12.1978	PNE Coliseum	Vancouver, CAN
16.12.1978	Coliseum	Oakland, CA
18–20.12.1978	Forum	Inglewood, CA

Tour dates and tickets courtesy Martin Skala, QueenConcerts.com

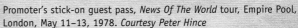

Promoter's stick-on guest pass, *News Of The World* tour, Empire Pool, London, May 11–13, 1978. *Courtesy Peter Hince*

PHILIPS HALLE DÜSSELDORF-OBERBILK
SIEGBURGER STRASSE 15

Gültig gemäß der Hausordnung

Fritz Rau + Michael Scheller + John Reid
present

Philips-Halle Düsseldorf

A NIGHT WITH QUEEN

16.5.77

Montag
16. 5. 77
20⁰⁰ Uhr

Keine Haftung für Personen- und Sachschäden.
Beim Verlassen der Halle verliert die Karte ihre Gültigkeit.
Kartenrückgabe ausgeschlossen.

Einheitspreis
Abendkasse (unnumeriert)
DM 20,00 incl. 5,5 % MWSt.

00919

Einheitspreis
Abendkasse (unnumeriert)
DM 20,00 incl. 5,5 % MWSt.

Haubold, Eschwege

AMK BERLIN – DEUTSCHLANDHALLE
Messedamm 26 Autobus 4, 10, 65, 66, 69, 92, 94 U-Bahn Kaiserdamm (Zubringer)

Deutschlandhalle

Freitag, 28. April 1978

Beginn siehe Rückseite

A Night With QUEEN Concert '78

DM 17,–

Veranstalter: Concert Büro Lippmann + Rau, Frankfurt/Main – Konzertdirektion Wolfgang Jänicke GmbH, Berlin

Programmänderung vorbehalten

Kartenrücknahme ausgeschlossen

Buchdruckerei Bree Schöneberg
Kontrollabschnitt
28. April 1978

Vorverkauf: DM 17,–
+ Vorverkaufsgebühr incl. Mehrwertsteuer

28. 4. 1978

5095 *

capital centre

G 559357

CONCERT
QUEEN

CAPITAL CENTRE

MON NOV 6.1978

enter portal

28|025|652

14 8:00

125 U 13 ADULT

125 U 13 $ 7.70

SEC ROW SEAT TAX INCL

EMPIRE POOL, WEMBLEY

MAY 11 ENTER AT NORTH DOOR

HARVEY GOLDSMITH ENTERTAINMENTS present

Queen

A ROW 10 SEAT 4

THURSDAY, MAY 11, 1978 at 8pm

ARENA £4.25

see conditions on back

MAY 11 1978

£4.25

A ROW 10 SEAT 4

TO BE RETAINED

TO BE GIVEN UP

Courtesy Martin Skala, QueenConcerts.com

Spectrum

AT THE SPECTRUM
SPECTRUM CONCERTS PRES

QUEEN

MON NOV 20 1978
8:00P

SEC.

$8.50

SEAT ROW

Spectrum

AMERICA'S SHOWPLACE

NO REFUNDS/EXCHANGES

329454838X5193

6 PLAYING THE GAME

Japan, 1980.

SHOWMEN THAT THEY WERE, Queen always made success look easy, their natural state of grace. But in the *Jazz* era, the joy among them had faded somewhat. Roger Taylor recalled to Mark Blake for *Mojo* in 2008, "My songs were very patchy . . . [and] *Jazz* never thrilled me. It was an ambitious album that didn't live up to its ambition." For the same feature, May ruminated on the deleterious effect of tax exile—"We weren't as much of a group when we started living in a different country"—and how their next move wrought further damage: "It was when we went to Munich that it started to fall apart."

They started 1979 with a long, routine European tour—twenty-eight shows, seven countries, January 17 to March 1. Routine as it may have been by then, it provoked some dissension. In Laura Jackson's *Brian May: The Definitive Biography*, tour manager Pete Brown described arguments about the equality of their accommodations, even though they had a house each, he said. Still, work never slackened. They put in a month's intensive labor at Mountain in Montreux, choosing and mixing tracks from sixteen of the European shows for the double vinyl *Live Killers*. Released that June, it sold solidly: U.K. No. 3, U.S. No. 16.

Meanwhile, ultra-Queenly, they offloaded some cash before it could be repatriated to the U.K. and taxed: they bought Mountain. "We did like the place," said May, later. "We ran it at a break-even level and it's nice to have it available." Of course, they promptly started recording somewhere else.

The band had sometimes discussed the possibility of making a movie soundtrack. The notion, Taylor recalled to Blake, was, "We wanted to write the first rock 'n' roll soundtrack to a non-music film." Before they left for another screamy Japanese sojourn in April, business manager Jim Beach visited Italian Hollywood film producer Dino De Laurentiis (*Serpico*, *Three Days Of The Condor*, *Death Wish*) and pitched for his upcoming science-fiction epic *Flash Gordon*. The mogul, pushing sixty, hesitated, then went for it.

"Play The Game" video shoot, London, summer 1980. Another photo of Peter Hince's very similar to this was used for the cover of "Another One Bites The Dust" and for concert posters and other worldwide promotions. © *Peter Hince*

133

QUEEN

134

Jazz tour, France, 1979. *Georges DeKeerles/Getty Images*

Jazz tour, 1979. © *Denis O'Regan/Corbis*

Fritz Rau + Michael Scheller present

QUEEN
ON TOUR '79
IN GERMANY

17.1. Hamburg - Ernst-Merck-Halle · 18.1. Kiel - Ostseehalle ·
20.1. Bremen - Stadthalle · 21.1. Dortmund - Westfalenhalle ·
23.1. Hannover - Messe Sportpalast · 24.1. Berlin - Deutschlandhalle · 1.2. Köln - Sporthalle · 2.2. Frankfurt - Festhalle ·
10.2. + 11.2. München - Rudi-Sedlmayer-Halle · 13.2. Böblingen -
Sporthalle · 15.2. Saarbrücken - Saarlandhalle

LR Der Vorverkauf hat begonnen!

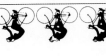

JAZZ – das
neue Album von
QUEEN

Die LP: 1C 064-61820
Die MC: 1C 264-61820

EMI ELECTROLA

QUEEN

Q

DIAS
19 Y 20
FEBRERO
22 HORAS
PALACIO
MUNICIPAL
DEPORTES
BARCELONA

Venta anticipada
de localidades:
GAY & COMPANY,
Hospital 94
y Rosellón 222
DOMUS BAR,
Mariano Cubí-A...
CLUB DE VANGU...
Corpe 23 (edis...

En
discos
E.M.I.

EUROPEAN
TOUR 1979

QUEEN

Crew and staff laminate, Jazz European tour,
1979. Courtesy Peter Hince

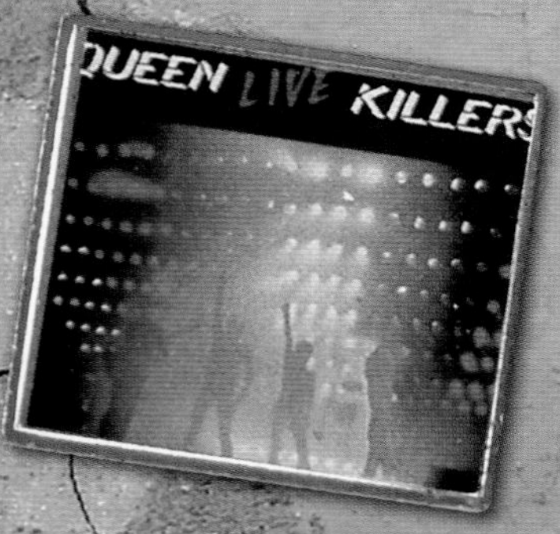

QUEEN LIVE KILLERS

Courtesy Martin Skala, QueenConcerts.com

Jazz tour, Budokan, Tokyo, April 1979.
Courtesy Ferdinando Frega,
Queenmuseum.com

Crew and staff luggage tag, Jazz Japan tour, 1979. Courtesy Peter Hince

Queen gathered at Musicland Studios, Munich, in June—just after the birth of John Deacon's third child, Laura—with almost none of their usual advance writing or preparation done and two albums to work on: the soundtrack and *The Game*.

Progress proved slow. Accounts of the atmosphere vary considerably. In *More Of The Real Life . . . Freddie Mercury*, roadie Chris Taylor wrote, "Once we got to Munich . . . we became once and for all what Fred called 'the family.'" He described how at the end of a night's recording, maybe 3 a.m., they'd hit the clubs, probably the straight Sugar Shack or the gay Mrs. Henderson's. Then back at their hotel (usually the Hilton or the Arabellahaus, under which Musicland had been built), they'd get together either in the suite Brown shared with Roger Taylor ("the HH," or Hetero Hangout), or in Freddie's

rooms ("the PPP," Presidential Poufter Parlour) for more drinking, drugging, or even playing board games until 8 a.m.

But May saw it very differently. "Emotionally, we all got into trouble in Munich," he told Blake. "'Hey, let's have a drink after the studio.' It was nice to start with."

Their new producer, Reinhold Mack, known by his surname, had his own problems with the band. Highly regarded through engineering with Giorgio Moroder at Musicland, he had never met Queen before. In 2007, he told izotope.com he found them "set in their ways like pensioners. Their credo was, 'This is how we are used to doing things. . . .' There were two camps of songwriting: Freddie and Brian. Fred was easy. We thought along similar lines and it took him fifteen to twenty minutes to come up with something absolutely

The Real Craziness Behind "Crazy Little Thing. . ."

SETTING THE RECORD STRAIGHT ON ANOTHER QUEEN LEGEND

By Peter Hince

DURING THE SUMMER OF 1979, Queen were finishing a "year out" to avoid the wicked tax man of the Labour government by recording some new ideas in Munich. During the sessions I briefly went back to London to clear through customs the balance of the gear that had arrived back by sea from Japan. Having done my professional duties and picked up various items and paperwork from our office to courier back to Munich, I received a phone call from Musicland.

"Ratty?" The chirpy office voice sounded a bit too friendly.

"Yes. . .?"

"There's something else for you to take back to Munich."

"What a surprise. What is it? Is it heavy? And will I have to get it through customs?"

"It's Freddie."

Fred, who was also in London for a few days, had nobody to accompany him back to Munich. Would I mind? Fred never traveled alone; there was always somebody with him and always somebody in the next hotel room. Somebody to talk to. Well, a first-class seat on British Airways was not too shabby, so I agreed. However, due to a strike at Heathrow, flights were

severely delayed. There was an anxious air to the situation, as Fred had used his allotted days in the U.K. and needed to leave our shores rather imminently. I hung around Heathrow's Terminal One until I got some positive news about our flight. Fred was phoned and sped down the M4 from Kensington to join me. It was a sunny summer's day in both London and Munich, and several glasses of in-flight bubbly were well-received.

At the Munich airport we were met by Peter, a local German who drove Fred in a hired Mercedes, and we cruised into the east of the city and our Hilton home. Fred was reinstalled in his grand suite and wanted to take a bath before going to the studio. I called Musicland and gave the other bandmembers the news that "his self" was back in Munich and would arrive shortly. Fred was humming and tapping in the bath and shouting out the names of chords: "D—yes! And C and G . . . Ratty, quick, come here!"

"Uhh, you want me to come into your bathroom, Fred? I'm not sure about this."

"No, no! Get me a guitar! Now!"

He emerged from the bathroom wrapped in towels, still dripping, and scurried into the living room of the suite where I gave him the battered acoustic that had

"Crazy Little Thing Called Love" video shoot, London, autumn 1979. © *Peter Hince*

brilliant. Brian . . . would come up with a great idea, but get completely lost in insignificant details after the first rush of creativity."

Taylor confirmed to *Mojo* in 2008 that, "We had massive rows in the studio . . . usually about how long Brian was taking." In the same article, May more or less accepted the complaints: "I have an unusually long attention span. I seemed to be on this eternal quest for perfection." In 1991 he recalled, "We did hate each other for a while. In the studio the differences in musical opinions can get very accentuated, you can end up quibbling over one note. We got very angry with each other [during] *The Game* and *The Works*. I left the group a couple of times. Only for a day, you know. A bit of, 'I'm off and I'm not coming back!'"

"Recording *Jazz* and those albums we did in Munich, *The Game* and *The Works*, we got very angry with each other. I left the group a couple of times just for the day, you know. I'm off and I'm not coming back! We've all done that. You end up quibbling over one note."
—Brian May, quoted by Phil Sutcliffe, *Q*, 03.1991

Legend has it Mercury got *The Game* under way when, while taking a bath in his Arabellahaus suite, he suddenly yelled "Bring me the tape recorder—quick!" and hummed and chuntered out a rough "Crazy Little Thing Called Love." Next day, the popularized version of the tale continues (see Peter Hince's sidebar, "The Real Craziness Behind 'Crazy Little Thing. . .'" for the longtime crewmember's version), he got down to the studio early and told Mack, "Let's do this before Brian comes." On an Ovation twelve-string

been put there for these creative emergencies. Despite the guitar being out of tune, Fred strummed away for a short time with his fingers—he never used a pick, even on stage.

Seizing the urgency of the moment, Fred insisted we dash to Musicland where a halt was firmly called to whatever work was in progress. He summoned Brian, John, and Roger into the studio room and enthused about this new idea, which they started to work on and record immediately. The song was "Crazy Little Thing Called Love," one of Queen's most successful worldwide singles.

That's how hit records are written. ⚜

The Game tour, Madison Square Garden, September 1980. *Arthur D'Amario/Retna Ltd.*

"When I heard 'Crazy Little Thing Called Love' the first time, I was in my car and I listened and I went, 'Wow, those sons of guns really did that right'. . . . You listen to the guitar and the sound and Brian's solo, the way the whole thing was done, I had a big thumbs-up. I thought, 'Wow, those guys are really good.'"

—John Fogerty

guitar he could barely play, he knocked out the Elvis/Eddie Cochran basics in no time. Later, May added his '50s-style solo and, with Mercury and Taylor, did Queen's impression of Elvis' Jordanaires on the harmony "woo woos" and "ready Freddies."

In June and July 1979, they completed just four album tracks: "Crazy Little Thing Called Love," Taylor's "Coming Soon," and May's "Sail Away Sweet Sister" and "Save Me." But it seems they did start work on *Flash Gordon* during this period. And, although *The Game*'s sleeve states that it "includes the first appearance of a synthesizer on a Queen album," May has said they first *recorded* one for the soundtrack.

Taylor had always favored the bans on both synthesizers and outside musicians because they imposed the ultimately more satisfying need to "drag it out of *ourselves*." But in Munich it was the drummer who brought along an Oberheim OB-X (an analog polyphonic synthesizer launched that year) and won over his bandmates. No ideological debate at all. Taylor said Mercury waved it through with a blithe, "Oh, this looks good, dear." Arch-techie Deacon told Jacky Gunn and Jim Jenkins for *Queen: As It Began*, "We wanted to experiment with all that new studio equipment. . . . The synthesizers then were very advanced compared to the early Moogs, which did little more than make a series of weird noises." (Stevie Wonder could show reason to dispute that last remark.)

By August they'd left the studio to rehearse for a one-off festival at Saarbrücken, Germany, and they didn't return for six months. During their downtime Mercury flew a hundred people to New York on the Concorde for his thirty-third birthday party and made a guest appearance dancing, after a fashion, with the Royal Ballet in London at a gala charity show. One of the tracks he pranced about to was "Crazy Little Thing Called Love," which, as soon as it came out in October, revived Queen's somewhat dormant fortunes. In the U.K. it went to No. 2. In America (and six other countries) it topped the chart, breaking a run of flop U.S. 45s: "Don't Stop Me Now" had reached only 86, while "Jealousy" and the *Live Killers* version of "We Will Rock You" failed to make the Top 100.

Mercury's Royal Ballet adventure brought a new face to his entourage when he hired one of the company's wardrobe men, Peter Freestone, for the band's November–December U.K. tour (which featured several smaller back-to-the-roots venues). Freestone's first stage-wear purchases, noted in his *Freddie Mercury* memoir, indicated a significant new look: three pairs of red PVC trousers, skateboarder's knee pads in blue and red, and white boxing boots—an

Hammersmith Odeon, London, December 26, 1979.

Stick-on passes, *Crazy* U.K. tour, 1979. *Courtesy Ferdinando Frega, Queenmuseum.com (red) and Peter Hince (blue)*

TOMMY LEE OF MÖTLEY CRÜE ON ROGER TAYLOR

"Just An All-Around Talented Dude"
As told to Gary Graff

I GREW UP WITH QUEEN, man. That band has been highly influential in my life, not only the band as a whole but as a big fan of all the guys individually. For me, as a drummer, watching Roger Taylor sing and play drums was like, "Oh, man, I want to do *that*!" Roger did all the high harmonies on those songs, on all that crazy-sounding, operatic stuff. His voice was really prominent, so he was just an all-around talented dude. And he had some great tracks on those records.

Roger is just a super big-beat drummer. We have somewhat similar styles—simple, which I fly the flag for because there's nothing worse than a drummer who overplays. He's just a real solid drummer who played exactly what the song needed—nothing more, nothing less—which to me is a talented drummer. He also got a really cool sound. And "We Will Rock You"—dude, that's epic. That plays at every hockey game, basketball game, you name it. That's right there as an anthem. It's the most simple beat on the planet, but everyone knows it. You could be paraplegic in a wheelchair and still clap your hands and stomp your feet to that one. ⚜

> *"Roger is the most extreme [bandmember] in extravagance and the rock 'n' roll lifestyle."*
>
> —BRIAN MAY, QUOTED BY
> PHIL SUTCLIFFE, Q, 03.1991

Roger at Musicland Studios, Munich, during recording of *The Game*, spring 1980. These stickers were put on the road cases for identification. © *Peter Hince*

CHRIS SQUIRE OF YES ON JOHN DEACON

"Prog, Funk, And Pure Pop"
As told to Gary Graff

JOHN WAS REALLY GOOD. There are a lot of good bass parts in [Queen's] music . . . and they had a wide vocabulary, no doubt about it. A lot of it is proggy and some of it was bordering on funk and a lot of it was pure pop, as well. They certainly had a big mixture of styles and, as a bass player, I would've been happy to have had that freedom to go between styles and just be inventive, as I'm sure John was. John wrote some of their biggest songs as well.

I would've thought that after a while, John would have had some kind of itch to want to play with them again. I know he had that kind of not wanting to be in the limelight personality, hence his reasons for his non-appearance with them these days. I personally can't understand how, if you've been part of something that was such an important musical statement, you wouldn't want to take the chance to do it again. I think in the States people don't realize how much more stature Queen have in Europe. They're just giant, still to this day. It was an incredible impact. ⚜

"John is reserved, almost nonchalant on stage, as if it's all in a small, personal joke. When asked how he saw himself within the framework of the band he replied, with a small smile, 'I'm the bassist.'"

—JONH INGHAM, *Sounds*, 29.11.1975

John Deacon is reflected in Freddie's Steinway at rehearsals for the 1980 European leg of *The Game* tour. Hallenstadion, Zurich, November 22, 1980. © *Peter Hince*

extreme contrast to John Deacon, who simultaneously switched from ornate Queen gear to suit, collar, and tie.

Back in Munich from February to May 1980, they slogged through six more tracks for *The Game* and, no doubt, some more *Flash Gordon* ideas. By his own account to izotope.com, producer Mack hauled them toward radical new techniques, most memorably on Deacon's disco/Chic-influenced "Another One Bites The Dust," where they built up from a drum loop and used backward piano, cymbals, and handclaps. "The idea was less is more," said Mack. "[Before *The Game*] the band would have never contemplated going about recording in this manner."

In this case, Roger Taylor emerged as a voice of conservative caution. A little later, in August, 1982, he conceded to the *Detroit Free Press* that "Another One Bites The Dust" was "so un-me." At greater distance, May told *Mojo* in 2008, "[Roger] hated it. He said, 'This isn't rock 'n' roll, what the hell are we doing?' He didn't want Queen to become funky whereas John did. . . ." But Taylor lost the argument. "And Freddie sang till his throat bled on that song," said May.

Freddie at dining table in Musicland Studios, Munich, during recording of *The Game*, spring 1980. © *Peter Hince*

Among the Mercury undercurrents in 1980 was a public indication of his sexuality. In March, he guested on his similarly semi-closeted DJ friend Kenny Everett's TV show. In an unscripted skit, Mercury silently sidled on in gay-biker cap and leathers then jumped on Everett and dragged him to the ground.

On the same trip back to London, he impulse-bought Garden Lodge, 1 Logan Place, Kensington, for £500,000 cash on the barrelhead. With eight bedrooms and a quarter-acre garden, it represented settling down, but he kept that for the future, staying on at his nearby Stafford Terrace flat—with his new live-in male lover, Tony Bastin, whom he'd met on the road in Brighton before Christmas. Then, that May, Mercury appeared in Queen's "Play The Game" promo video wearing the complete '80s macho "gay clone" look—hair cropped, black moustache, no more nail varnish.

Minor, mostly good-natured bombardments of razors and nail-varnish bottles followed during Queen's huge June-to-September tour of North America. Mercury responded with humor. "Do you think I should keep this moustache?" he'd holler. "Do you say *no*? Fuck off!" He seems never to have discussed any of this with the band, but they stood behind him. Taylor told *Mojo* in 2008, "We couldn't give a shit. We

refused to worry about people being small-minded."

Offstage, Mercury diligently studied the *Spartacus Guide* to gay nightspots and sought them out in every town. Meanwhile, according to Freestone, he summoned Bastin over to Charleston, South Carolina (where they had a show on August 16), just to dump him because of reported infidelities. Mercury promptly fell in with a new foursome of long-term male friends and partners whom he dubbed "my New York daughters."

Commercially, Queen evidently suffered no damage from Mercury's body language. An influential black music radio station, WBLS in New York, started playing "Another One Bites The Dust." About the same time, in July, the band had a visitation from Michael Jackson and his brothers backstage at the Los Angeles Forum; Michael told them it was "a fantastic track. You must release it." Taylor admitted to *Mojo*, "I was like, 'I don't know about that.' How wrong was I?"

Elektra got the drift. They released the track as a single in August, and it climbed steadily to No. 1 in the U.S. that October. In America, like "We Are The Champions" and "We Will Rock You," it developed into a sports anthem. *The*

Crew and staff
luggage tag, *The
Game* U.S. tour,
1980. *Courtesy
Peter Hince*

Playing The Game

The Darth Vader gag that ran afoul of George Lucas and company. *The Game*
tour, CNE, Toronto, August 30, 1980. *www.photosets.net, Brannon Tommey*

Rock 'N' Roll Comics recounts The Game–era events, including the oft-reported meeting with Michael Jackson at the L.A. Forum. Rock 'N' Roll Comics No. 4, Revolutionary Comics, June 1992. Courtesy Jay Allen Sanford

Game, which topped the U.K. chart as soon as it came out in July, climbed more gradually in America, alongside "Another One Bites The Dust," but reached No. 1 in late September.

The band's year closed frantically with the conclusion of the *Flash Gordon* sessions at Advision Studios, London, with European and British tours, and even with a threatened lawsuit from *Star Wars* creator George Lucas over their joke use of a bodyguard clad in Darth Vader gear to carry Mercury onstage (settled out of court). The only somber interruption amid the helter-skelter came on December 9 when, grieving like every other musician, they responded to overnight news from America of John Lennon's assassination by playing "Imagine" at their Wembley Arena concert. May lost it and got the chords wrong, but nobody minded.

Released in December, the movie *Flash Gordon* generally was panned, but film and music critics reviewed the soundtrack with unexpected appreciation.

The Game tour, Sports Arena, San Diego, July 5, 1980. *George Rose/Getty Images*

Yet the malaise dogging Queen since *Jazz* persisted. The least of their worries was Taylor's endeavour to become the first member to make a solo album. Having become a father for the first time in May (a boy, Felix), he'd started recording at the band's own Montreux studio during a late-July break from the American tour. In 1978, Mercury had told *Record Mirror*'s Rosie Horide, "If anyone left . . . that would be the end of Queen. We are four equal, interwoven parts." But Taylor allayed any such concern by portraying his venture as a hobby, a matter of using his many surplus songs.

May, meanwhile, was looking distinctly wobbly. For instance, in Laura Jackson's *Queen: The Definitive Biography*, Pete Brown said May felt almost allergic to the private plane, hotel, gig, and back again hamster-wheel of rock star lifestyle: "The rarefied atmosphere was driving Brian mad . . . what he missed dreadfully was normality. He used to say to me: 'What can I honestly say I know about anything, living the way we do?'" He wanted to go back to scheduled flights because "I'd feel I've been somewhere!"

Looking back with Dave Thomas of *Mojo* in 1999, May summed up his feelings about Queen at that time: "We struggled bitterly with each other. We were all frustrated with each other. I remember John saying I didn't play the kind of guitar he wanted on his songs. . . . We all tried to leave the band more than once. But then we'd come back to the idea that the band was greater than any of us. It was more enduring than most of our marriages."

♔

The Game tour, Joe Louis Arena, Detroit, September 20, 1980.
© *Robert Alford*

fot. A. Pisarski

POCZTÓWKA DŹWIĘKOWA

R-1069

PLAY THE GAME

Wykonawca: QUEEN

NIE ZGINAĆ
CENA ZŁ 12.—

tonpress

ансамбль КУИН великобритания

PATHETIC EARTHLINGS...
WHO CAN SAVE YOU NOW?

Music by QUEEN

DINO DE LAURENTIIS Presents
FLASH GORDON
SAM J. JONES ★ MELODY ANDERSON ★ ORNELLA MUTI
MAX VON SYDOW ★ TOPOL ★ TIMOTHY DALTON
MARIANGELA MELATO as Kala ★ BRIAN BLESSED
PETER WYNGARDE ★ Screenplay by LORENZO SEMPLE, JR.
Produced by DINO DE LAURENTIIS ★ Directed by MIKE HODGES
Filmed in TODD-AO® A UNIVERSAL RELEASE

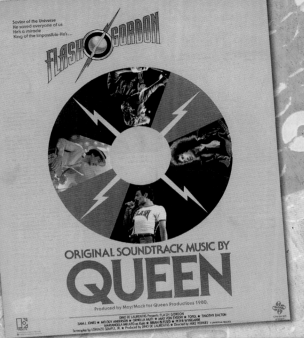

Savior of the Universe
He saved everyone of us
He's a miracle
King of the Impossible-He's...

FLASH GORDON

ORIGINAL SOUNDTRACK MUSIC BY
QUEEN

Produced by May/Mack for Queen Productions 1980.

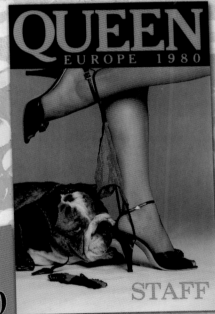

QUEEN
EUROPE 1980

STAFF

Crew and staff laminate, *The Game*
European tour, 1980. *Courtesy Peter Hince*

QUEEN
Christmas 1980

Fan club publication, Christmas 1983.

The Game
by Garth Cartwright

AT THE BEGINNING OF 1979 Queen were among the world's most successful and wealthy entertainers, but things weren't all smooth. Their last album, 1978's *Jazz*, attracted even more vitriolic reviews than usual while the publicity stunt of launching "Fat Bottomed Girls" b/w "Bicycle Race" with a few dozen naked women cycling around a velodrome gave those who wished to beat the band an even bigger stick than usual. Many openly professed their dislike. Punk and new wave, reggae and funk were the commanding sounds of the time; as Led Zeppelin and Black Sabbath disintegrated, so it appeared time might be up for the remaining hard rock superstars of the early 1970s. While the likes of the Sex Pistols attacked the establishment, Freddie Mercury claimed, "Our songs are utterly disposable. I don't want to change the world with our songs. People can discard them like a used tissue." That Queen were tax exiles only added to the contempt with which many viewed the band. All this gave critics the opportunity to snipe that the band was over. Instead, Queen was about to reinvent themselves and achieve their greatest success.

In June 1979, Queen checked into Munich's Musicland Studios. While previous albums had been produced by either Roy Thomas Baker or the band (with engineer Mike Stone), in Munich, Queen settled down to work with engineer and co-producer Reinhold Mack. The resulting album, *The Game*, proved to be an album of two halves.

The initial June–July 1979 sessions produced four songs: "Crazy Little Thing Called Love," track 5, reportedly written by Mercury in five minutes while enjoying a bubble bath, is an infectious rockabilly-tinged song that became a huge international hit. Recorded in two takes by Mercury-Taylor-Deacon ("Quick, let's do it before Brian comes," the vocalist told Mack), with May later adding backing vocals and a guitar solo, "Crazy Little Thing" could be Mercury paying tribute to Elvis (a personal hero) or referencing the then hugely popular movie *Grease*.

The other three songs from the June–July 1979 sessions— the May efforts "Sail Away Sweet Sister" and "Save Me," along with Roger Taylor's "Coming Soon"—hark back to Queen's pomp-rock past and ended up as the album's final three tracks.

That they were buried at the end of the vinyl album suggests the band recognized them as weak material.

The Queen that resumed recording in February–May 1980 sounds refreshed. Album opener "Play The Game" starts with an aggressive, distorted tape loop of the kind many new-wave bands were experimenting with at the time. The track challenges listeners, while allowing elements of a traditional power ballad to keep the fans in check. Indeed, the album's eclectic nature—attuned to contemporary club culture, while showing off the band's stadium pedigree—makes *The Game* a curious, almost postmodern artifact. No one else would attempt such a feat until U2 did so on *Achtung Baby*, an album that is, in its own way, an offspring of *The Game*.

Track 2, "Dragon Attack," presents an aggressive, almost punk feel. May has complained since that he later felt sidelined by the more funky material Queen went on to explore in the early 1980s, but here his playing is fierce, the band aggressive and raw.

"Another One Bites The Dust," track 3, divided old fans and caused some disunity within the band. Disco ruled the late 1970s charts, and The Rolling Stones, Rod Stewart, and Kiss, among other rock acts, had employed it to achieve huge international hits. Written by bassist John Deacon, "Another One Bites The Dust" builds on the bass line from Chic's 1979 hit "Good Times," making it more minimalist and functional, while Mercury's vocal adds a level of hysteria. A huge international hit—No. 1 in the United States!—it demonstrates how Mercury and Deacon were embracing the funk sounds heard in clubs around the world, while May's and Taylor's songs still favored heavy rock.

"Dust" was the fourth single off *The Game*, suggesting that few initially saw its massive potential. Taylor admits he was unenthusiastic about playing disco and never wanted "Dust" released as a single, but black U.S. radio stations began playing the track, and Michael Jackson, dropping in on the band backstage after a Los Angeles concert, urged them to release the song as a single. "Dust" filled dance floors, crossed genres, and helped make Queen the biggest-selling band of 1980.

Track 4, "Need Your Loving Tonight," was another Deacon composition, further suggesting the bassist had a canny ear for what would work on U.S. pop radio. This slick, empty hard rocker set a format for much of what would succeed in the United States until Nirvana arrived to reinvent rock.

Track 6, "Rock It," could be drummer Taylor's answer to Mercury's "Crazy Little Thing," employing a '50s riff wrapped in a slick, new-wave production. Here, May demonstrates metal guitar licks à la Eddie Van Halen.

While *The Game* features several outstanding songs, it also features some that Mercury surely had in mind when describing Queen's songs as "disposable," most notably track 7. "Don't Try Suicide" opens with the guitar lick from The Police's "Walking On The Moon," then descends into a camp bitchfest with Mercury slating a former lover as a "prick teaser." Song's moral? Don't try suicide, as no one would care.

In many ways, *The Game* was a breakthrough album for Queen. They broke their "no synthesizers" rule, left much of their hard-rock leanings behind for pop, and lost some of their oldest fans with their appropriation of disco (while winning countless more fans for this very reason). At thirty-five minutes, it is their shortest album. And in international sales, *The Game* was also Queen's most successful. ❧

Japan, 1979.

 "As a DJ, I still play 'Another One Bites The Dust.' It's a great funk song."

—NORMAN COOK, AKA FATBOY SLIM

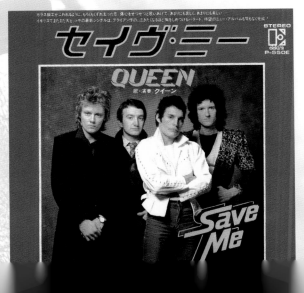

Japan, 1980. *Courtesy Christian Lamping*

Flash Gordon
by David Dunlap Jr.

ORIGINAL SOUNDTRACK MUSIC BY QUEEN

QUEEN'S FLASH GORDON *SOUNDTRACK* has been viewed as a surprising anomaly within the band's discography by fans and critics alike. The eye-straining cover doesn't help matters. Dominated primarily by a cosmic egg-yolk yellow, it's so bright that a glaucoma patient would have no trouble plucking it from the bin. Furthermore, the album is hardly recognizable as a proper Queen release because the band's name only appears at the bottom in relatively small print. Photos of the band were relegated to the inner sleeve, although the shot of Freddie looking resplendent in a form-fitting Flash tee and red leather trousers makes up for the oversight.

In addition, *Flash Gordon* showed that Queen had finally lost its battle against that dreaded instrument, the synthesizer. For seven straight studio albums (until *The Game*), Queen had proudly and overtly resisted its electronic siren call. If, however, *The Game* was an example of the band tentatively dipping its collective toe into the pool of electronic keyboards, *Flash* found the lads tits-high in spacey synth sounds. Queen took to synthesizer with the fervor of a convert; every single member gets in on the act. In context, however, it's easy to forgive Queen for using synths. The album, apart from the standout rock tracks, "Flash's Theme" and "The Hero," is actually composed of instrumental music intended to accompany scenes from a science fiction film, and nothing connotes interplanetary misadventures like the whooshes, gurgles, and bleeps of a synthesizer.

Admittedly, the choice to release a soundtrack album seems like an odd one. The band was coming off *The Game*, a quadruple platinum smash. Releasing *Flash Gordon* meant a yearlong delay of a *Greatest Hits* package that ultimately sold over eight million copies. Although the *Flash* soundtrack had more than respectable sales, it fell far short of its predecessor and successor. A Mad Peck comic strip for the rock magazine *Creem* summed up the commercial and artistic dilemma. The comic depicts Abbott and Costello (for no apparent reason) discussing the album. Costello: "But, I think when the kids who are used to getting a dozen hits on a movie LP find out that this really *is* a soundtrack, with only one cut that remotely resembles a single, it'll be cut-out city!" Abbott: "Well, I

disagree! I found the music to be the kind of kissie-poo mock opera that made Queen number one on the 'America's Top 10' viewers poll!" The best explanation for why Queen agreed to record Flash when movie producer Dino De Laurentiis asked them during the recording of *The Game* was that the band members thought it would be fun.

For years, critics had written that Queen's music was just mindless fluff and adolescent wish-fulfillment fantasies. Recording over-the-top songs for a silly sci-fi popcorn flick allowed the band a sly retort, as if to say "Oh, so you really want to see puerile antics and schlocky space operatics?" Thus was born the absolutely beautiful and only slightly absurd "Flash's Theme." The high-energy song is peppered with campy dialogue from the movie (screenwriter Lorenzo Semple Jr. had previously worked on the '60s *Batman* TV show). It begins with a sample of Max Von Sydow, as Ming the Merciless, expressing his contempt for Earth, before John Deacon's pulsating bass line takes over. Just as the rhythm builds to a climax, Freddie releases a triumphant shout of "Flash . . . A-Ah!" The theme is certainly a million times more memorable than the movie for which it was written.

フラッシュ・ゴードンのテーマ

FLASH GORDON

FLASH GORDON

QUEEN

フットボール・ファイト
FOOTBALL FIGHT

45RPM ¥600

Promo copy, Japan, 1980.

"Flash Gordon is like a fairy tale set in a discothèque in the clouds. . . . There are no hidden themes in this comedy fantasy; everything is on the luscious surface."

—Pauline Kael, *The New Yorker*, May 1, 1981

While some may deride the song's silliness, no one can deny the song's staying power or infectiously fun nature. Empirical evidence has shown this writer that "Flash's Theme" is one of the best candidates of all of Queen's songs to start a drunken, spontaneous sing-along.

The songs on *Flash* aren't all bombast and extravagance. Several of the instrumentals—Taylor's "In The Space Capsule (The Love Theme)" and "The Ring (Hypnotic Seduction Of Dale)," in particular—are subtle and nuanced. Deacon's "Arboria (Planet Of The Tree Men)" sounds like funky beat-based art rock, similar to the songs on David Byrne and Brian Eno's *My Life In The Bush Of Ghosts*. However, Queen is all about its bigger-than-life sound, and "Battle Theme" and "The Wedding March" are perfect rock showcases for May's sense of drama and imperial pomp. May's underrated, album-ending "The Hero" is also a perfect anthemic counterweight to "Flash's Theme." Critics had often mistaken Queen's members' ostentatious personas as signs of egotism, but *Flash* is evidence that the bandmates were more than willing to sublimate their egos for a common artistic goal. *Flash* is undeniably a Queen record, and it's also apparent that Freddie and the rest of the boys were having a blast.

Creem writer Rick Johnson had written that Queen's albums "packed all the wallop of a wet teabag," but the catchy, powerful *Flash Gordon* hits more like one of Ming's planet-shattering death rays. *Flash* is a record that all Queen fans should cherish and that should not be ostracized either like the black sheep in the band's discography or, in this case, like an irradiated yellow one. ⚜

SNEAKY REVIEWS

QUEEN
FLASH GORDON SOUNDTRACK
(ELEKTRA)

JEFF BARRY ET AL.
THE IDOLMAKER SOUNDTRACK
(A&M)

BY THE MAD PECK & ROBOT A HULL

© MAD PECK STUDIOS 1981

Playing The Game

157

© The Mad Peck

Tour Dates

Jazz[1]

17.01.1979	Ernst-Merck Halle	Hamburg, FRG
18.01.1979	Ostseehalle	Kiel, FRG
20.01.1979	Stadthalle	Bremen, FRG
21.01.1979	Westfallenhalle	Dortmund, FRG
23.01.1979	Messesportspalace	Hanover, FRG
24.01.1979	Deutschlandhalle	Berlin, FRG
26–27.01.1979	Forest National	Brussels, BEL
29–30.01.1979	Ahoy Hall	Rotterdam, NLD
01.02.1979	Sporthalle	Cologne, FRG
02.02.1979	Festhalle	Frankfurt, FRG
04.02.1979	Hallenstadium	Zurich, CHE
06.02.1979	Dom Sportova	Zagreb, YUG
07.02.1979	Tivoli Halle	Ljubljana, YUG
10–11.02.1979	Rudi Sedlmayer Halle	Munich, FRG
13.02.1979	Sporthalle	Boblingen, FRG
15.02.1979	Saarlandhalle	Saarbrücken, FRG
17.02.1979	Palais Des Sports	Lyon, FRA
19–21.02.1979	Palacio De Deportes	Barcelona, ESP
23.02.1979	Pabellon De Real Madrid	Madrid, ESP
25.02.1979	Les Arenes	Poitiers, FRA
27–28.02.1979	Pavillon de Paris	Paris, FRA
01.03.1979	Pavillon de Paris	Paris, FRA
13–14.04.1979	Nippon Budokan	Tokyo, JPN
19–20.04.1979	Festival Hall	Osaka, JPN
21.04.1979	Practica Ethics Commemor. Hall	Kanazawa, JPN
23–25.04.1979	Nippon Budokan	Tokyo, JPN
27.04.1979	Central International Display	Kobe, JPN
28.04.1979	International Display	Nagoya, JPN
30.04.1979	Kyuden Kinen Taikukan	Fukuoka, JPN
01.05.1979	Kyuden Kinen Taikukan	Fukuoka, JPN
02.05.1979	Prefectural Athletic Association	Yamaguchi, JPN
05–06.05.1979	Makomani Ice Arena	Sapporo, JPN
18.08.1979	Ludwigsparkstadion	Saarbrücken, FRG

Crazy

22.11.1979	RDS Simmons Hall	Dublin, IRL
24.11.1979	National Exhibition Centre	Birmingham, GBR
26–27.11.1979	Apollo Theatre	Manchester, GBR
30.11.1979	The Apollo	Glasgow, GBR
01.12.1979	The Apollo	Glasgow, GBR
03–04.12.1979	City Hall	Newcastle, GBR
06–07.12.1979	Empire Theatre	Liverpool, GBR
09.12.1979	Hippodrome	Bristol, GBR
10–11.12.1979	Centre	Brighton, GBR
13.12.1979	Lyceum Ballroom	London, GBR
14.12.1979	Rainbow Theatre	London, GBR
17.12.1979	Purley Tiffany's	London, GBR
19.12.1979	Tottenham Mayfair	London, GBR
20.12.1979	Lewisham Odeon	London, GBR
22.12.1979	Alexandra Palace	London, GBR
26.12.1979[2]	Hammersmith Odeon	London, GBR

The Game

Date	Venue	City
30.06.1980	PNE Coliseum	Vancouver, CAN
01.07.1980	Coliseum	Seattle, WA
02.07.1980	Coliseum	Portland, WA
05.07.1980	Sports Arena	San Diego, CA
06.07.1980	Compton Terrace	Phoenix, AZ
08–09.07.1980	Forum	Inglewood, CA
11–12.07.1980	Forum	Inglewood, CA
13–14.07.1980	Coliseum	Oakland, CA
05.08.1980	Mid-South Coliseum	Memphis, TN
06.08.1980	Riverside Centroplex	Baton Rouge, LA
08.08.1980	Myriad	Oklahoma City, OK
09.08.1980	Reunion	Dallas, TX
10.08.1980	Summit	Houston, TX
12.08.1980	Omni	Atlanta, GA
13.08.1980	Coliseum	Charlotte, NC
14.08.1980	Coliseum	Greensboro, NC
16.08.1980	Civic Center	Charleston, SC
17.08.1980	Riverfront Coliseum	Cincinnati, OH
20.08.1980	Civic Center	Hartford, CT
22.08.1980	The Spectrum	Philadelphia, PA
23.08.1980	Civic Center	Baltimore, MD
24.08.1980	Civic Center	Pittsburgh, PA
26.08.1980	Civic Center	Providence, RI
27.08.1980	Spectrum	Portland, ME
29.08.1980	Forum	Montreal, CAN
30.08.1980	CNE	Toronto, CAN
31.08.1980	Convention Center	Rochester, NY
10.09.1980	Mecca	Milwaukee, WI
11.09.1980	Market Square Arena	Indianapolis, IN
12.09.1980	Kemper Arena	Kansas City, MO
13.09.1980	Civic Center	Omaha, NE
14.09.1980	Civic Center	St. Paul, MN
16.09.1980	Hilton Coliseum	Ames, IA
17.09.1980	Checkerdome	St. Louis, MO
19.09.1980	Rosemont Horizen	Rosemont, IL
20.09.1980	Joe Louis Arena	Detroit, MI
21.09.1980	Coliseum	Richfield, OH
23.09.1980	Civic Center	Glens Falls, NY
24.09.1980	War Memorial Auditorium	Syracuse, NY
26.09.1980	Garden	Boston, MA
28–30.09.1980	Madison Square Garden	New York, NY
23.11.1980	Hallenstadion	Zurich, CHE
25.11.1980	Le Bourget La Rotonde	Paris, FRA
26.11.1980	Sporthalle	Cologne, FRG
27.11.1980	Groenoordhallen	Leiden, NLD
29.11.1980	Grugahalle	Essen, FRG
30.11.1980	Deutschlandhalle	Berlin, FRG
01.12.1980	Stadthalle	Bremen, FRG
05–06.12.1980	National Exhibition Centre	Birmingham, GBR
08–10.12.1980	Wembley Arena	London, GBR
12–13.12.1980	Forest National	Brussels, BEL
14.12.1980	Festhalle	Frankfurt, FRG
16.12.1980	Hall Rhenus	Strasbourg, FRA
18.12.1980	Olympiahalle	Munich, FRG

Notes

1. European dates provided the material for the band's first live release, *Live Killers*.
2. Concerts for the People of Kampuchea.

Tour dates and tickets courtesy Martin Skala, QueenConcerts.com

7 UNDER PRESSURE

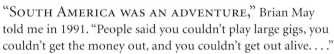

"SOUTH AMERICA WAS AN ADVENTURE," Brian May told me in 1991. "People said you couldn't play large gigs, you couldn't get the money out, and you couldn't get out alive. . . .'"

Jokey nervousness and rock 'n' roll rumor met military *junta* paranoia when Argentinean security police asked Queen's local representative, Jose Rota, what he would do if some miscreant got on stage mid-show, put a gun to Freddie Mercury's head, and ordered him to shout, "Viva, Perón!"? (Or maybe "Viva Perón, dear.") But Queen's advance guard of lawyer/business manager Jim Beach and tour organizer Gerry Stickells kept the project moving—in Brazil, Venezuela, and Mexico too. "Gerry achieves things which no one else can," said May. "Most people shout if things go wrong, but he walks in and says, 'Do we have a problem? Well, you do this for us, we'll do that for you'—and it's solved."

With South America pending, Queen enjoyed another Japanese jaunt: sixty thousand attending five sell-outs at the Budokan February 12–18, 1981, a motorcade to the premiere of *Flash Gordon*, and a Mercury shopping spree facilitated by department store Seibu closing whole floors so he could spend a fortune unimpeded by fans.

After that, Stickells had forty tons of gear flown from Japan to Argentina and more sent down from the United States. When the band arrived in Buenos Aires, they quickly discovered why all the effort was worthwhile. "We didn't really believe it when the local promoter said we could do football stadiums," said May. After all, their only immediate rock predecessors in the country, The Police, had played smaller indoor venues a couple of months earlier. But, on February 24, as they disembarked at Ezeiza International Airport, normal flight announcements on the PA were replaced with the band's hits.

Escorted by military police outriders and, often, armored troop carriers wherever they went, Queen felt both protected and edgy. "There were a lot of guns around and a tendency

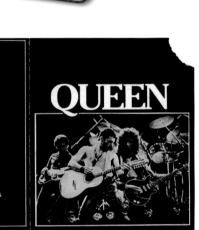

Courtesy Ferdinando Frega, Queenmuseum.com

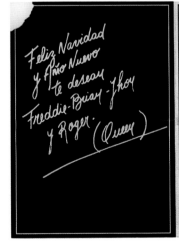

CLUB VELEZ SARSFIELD
SÁBADO 28
DIA ....
HORA ....

SECTOR **T**

Platea Norte
BAJA

FILA **4**   ASIENTO **33**

The band is introduced at the first South American show at the Vélez Sarsfield soccer stadium, Buenos Aires, February 28, 1981, on the South America Bites The Dust tour. Note the clock at the upper right: the show started at 11:30 p.m. © *Peter Hince*

Rock 'N' Roll Comics No. 4, Revolutionary Comics, June 1992.
Courtesy Jay Allen Sanford

The band takes their bows at the end of the show,
Budokan, Tokyo, February 16, 1981. © Peter Hince

Stick-on guest pass, Japan and South America
Bites The Dust tours, 1981.

QUEEN

PARCO QUEEN JAPAN TOUR '82

Courtesy Ferdinando Frega,
Queenmuseum.com

Overhead shot at end of show, *Hot
Space* tour, Seibu Lions Baseball Stadium,
Tokorozawa, November 3, 1982. Fred and
Roger are fighting over bunches of flowers to
throw into the audience. Peter Hince rigged a
camera into the rear lighting truss and fired it
by remote control. © *Peter Hince*

to overreact," said May. "One gig, Rosario I think [March 6], along the front of the stage there were guys with machine guns and we said that was a little bit much and got them taken away. I never saw any violence used, it was just implied."

However, the band felt at home onstage, at least, from the moment bandmembers stepped out in front of fifty-four thousand at Vélez Sarsfield stadium on February 28. "We thought maybe the tickets had sold on novelty, but the audience were true fans and they sang every word," said May. "The whole feeling was so electric, like they understood exactly what we were about. You could feel it surging out of them, that release."

Otherwise, history caught Queen at a strange moment. They met Argentina's soccer legend Diego Maradona, and May swapped a Union Jack T-shirt for the football star's national team shirt; during the 1986 World Cup, Maradona would perpetrate soccer's most infamous and successful act of cheating by deliberately handballing a goal that would allow Argentina to beat England 2–1. At the end of the three Buenos Aires shows, Argentinean and British flags were raised in fellowship; just over a year later, in April 1982, the bloody Falklands War between the two nations began. And then there was the matter of Queen's dinner with the president (or not).

Jorge Videla seized power in a 1976 coup d'état, establishing the *junta* that conducted the so-called "Dirty War" against its opponents, *Perónistas* and others, murdering thousands. In 1991, May told me Queen knew this made the tour "controversial" because "It wasn't long after all the massacres." But his recollection was of meeting President Roberto Viola— although Viola didn't replace Videla until March 29, three weeks after Queen left Argentina. Perhaps it was the president-in-waiting they dined with. May, genuine as always, added that Viola was "put up as someone who was going to moderate the violence" (but later he served time for his role in the *junta*'s atrocities).

Without apparent intra-band conflict, Taylor did refuse to attend the Videla (or Viola) dinner. He's quoted in Laura Jackson's *Queen: The Definitive Biography*: "I didn't want to meet [the president] because that would have been playing into their hands."

May's 1991 summing up suggested the enduring, well-meant naïveté about international politics which shortly landed the band in much greater difficulty: "People are people no matter what regime is on top of them, and we thought it was very important to play to those people at that time. You can't be a judge of things that have nothing to do with you."

Queen left Argentina with all their albums in the national Top 10 and "Love Of My Life" en route to a year on the singles chart.

Brazil, at least, offered no such conspicuous moral conundrums, only frustration and thrills. The Rio de Janeiro authorities refused Queen permission to play the biggest stadium in the world, the 200,000-capacity Maracanã, because they were not deemed to constitute the requisite "cultural" event. So the band flew to São Paulo and two triumphant shows—combined audience 251,000—at the Estádio do Morumbi (Mercury's performance fired up, according to Peter Freestone's *Freddie Mercury*, by the tempestuous termination of his latest romance, with bodybuilder Peter Morgan).

Looking back on this first leg of their South American venture, May said, "It was wonderful—and we got the money out." A cool $3.5 million, allegedly.

May 1981.

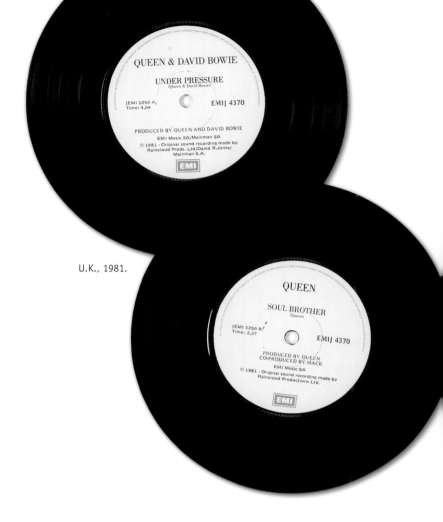

U.K., 1981.

Queen took a break, except that Taylor released *Fun In Space*, the first solo album by any bandmember. It did well enough domestically (No. 16). Asked about the next Queen album while doing his promotional interviews, he promised "Most of the songs are already there." Soon after the birth of May's second child, Louisa, on May 22, 1981, they repaired to their Montreux studio.

Almost immediately they struck lucky. Their engineer, Dave Richards, heard another of his regular clients, David Bowie, was in town and called him. "Dave asked me to come down to see what was happening," Bowie told Daryl Easlea for *Mojo Classic: Queen*. "Suddenly you're writing something together. It was totally spontaneous."

And a noisy twenty-four-hour clash of peacock egos. As "People On Streets" developed through the night into "Under Pressure," Bowie "took over the song lyrically," May told Mark Blake for *Mojo* in 2008. But the mixing provoked a "fierce battle," he said, probably not resolved until a further session in New York that October.

It was the first time Freestone, now redeployed from band wardrobe master to Mercury's personal assistant, had observed a Queen album built from the ground up. In his memoir, he noted Mercury's continuing openness to other people's ideas: "Freddie always liked input from the rest of the band. He never believed his was the only perfect way." Freestone even experienced Mercury's cooperative ways firsthand on a flight from New York to Montreux that summer. Mercury demanded paper and pen and started jotting down the lyrics to "Life Is Real (Song For Lennon)." He read them out, and Freestone's reactions steadily steered the first line away from "Cunt stains on my pillow" and then "Cum stains" to the more appropriate "Guilt stains."

September brought a lengthy, planned interruption to the *Hot Space* sessions. First, Mercury held a five-day thirty-fifth birthday party in his suite at the Berkshire Hotel, New York (perhaps not wishing to mess up the apartment he'd recently bought in the Sovereign Building on East 58th Street). Then the band rehearsed for South America, part two.

(continued on pg. 168)

Freddie at the christening of Mack's son, John-Frederick ("Little Freddie"), Munich, May 1982.

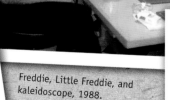
Freddie, Little Freddie, and kaleidoscope, 1988.

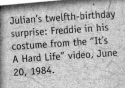
Julian's twelfth-birthday surprise: Freddie in his costume from the "It's A Hard Life" video, June 20, 1984.

Freddie and Little Freddie with birthday gift, February 16, 1985.

MACK LOOKS BACK

Words and Photos by Reinhold Mack

"DARLING, IT IS LOVELY OUTSIDE, WHERE CAN WE GO FOR A DRINK?"

Strolling arm in arm down the main concourse of Munich's English Garden with a man I just met was not entirely what I had envisioned for the first day of recording Queen. Concerned with who might be out there to spread the word of my "outing," it took some effort on my part to look cool and casual,

Freddie was wearing a Hawaiian shirt, matching short-shorts, and ballerina slippers. We caused quite a stir, and the entourage of about eight did nothing to lessen the impact on the natives.

How did I get there?

I was working with an artist in Los Angeles, or at least trying to, when I received a message: "Please call Musicland Studios in Munich—are you available for a recording session with Queen?" Alrighty then, that's something. Because of the nine-hour lag, my curiosity had plenty of time to increase tremendously. I conjured up a variety of scenarios, only to have them wiped blank come Munich office hours. Nobody seemed to have any idea of what I was talking about—certainly no such message was sent. Was the "message," and the fame and glory that might come with such a job, someone's cruel joke?

A few days passed, the message was forgotten. Then the same thing. Another message. I bought a plane ticket on the off chance that this was real. Stranger things had happened, and I could not wait for a prepaid ticket to appear out of nowhere.

Sixteen hours later I arrived at Musicland Studios. Deep down, I was prepared to be greeted by an empty studio or to walk in on the crooner du jour. Instead, a sea of flight cases and boxes:

Queen had arrived. A little chitchat and answers to where would I like equipment to be set up, a little paint, a few flowers, and we were ready to roll. But first, the aforementioned drink with Freddie.

Later that day, Roger and John came by to see the studio setup. Freddie picked up an acoustic guitar and, sensing my puzzled look, said, "Don't worry, darling, I can't play guitar. I just want to show the others something I was doodling with." It happened to be the opening chords to "Crazy Little Thing Called Love."

In a recording studio, it is always good to anticipate that, eventually, some recording will take place. My basic setup allowed me to lay down something for reference. When Freddie asked if I was ready to record, he liked my answer: "I can play back what you just did."

This piece of tape remained the basic track to "Crazy Little Thing." It also gave me a front-row seat to the balance of power, diplomacy, likes and dislikes, and various ways of writing within the band.

Brian is the most meticulous bandmember—in some cases, so meticulous that the details he sees become exponentially more important to him than the overall picture. He never forgets anything, and everything is personally quadruple-checked. Brian arrived a few days later. Freddie said: "I tell you, Brian is not going to like it."

Sure enough, one listen and the verdict was in: "I don't like it!" Having not yet learned that every note played was precious and must be preserved, I had kept the one take I felt was worth keeping, recording over the previous ones. On top of that,

John, Freddie, and the entire Mack family, Munich, May 1982.

25.10.1985

Felix's ninth birthday, Munich, 1985.

Christmas card from Freddie to Little Freddie, December 1986.

POST CARD

My dear F. M. Junior
Well What Can I Say!

財団
法人 栗田美術館 KURITA PORCELAIN MUSEUM

Just go for it —
My Love is With You
Always —
Your Godfather
Freddie
xxx

I committed the cardinal sin of asking Brian to try a Fender Telecaster and Fender amp on the song, for authenticity's sake. This remains an issue with Brian to this day. Having recorded the entirety of his musical career on his rightfully famous Red Special, it is as though this episode was a blemish on the instrument's otherwise perfect record, though my comment, "That was good! Check it out!" did turn the mood a little.

Freddie was the direct opposite. "Give me twenty minutes— you don't like it, I can change it." A waterfall of ideas with rivulets of thought cascading into a sea of brilliant alternatives. (That's borrowed from somewhere.)

Freddie appreciated the fact that he never had to wait to do something creative. He did not mind my "placeholders," like the backward piano in "Another One Bites The Dust," the guitar slide down in "Princes Of The Universe," the intro to "One Vision," or Fred Mandel's keyboard solo in "I Want To Break Free" years later. (Since nobody other than John and Mandel were around, I asked Mandel to put down a little something where the "real" solo should go, presumably to be replaced by Brian's guitar work. Mandel's keyboard is still there today.)

Freddie also had the talent to instigate discussions that could turn into fights, as well as the more important gift to give everybody the feeling that something had been achieved, and that it was high time to celebrate over a fabulous dinner.

Roger was always very likable, very well-dressed, and an exceptionally good drummer. His talent may, on occasion, have taken a backseat to an emerging hip thing called the "drum machine." To top it off, he had an unbelievable vocal timbre and

range. I take the blame for introducing drum loops ("Another One Bites The Dust" and a lot of *Hot Space*).

John is the walrus, with built-in funk, one eye on accounting, the other one on worrying. He also has to take the blame for the use of drum machines, not that there is anything wrong with it (*The Works* and *A Kind Of Magic*). Ours was a straightforward and honest relationship (John babysat the night I took my wife Ingrid to the maternity ward).

My not calling in the Shaman or doing a tap dance routine to shine a light on technical difficulties helped smooth the workflow, but over time, sessions turned more individualistic and more long-winded. Working on *Hot Space*, it came to the point that I said to Freddie, "It is quite possibly easier to conceive and give birth to a child than to get this record done." Little Freddie, my third child, was born a couple of weeks before *Hot Space* was put to bed (John and Freddie became his godfathers). Both were labors of love.

Little Freddie got the most out of it: a tremendously caring, concerned, and over-the-top generous godfather. That godfather, Freddie, enjoyed kids' birthdays, family dinners, and a home away from home.

Although quite controversial then, *Hot Space* was way ahead of its time. A whole disco revival followed suit. That pattern of Queen albums was typical: a really popular release followed by a more modern one. Nevertheless, the band managed to persevere for the greater good. Rock 'n' roll and glamour at their finest.

Good thing I bought that ticket.

(continued from pg. 165)

Big-picture malignant fate nailed them at once. With five shows scheduled for September 25–30 at Venezuela's Poliedro de Caracas, a Buckminster Fuller–inspired thirteen-thousand-seat dome, Queen arrived to find its schedule threatened because the country's "father of democracy," ex-President Rómulo Betancourt, was on his deathbed in a New York hospital. His demise would trigger immediate national mourning.

They managed three performances. On the 28th, a day off, Deacon, May, and Taylor appeared on a live TV pop show. Just as the host introduced them, one of the production crew rushed up and grabbed the mic to announce Betancourt's death and declare two minutes silence. This was truncated by a second announcement that the ex-president still clung to life after all. In fact, Betancourt did pass away later that night, so Queen's last two concerts never happened. Consequent closure of the airport at least gave their financial team time to secure their minimum guarantee for the missing shows.

Mexico rattled them even more. Following a successful night at the Monterrey Estádio Universitario on October 9, Queen played the forty-six-thousand-capacity Estádio Cuauhtémoc at Puebla on October 16–17. There, tequila-fueled fans bombarded them with a selection of missiles—shoes, bottles, batteries. Despite assurances that, locally, this indicated appreciation, after a second night under fire in Puebla, they ran for it, blowing smoke about "next stop Guadalajara!" while actually making for the airport (Queen) and the U.S. border (crew and equipment) with all haste.

"It was really hard," May recalled in 1991. "So much violence. Very uncontrolled. A tequila bottle hit me on the hand while I was playing. . . ." In 2008 Taylor told *Mojo*, "It was a miracle we made it." They vowed never to play Mexico again.

Back home, orderly business resumed. In November 1981, marking ten years since Deacon finalized the line-up, Queen released their *Greatest Hits* album, along with video and photographic collections, *Greatest Flix* and *Greatest Pix*, all three carrying cover portraits shot by Lord Snowden, former husband of the late Princess Margaret. The album reached No. 1 in the U.K. (becoming a chart fixture for more than 450 weeks) and No. 14 in America.

From December to March they consigned themselves to Musicland and Munich, where the fight for Queen's musical heart reached a crescendo. At one point even Deacon up and left with no debate, just a note stuck to his bass saying "Gone to Bali for 10 days."

In these skirmishes May nearly always ended up the loser; his guitar was little heard on *Hot Space*. He told Mark Blake for *Q* in 1998, "We were all going, mad. Even John could break out and be wonderfully unpredictable. It was such a competitive situation. Freddie was up for taking the music into different areas that Roger didn't think was part of our world . . . and on it went."

Crew and staff laminate, Gluttons For Punishment tour, Venezuela and Mexico, 1981. *Courtesy Peter Hince*

"I thought Queen was great music, very well-produced. It was a niche that needed to be filled. They had a very recognizable sound, very well-produced, and I love that. I heard it and thought, 'Man, if you can do that and be that good, this is what needs to happen. This is the direction music needs to go.' There were a lot of innovative people who picked up on Queen's music, so in that respect they were very influential on the rock scene in general."

—Mark Farner, Grand Funk Railroad

But the conflict obviously flowed in all directions. In Blake's 2008 *Mojo* interview, while Taylor agreed with May that *Hot Space* "went too far down the road" of disco/dance, May reckoned the "big difference" lay between him and the drummer, with Mercury appearing as peacemaker: "In Munich Roger and I had some incredible disagreements. Fred was always the one who would come along and mediate: 'Now, dears, we can do this *and* do that, so just fucking do it!' He was the best diplomat ever in the studio."

Despite all the intensity the others admitted to, and Mercury's own seismic shifts from problem-solving to tantrum-throwing, in the singer's early-'80s interviews he seemed to strive for offhandedness about Queen's music and even his own songwriting. Outside work the band would go their "separate ways," he said. He could write "to order, like a job" whenever "product" was required. It was "a bit of a joke" really. He used to tape his melodic ideas, but now "I just store them in my head," and "If they're worth remembering, I will; if I lose them, I lose them." Most notoriously, in June 1981, he told *Melody Maker* (interviewer not credited): "I think Queen songs are pure escapism. . . . I like

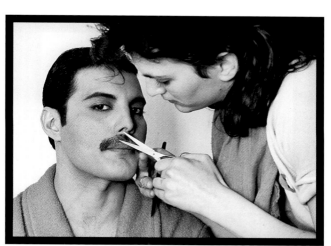

Grooming the 'stache, 1982. *Steve Wood/Hulton Archive/Getty Images*

to write songs for fun, for modern consumption. People can discard them like a used tissue [or 'a tampon,' as he sweetly put it in one radio interview]. Disposable pop, yes."

But May firmly believed those lines, and kindred remarks, should be understood as subterfuge, not candor. "That was just Fred being very clever," he told *Mojo* in 2008. "[It] stopped him having to talk about it. I knew Fred pretty damn well and there's a lot of depth in his songs. . . . [The only problem was] he didn't have the greatest attention span. He would peak, then you'd hear, 'Oh look, dear, I have to go now.'" The guitarist's comments suggest a significant change from the singer's earlier omnipresence on studio sessions.

When *Hot Space* emerged in May 1982, just after Queen signed with EMI for six more albums, disco-related tracks dominated, including "Under Pressure" (U.K. No. 1 already the previous November and U.S. No. 29 in January), "Body Language" (U.K. No. 25, U.S. No. 11, probably boosted by the Lennon tribute B-side and the banning of a sleeve featuring naked bodies), and "Staying Power" (flown to New York for Arif Mardin to overdub a horn arrangement).

Crew and staff laminate and luggage tag, *Hot Space* European tour, 1982. *Courtesy Peter Hince*

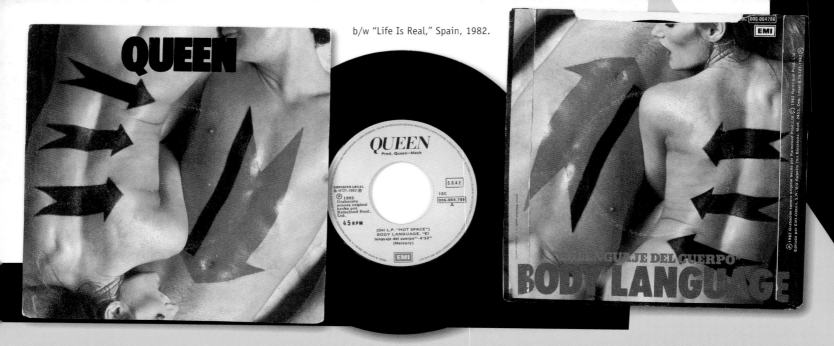

b/w "Life Is Real," Spain, 1982.

The album reached only No. 4 in the U.K. and 22 in America—a key downturn moment. Taylor and May never liked it much. Yet in 2007, producer Mack told izotope.com that *Hot Space* was his favorite work with Queen: "Very underrated, really hi-tech [although it was] still all analog." Michael Jackson is said to have declared its influence on *Thriller*, released in December 1982—not inconceivable given his previous interest in Queen.

Queen had a weird spring and early summer. Despite their wish to remain apolitical, they found themselves banned for "life" by Argentina's *junta* for topping the charts with "Under Pressure" during the Falklands War. And then their European tour—their first with an extra player, Morgan Fisher, ex–Mott

The Hoople, on keyboards—caught them in a rare state of musical turmoil. May feared loyal fans would be "shocked" by their shift to dance rhythms and resolutely thrust his guitar into a lot of those new hot spaces. "I wish we could have made some of those studio songs sound more like they did live," he told *Mojo* in 2008.

Closing their British dates at Milton Keynes Bowl on June 5, 1982, Mercury felt sufficiently out of kilter to play out his arguments with the band, reviewers, and fans on stage. "We're gonna do a few songs in the black/funk category, whatever you call it," he announced awkwardly. "That doesn't mean we've lost our rock 'n' roll feel, OK? I mean it's only a bloody record. People get so excited about these things."

Promoting *Hot Space* in North America, July 1982.
Ebet Roberts/Redferns Collection/Getty Images

SHOW #302

AIR: SEPTEMBER 25, 1982

HOST: CHEVY CHASE

SHOW RUNDOWN FOR AIR:

AIR

CHEVY COLD OPENING (L.A.)
MONTAGE (VT)
CHEVY BROKEN MONITOR (L.A.)
ART OPENING
JOE TAKES A BRIDE (w/ VT)
        Commercial #1

HINCKLEY
THE WEB (VT)
MYSTERY THEATRE /CHEVY SHARK (L.A.)
        Commercial #2

INTRO (L.A.)
QUEEN "Crazy Little Thing Called Love"
VIDEO VICTIMS (VT)
POPIEL
        Commercial #3
        N.I./Station Break

SNL NEWS (L.A. & Live)
        Commercial #4

LETTERMAN (w/ VT)
        Commercial #5

PTC CLUB
        Commercial #6
CHEVY - THE GOLDEN YEARS
        N.I./Station Break

SISKEL & EBERT
        Commercial #7

INTRO (L.A.)
QUEEN "Under Pressure"
        Commercial #8
        Berkshire Place

DON'S BACK
        Commercial #9

SHOW CLOSE (L.A. & Live)
GOODNIGHTS &
CREDITS

CUT:

MIME ROOM-MATE
TRASHING JERRY

BOTH: The last U.S. concert date, *Hot Space* tour, Forum, Inglewood, September 15, 1982.
© *Robert Matheu*

Hot Space

by Jeffrey Morgan

THIS IS IT, FIGHT FANS: the moment you've all been waiting for! Vegas touts have bet fat bundles of bucks that most of you machismo mustachioed Mustaphas turned to this page first just to see which unlucky pug drew the short straw and was dragged into the ring to tackle this, the most contentiously divisive long player in the entire history of Queen's decades-long heavyweight reign.

Well, get ready to take a back-catalog bath if you bet the farm expecting a first-round canvas-kissin' dive because not only did I *ask* for this undertaking, I'm more than eminently qualified to wax rhapsodic about it, seeing as how I was first on the front lines when I similarly assigned it to myself for review in the October 1982 issue of *Creem: America's Only Rock 'n' Roll Magazine.* You could look it up—but just in case you're still too 'luded out *to* look, I'll save you the trouble and reiterate for ya what I wrote over a quarter of a century ago:

> *Hot Space* is Queen at their high-techiest: a chrome 'n' glass altar paean to contemporary, vacuous lifestyles. Side one preaches a fairly cool gospel of dance 'n' sexuality which can be sung to any gender, age or species you choose to name, while side two is a moral exercise in "keep yourself alive" polemics, capped by the nth appearance on vinyl of "Under Pressure," the survivalists' anthem of the "ME" decade—a decade too late.
>
> This is (no snickering please) a *concept* album, whose central core suddenly becomes clear when one realizes how the last song on side one musically reiterates the previous melodic passages while its lyrics foreshadow those about to be heard on side two.

What a load of malarkey, right? Mebbe so, but I'm willing to wager that those two breathless paragraphs gave *Hot Space* far more respect than an unsympathetic listener like *you* ever did. Besides, any album that can so thoroughly

polarize a populace has got to have *something* going for it. I could go on, so I will.

The key to decoding this vexatious vinyl lies in its cover design—an ostensibly innocuous pattern that nevertheless was deemed important enough to merit its own special credit: *Album package concept by Freddie Mercury.* And although the untutored eye might very well wonder just exactly what kind of concept could possibly be divined in such a deceptively simple squaring off of four primary colors, the answer becomes apparent when one realizes that the cover of *Hot Space* is nothing less than Queen's enthrallment with the 1978 Milton Bradley game Simon made manifest.

Simon was an electronic musical memory game that became an immediate worldwide pop culture phenomenon that lasted well into the '80s. It's no coincidence that Milton Bradley was prescient enough to unveil the subliminally seductive Simon at New York's notorious discothèque Studio 54, which was disco's hedonistic headquarters for

rampant drug ingestion and promiscuous public sex—and it's no coincidence that pop culture vultures Queen latched onto that hip happening as an apposite means of expressing themselves both musically as well as stylistically.

Talk about playing the game: by cleverly crafting the cover of *Hot Space* as a Simonesque simulacrum that precisely duplicated the game's color coding and sequencing, Queen was signalling their use of Simon's capricious flashing lights and repetitive robotic tones as an aesthetic template for their own foray into the increasingly extreme hedonistic characteristics of the genre—a fearless infusion of buxom beats and overly endowed sounds coupled with an overtly socio-sexual subtext of calculated carnality.

Paradoxically, *Hot Space*'s one flaw is that it demurely holds back instead of lustfully going all the way. By prematurely pulling its punches and hedging its bets with a second-side serving of servile rock songs, the band strays from their salacious source material and opts instead to placate their audience by adhering to a public persona as preeminent pop purveyors rather than staying faithful to their true nature as aural carousers.

Of course we can only imagine what an unfettered and unabridged version of *Hot Space* would've sounded like; one that bawdily broke free from societal customs and held no truck nor trade with the staid conventions of classic rock. But let's be thankful for what we *do* have: a ribald record with a licentious legacy that rarely receives any respect; a debauched disc whose unfortunate fate can best be summarized in two words: No sympathizers. ⚜

Japan, 1982.

b/w "Put Out The Fire," U.S., 1982.
Courtesy Christian Lamping

Tour Dates

Japan 1981

12–13.02.1981	Nippon Budokan	Tokyo, JPN
16–18.02.1981	Nippon Budokan	Tokyo, JPN

South America Bites The Dust

28.02.1981	Estádio Jose Amalfitnai de Vélez Sarsfield	
	Buenos Aires, ARG	
01.03.1981	Estádio Jose Amalfitnai de Vélez Sarsfield	
	Buenos Aires, ARG	
04.03.1981	Estádio Jose Maria Minella	
	Mar del Plata, ARG	
06.03.1981	El Gigante de Arroyito (Estádio Rosario Central)	
	Rosario, ARG	
08.03.1981	Estádio Jose Amalfitnai de Vélez Sarsfield	
	Buenos Aires, ARG	
20–21.03.1981	Estádio do Morumbi	
	São Paulo, BRA	

Gluttons For Punishment

25–27.09.1981	Poliedro De Caracas	Caracas, VEN
09.10.1981	Estádio Universitario	Monterrey, MEX
17–18.10.1981	Estádio Cuauhtémoc	Puebla, MEX

We Will Rock You

24–25.11.1981[1]	Forum	Montreal, CAN

Hot Space

09.04.1982	Scandinavium	Gothenburg, SWE
10.04.1982	Ice Stadium	Stockholm, SWE
12.04.1982	Drammenshallen	Drammen, NOR
16–17.04.1982	Hallenstadion	Zurich, CHE
19–20.04.1982	Palais Des Sports	Paris, FRA
22–23.04.1982	Forest National	Brussels, BEL
24–25.04.1982	Groenoordhallen	Leiden, NLD
28.04.1982	Festhalle	Frankfurt, FRG
01.05.1982	Westfallenhalle	Dortmund, FRG
03.05.1982	Palais Des Sports	Paris, FRA

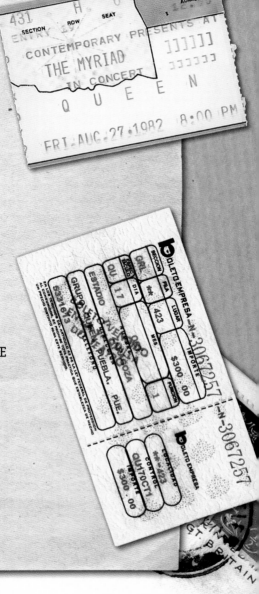

05.05.1982	Eilenriedehalle	Hanover, FRG
06–07.05.1982	Sporthalle	Cologne, FRG
09.05.1982	Carl-Diem Halle	Wurzburg, FRG
10.05.1982	Sporthalle	Boblingen, FRG
12–13.05.1982[2]	Stadthalle	Vienna, AUT
15.05.1982	Waldbuhne	Berlin, FRG
16.05.1982	Ernst-Merck Halle	Hamburg, FRG
18.05.1982	Eissporthalle	Kassel, FRG
21–22.05.1982	Olympiahalle	Munich, FRG
29.05.1982	Elland Road Football Stadium	Leeds, GBR
01–02.06.1982	Ingliston Showground	Edinburgh, GBR
05.06.1982[3]	Bowl	Milton Keynes, GBR
21.07.1982	Forum	Montreal, CAN
23.07.1982	Garden	Boston, MA
24.07.1982	The Spectrum	Philadelphia, PA
25.07.1982	Capital Centre	Washington, DC
27–28.07.1982	Madison Square Garden	New York, NY
31.07.1982	Coliseum	Richfield, OH
02–03.08.1982	Maple Leaf Gardens	Toronto, CAN
05.08.1982	Market Square Arena	Indianapolis, IN
06.08.1982	Joe Louis Arena	Detroit, MI
07.08.1982	Riverfront Coliseum	Cincinnati, OH
09.08.1982	Brendan Byrne Arena	East Rutherford, NJ
10.08.1982	Coliseum	New Haven, CT
13–14.08.1982	Poplar Creek Music Theater	Hoffman Estates, IL
15.08.1982	Civic Center	St. Paul, MN
19.08.1982	Mississippi Coast Coliseum	Biloxi, MS
20.08.1982	Summit	Houston, TX
21.08.1982	Reunion	Dallas, TX
24.08.1982	Omni	Atlanta, GA
27.08.1982	Myriad	Oklahoma City, OK
28.08.1982	Kemper Arena	Kansas City, MO
30.08.1982	McNichols Arena	Denver, CO
02.09.1982	Coliseum	Portland, OR
03.09.1982	Coliseum	Seattle, WA
04.09.1982	PNE Coliseum	Vancouver, CAN
07.09.1982	Coliseum	Oakland, CA
10.09.1982	Veteran's Memorial Coliseum	Phoenix, AZ
11–12.09.1982	Irvine Meadows	Irvine, CA
14–15.09.1982	Forum	Inglewood, CA
19–20.10.1982	Kyuden Auditorium	Fukuoka, JPN
24.10.1982	Hankyu Nishinomiya Stadium	Nishinomiya, JPN
26.10.1982	Kosusai Tenjijo	Nagoya, JPN
29.10.1982	Hokkaidoritso Sangyo	Sapporo, JPN
03.11.1982[4]	Seibu Lions Stadium	Tokorozawa, JPN

Notes

1. The shows that provided the material for the *Queen Rock Montreal* double-CD and DVD releases.

2–4. These shows, but principally the Milton Keynes date, of course, provided the material for the *Queen On Fire: Live At The Bowl* CD and DVD releases.

Tour dates and tickets courtesy Martin Skala, QueenConcerts.com

8 BREAK FREE

IT WASN'T MEANT TO BE THAT WAY, but on September 15, 1982, at the L.A. Forum in Inglewood, California, Queen played its last-ever concert in America. Longer-term responsibility lay with uncontrollable circumstance, but market forces started it. Queen had executed a hard-graft thirty-four-show tour to reinforce the standing *Jazz* and "Another One Bites The Dust" had won in North America. Then *Hot Space* stalled at No. 22 in the U.S. charts—a commercial damp squib and a rebuff to their ambitions.

Perhaps coincidentally, Mercury's conduct at the time seemed to symbolize the band's sense of drift away from America. While on the road Mercury broke up with his New Jersey boyfriend, Bill Reid. Then he quit his New York apartment, never to return. Further, over the coming months, his seething discontent at Queen's U.S. record label, Elektra, prompted the band to refuse to renew its deal; instead, Queen switched to its British record company EMI's North American wing, Capitol.

After another Japanese tour that fall, as one, Queen yawned. As Taylor said in one (unsourced) interview, "We got fed up and were lacking inspiration." Collectively, they admitted it and decided to take their first long break in nine years.

A lot of larking about ensued—one highlight, Taylor's arrest at the Monaco Grand Prix Formula One race and subsequent expulsion from the principality for reasons never specified. But soon—although this was definitely a rest, not a trial separation—Taylor (in Montreux), May (L.A.), and Mercury (Munich) all returned to the studio to record "solo."

Only Deacon spent most of their break at home—apart from a family trip to Switzerland, which detoured into playing some bass for Taylor. But while the bassist appeared steady and domestic, a 1985 interview with Martin Townsend of *The Hit* revealed his anguished frustration during Queen's nine-month

With Spike Edney, *The Works* tour, Wembley Arena, London, September 1984.
Phil Dent/Redferns Collection/Getty Images

John Deacon's Man Friday & Jive Junior collaboration with Robert Awhai, 7-inch, U.K., 1983.

"sabbatical" with both the band's development and his own limitations: "I need something to fill up my time, but I can't make a solo album because I can't sing. I mean basically I went spare, really, because we were doing so little. I got bored and actually quite depressed. . . ." When Mary Turner of Westwood 1 radio perceptively asked him whether this inability to sing left "a void" in his musical life, he replied, "Yes. It's awful. It's like being in a wheelchair because you can't actually express yourself in the way that you'd like to. . . . It's a handicap, a great handicap, in terms of writing songs."

Fortunately for him, the others missed working together too, and, given an offer of making the soundtrack to the movie of John Irving's novel *The Hotel New Hampshire*, Queen reconvened in mid-August 1983 in Los Angeles. After a band meeting, they flew Mack over from Munich and booked into the Record Plant.

However, the rush of enthusiasm didn't eliminate distractions. Peter Freestone wrote in his memoir that his employer plunged into the life of L.A.'s Boystown clubs, especially the Sunday-afternoon tea dances at Probe and Revolver. Away from all that, Mercury had one very unusual day writing songs with Michael Jackson, who invited him to his pre-Neverland mansion in Encino. The pair collaborated on three songs: "There Must Be More To Life Than This" (a Queen reject), "State Of Shock" (which Jackson later sang with Mick Jagger on The Jacksons' 1984 album *Victory*), and "Victory" (shelved, but maybe the source of an album title). Mercury concluded that his temporary writing partner was "a good lad."

After Mercury's birthday party in September, Queen decamped to Musicland in Munich once more and worked there until the new album's completion in January 1984. Meanwhile, May released his first solo single, "Starfleet," and a three-track "mini LP" *Starfleet Project*, notably featuring Eddie Van Halen; Deacon's fourth child, Joshua, arrived on December 13; and Mercury, who already had a boyfriend in Munich—restaurant owner Winnie Kirchberger—found a soulmate in German actress Barbara Valentin. A little later he told one interviewer, "Barbara and I have formed a bond that is stronger than anything I have had with a lover for the past six years" (unnamed web audio source).

SMOOTH COMPANY

WHEN I FIRST MET THE BAND in Boston on their first visit to the States in 1974, they were a very well-behaved lot: soft-spoken, mild-mannered, reserved (though not so much on stage). We went out to dinner after their show at the Orpheum in Boston, and I sat next to Freddie. As we stood at the table, he cast a furtive glance around the room, then unbuttoned his satin trousers and slid into his chair . . . his pants were too tight for him to sit comfortably. The whole band was quite serious and business-minded—they clearly wanted to make the most of their situation.

I first collaborated with members of the band while recording *Emotions In Motion* in 1982. Freddie and Roger were in New York and dropped by the Power Station, where Reinhold Mack (co-producer/engineer on *The Game*) and I were working. We had *Emotions* up, and Freddie immediately wanted to put down his heavy-breathing part. I've never seen anyone as spontaneously brilliant as Freddie Mercury. He had a wealth of free-flowing creativity. Roger came over to Munich while we were mixing and put on some well-suited harmonies.

Touring with the band in 1982 (the *Hot Space/ Emotions* tour) was a blast. The Queenies had loosened up considerably from the early days, and there was always a fair degree of merriment to be had. Those were excessive times, to say the least—we were always out to improve on the previous night's performance (both on and off the stage), and we managed to get pretty good at it.

On my next album, *Signs Of Life*, I coerced Brian into Capitol Studios in L.A. to put one of his signature solos on "(Another) 1984." Brian's a complete perfectionist and won't compromise his vision. I remember him putting all his bits together fairly quickly—to a point where I was pretty happy with it—and then reworking it endlessly to

ROCK ICON REFLECTS ON HIS COLLABORATIONS WITH FREDDIE AND QUEEN

By Billy Squier

get every nuance just so. I'm a bit of a perfectionist myself (no comments from those of you who know me), but I'd never seen anything like this. Needless to say, we got it. Brian has what I think is the most distinctive guitar sound ever, and he's a wonderful player.

The most memorable collaborations came with Freddie, when I was recording *Enough Is Enough* in London. We did two songs together. I'd pretty much finished "Love Is The Hero" when I played it for him at his house in Earls Court in spring 1986. As dawn broke, he sat down at his piano and threw off a new intro for the song that totally blew me away. I've never seen anything like it—it's a moment that's indelibly etched in my brain. Since we had no recording equipment at hand, it was up to me to remember what he'd done until I could get him down to the studio the following night to put it down properly. Capitol, fearful of image controversy, elected to

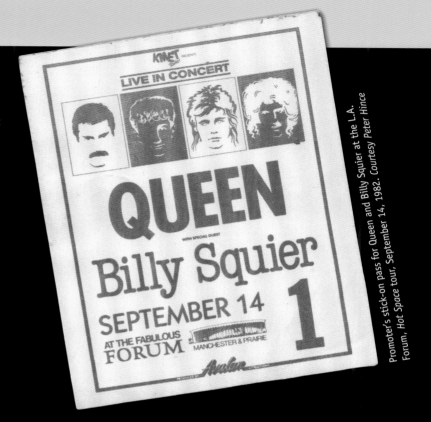

Promoter's stick-on pass for Queen and Billy Squier at the L.A. Forum, *Hot Space* tour, September 14, 1982. *Courtesy Peter Hince*

keep this mini masterpiece off of the album, but it does appear on my *Reach For The Sky* anthology and the Freddie Mercury box set. You can also hear Freddie and me duet throughout the body of the song.

"Lady With A Tenor Sax" was another spur-of-the-moment outburst. Freddie picked this title out of nowhere and threw down a bunch of scattered vocal lines in the studio. I then had the task of cobbling his (new) lyrics together and filling in the blanks. I wanted him to sing on the final, but he wouldn't have it: "You're a much better singer than I am," he said (oh, really?). My performance is inspired by his original guide vocal and words of encouragement. Freddie was magic to work with and a lot of fun just to be around. I miss him to this day.

Aside from the amount of raw talent in the band, Queen excelled because each member had a specific role to play and fulfilled it to the max. Everyone contributed as a songwriter. They had three lead singers who brought distinctly different attitudes to the songs they sang. They forged a unique collaborative vocal style. They had a sonic guitar presence that was unequaled and perhaps the most commanding frontman rock 'n' roll has ever seen. You don't get much better than that. ⚜

Budweiser & WMMS
— welcome —

QUEEN

WITH SPECIAL GUEST

Billy Squier

THIS SAT. JULY 31 8 P.M.

Coliseum
Tickets: $12.50 reserved. On sale now at the Coliseum & Ticketron.

PRODUCED BY Belkin
PRODUCTIONS

Break Free   179

Scene weekly, Cleveland, July 29–August 4, 1982.

Brian, loving L.A., with *Starfleet Project* co-conspirator Eddie Van Halen, circa 1983. *Ron Galella/WireImage/Getty Images*

Blake for *Mojo* in 2008, "The days drifted into the nights into this endless cycle." May said to Blake that, although he never took drugs, "Those later Munich days were lost in a haze of vodka," and "You end up emotionally distracted, trying to keep your life together away from the studio. I was married with two children by then, and it was a continual life-and-death battle to keep everything going."

Generally, it was left to Mercury, the one who really loved Munich, to haul those troubled husbands and fathers back into the rock 'n' roll mindset. Peter Hince, roadie and later photographer, wrote in *More Of The Real Life . . . Freddie Mercury*, "Anywhere and any time a Captain was required, it was always Freddie who fulfilled that role. He dragged it out of the others."

Despite all the stress, the music did the trick—except in America. After its release in January 1984, "Radio Ga Ga" reached No. 2 in the U.K., No. 1, it's reported, in nineteen other countries, and only No. 16 in the U.S. But for Queen it completed the cycle, in that all four members had now composed major hits. Titled *The Works* because they'd given everything they had—and maybe with a nod to a New York gay bar of that name—the new album went to No. 2 in the U.K., and No. 23 in the U.S. In April, "I Want To Break Free" made No. 3 in the U.K., Top 10s all over Europe and South America, and No. 45 in the U.S.

They "lost" America. In 1991, May argued that "Radio Ga Ga" got caught up in the record industry's payola "war," claiming it was blacked by corrupt independent pluggers who had come under attack from Capitol and other labels. Next came the "I Want To Break Free" video uproar. MTV and other stations banned it, or at least didn't show it because it featured Queen in drag with Mercury hamming it up in a leather miniskirt, false boobs, a wig, and his very own moustache.

While Queen toiled, the original inspiration for their return to the studio was snatched away when *Hotel New Hampshire* director Tony Richardson said he liked what they'd written, but he'd probably go with some classical music because it would be, well, cheaper. Still, the band salvaged a song triggered by and named after the film's catchphrase "Keep Passing The Open Windows" (meaning, don't jump).

Eventually the band put together some satisfying tracks, including Deacon's dance-beat anthem "I Want To Break Free," May's hard-rocker "Hammer To Fall," and Mercury/May's grand lament "Is This The World We Created?. . ." Before Christmas, though, they decided Taylor's synth-groover cum rabble-rouser "Radio Ga Ga" would make the killer first single they needed after *Hot Space*. They backed it with £110,000 worth of promo video featuring, at Mercury's suggestion following solo soundtrack work he'd been doing with Giorgio Moroder, a clip from Fritz Lang's silent 1927 sci-fi movie *Metropolis*. Taylor recalled in *Mojo Classic: Queen* in 2005, "I wrote 'Radio Ga Ga' after watching a lot of MTV in the States; it seemed to me there was far too much emphasis on a band's visual image and not enough on the music."

Still, amid all the creative work, Munich seemed always to exaggerate the band's self-destructive side. Taylor told Mark

QUEEN

Promo copy, b/w "Me Vuelvo Loco (I Go Crazy)," Argentina, 1984.

IT'S A HARD LIFE

I WANT TO BREAK FREE

The hostility puzzled Mercury. "It still makes me chuckle whenever I see it," he told BBC Radio 1 DJ Simon Bates in 1985. "For the first time in our lives we were just taking the mickey out of ourselves. But in America they said, 'What are my idols doing dressing up in frocks?'"

With no gigs until the summer, Mercury stayed in Munich to grind away at his solo album with Mack (and, incidentally, maintain his immunity to U.K. tax). But his friends were starting to worry about his "lifestyle." Freestone wrote that, in terms of drugs, Mercury "wouldn't touch anything" other than cocaine. But Lee Middleton, wife of his gay DJ and TV comedy star friend Kenny Everett, said in the TV documentary *When Freddie Mercury Met Kenny Everett* that it turned them into "monsters."

More important in the context of the times, AIDS—first reported by the U.S. Centers For Disease Control and Prevention in 1981 and given a name the following year—had become a matter of public alarm. And Mercury often boasted of having enormous amounts of casual sex throughout these years. As David Evans, a friend and co-editor of *More Of The Real Life . . . Freddie Mercury*, wrote, "Freddie certainly saw what was available, knew he could have whatever he wanted and went for it."

In *When Freddie Mercury Met Kenny Everett*, out gay BBC Radio 1 DJ Paul Gambaccini recounts how he returned from a harrowing visit to his native New York at about this time and, when he saw Mercury, asked him "whether he'd altered his behavior" because of AIDS: "He said with very theatrical arm gestures, 'My attitude is, Fuck it! I'm doing everything with everybody.'"

Roger Taylor's second solo album, *Strange Frontier*, released on June 25, 1984, carried an anti-nuclear-weapons theme—albeit "undirectly," as he put it, except for his cover of Bob Dylan's early protest song "Masters Of War." He told Jim Ladd of L.A. radio station KMET's *Innerview* he had joined the U.K.'s Campaign for Nuclear Disarmament (CND) and that, for ten years, he'd suffered a sporadic nightmare: "Being involved in a holocaust and trying to grab everybody I cared about." The album reached No. 30 in the U.K.

But the following month, Queen, obviously with Taylor's agreement, made the announcement that provoked the biggest controversy of their careers: they had scheduled a series of concerts for October in Sun City, Bophuthatswana, a "multiracial" resort in a South African "homeland" (semiautonomous area) set up by the country's apartheid system of racial segregation to attract high-rolling foreign visitors. Because of apartheid, the United Nations operated a cultural boycott against South Africa. In addition, since 1961, the U.K. Musicians' Union's policy had been that members—who included Queen—should not play in South Africa. Furthermore, the anti-apartheid campaign had widespread popular support.

June 1984.

Brian gives the Red Special a break and picks up a Telecaster on *The Works* tour, Wembley Arena, London, September 1984.
Phil Dent/Redferns Collection/Getty Images

Queen stood by the arguments they'd made regarding *junta*-period Argentina. After the announcement, May told Robin Smith of *Record Mirror*, "We've thought about the morals of it a lot. This band is not political, we are not out to make statements, we play to anybody who comes to listen."

Despite the political and media uproar, a twenty-three-date, eight-nation European tour passed off uneventfully, bar the installation of Spike Edney as regular touring keyboardist and Mercury hobbling on a knee injured in horseplay at the New York bar in Munich ("Some cunt kicked me," he explained to doctors).

They opened at the 6,230-capacity Sun City Superbowl on October 5—and stopped after fifteen minutes when Mercury's agonizing throat problem flared up. They missed five of the planned twelve shows. During the interruption, May accepted an invitation from some black musicians to attend an awards ceremony and festival eighty-five miles away in the Johannesburg township of Soweto, heart of the African National Congress movement to end apartheid. It wasn't quite like the Grammies. On an uncovered wooden platform in a field in the rain, May made the presentations and, moved by the welcome he received, vowed that Queen would come back some day and play for the Sowetans.

Aware that their Sun City audiences had been racially mixed but exclusively rich, Queen looked for a practical contribution they could make to the local people. They released a South Africa–only live album with all royalties and profits going to Bophuthatswana's Kutlwanong school for deaf and blind children.

When the band got home, facing possible expulsion from the union—which would have limited their radio and TV appearances internationally—May took responsibility for attending a meeting to state their case. "You have to respect the community you live in," he reflected to this writer in 1991, a

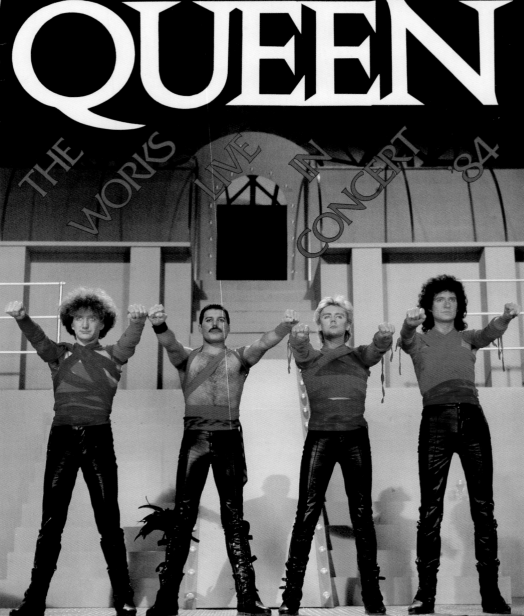

Crew and staff luggage tag, *The Works* European tour, 1984.
Courtesy Peter Hince

Ticket stub, Sportspalace, Milan,
September 15, 1984. *Courtesy
Ferdinando Frega, Queenmuseum.com*

PRESENTED BY FRITZ RAU & HERMJO KLEIN

QUEEN   THE WORKS

Aktuelle LP/MC
und Compact-Disc
»THE WORKS«
im Vertrieb der
Emi-Electrola

ELECTROLA

**Donnerstag 20 Uhr
27. September '84
Stuttgart
Schleyerhalle**

**27. Sept.
'84**

Karten an allen bekannten Vorverkaufsstellen.
Telefonische Kartenbestellungen: 0711-290349

Örtliche Durchführung: SKS Erwin Russ KG
Tourneeleitung: Lippmann + Rau GmbH + Co., KG

Stick-on guest pass, *The Works* European tour, 1984.
Courtesy Ferdinando Frega, Queenmuseum.com

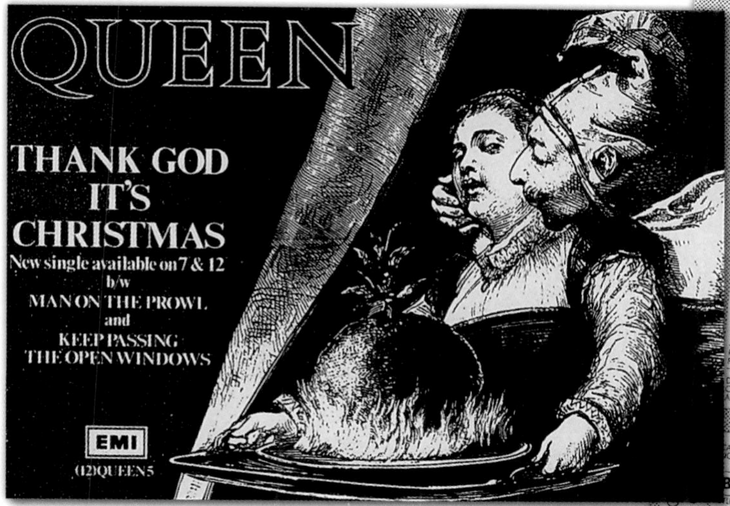

QUEEN

THANK GOD IT'S CHRISTMAS

New single available on 7 & 12
b/w
MAN ON THE PROWL
and
KEEP PASSING
THE OPEN WINDOWS

EMI
(12)QUEEN 5

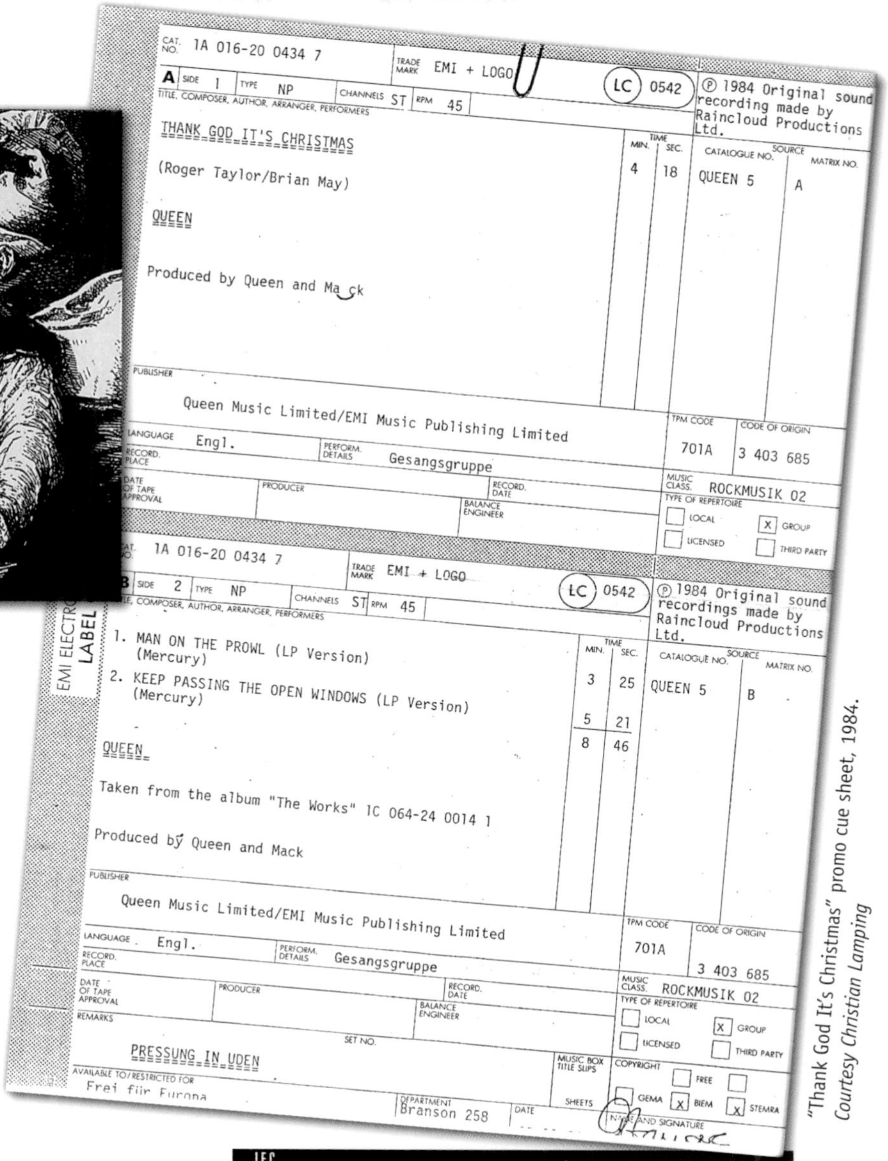

year after Nelson Mandela's release from Robben Island prison and three years before the elections that ended apartheid. "We broke one of their rules, there's no doubt about that, but I think we broke that rule with the best motives in mind. So I got up and made a speech to them. Afterwards, lots of members came up and said, 'Thanks, we understand now—but we still have to fine you because it's in the rules.' We have totally clear consciences, but I'm sure a lot of people still think we're fascist pigs. . . . It's a long story and it's one I feel very strongly about. Every time you get up and say what you believe you get into trouble because people misinterpret it.

"We are totally against apartheid and feel very strongly about it. At the time, having carefully considered all the pros and cons for a year, we decided we'd do more to achieve the end of apartheid by going than by staying away. A lot of people don't agree with that. But, having done it, I'm inclined to think that is the case because by being there we were able to say what we thought. We actually got quoted in South African newspapers saying apartheid should be ended—which was unusual—and we made contact with musicians there, all of whom said, 'Thanks for coming. Everyone ostracizes us because they think we're part of the system when we're not.'"

Queen must have wondered whether their South African venture caused their omission that December from Bob Geldof's Band Aid, whose U.K. single "Do They Know It's Christmas?" raised millions to relieve famine in Ethiopia. The star-studded cast included Bono, Sting, and George Michael, but Queen made light of it. Mercury told Robin Smith of *Record Mirror*, "I would have loved to have been on the record, but I only heard about it when I was in Germany. I don't know if they would have had me anyway, because I'm a bit old. I'm just an old slag who gets up every morning, scratches his head and wonders what he wants to fuck."

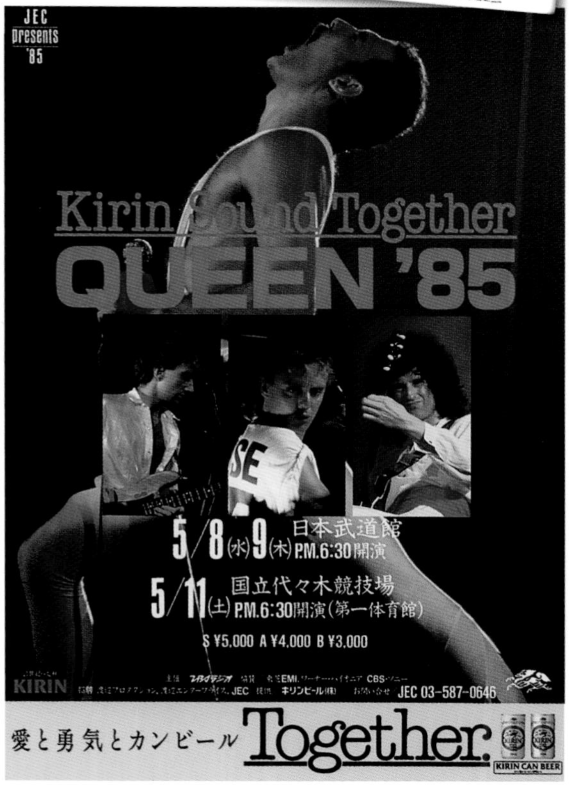

Handbill, *The Works* tour, Budokan and Yoyogi Taiikukan, Tokyo, May 8–9 and 11, 1985.

b/w "Rotwang's Party (Robot Dance)," Japan, 1984.

Promo copy, U.S., 1985.
Courtesy Christian Lamping

Promo copy, U.S., 1985.
Courtesy Christian Lamping

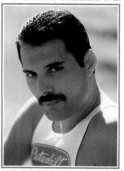

Japan, 1985.

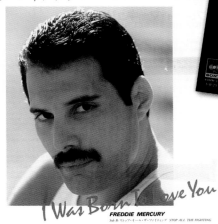

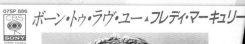

Japan, 1985.

b/w "She Blows Hot And Cold," 1985.

Promo copy, U.S., 1985.
Courtesy Christian Lamping

Freddie sports falsies, Barra da Tijuca (Rock in Rio), Rio de Janeiro, January 11, 1985.
Dave Hogan/Getty Images

David Bowie chats with Roger and Brian while Bob Geldof has a word with Prince Charles. Live Aid, Wembley Stadium, London, July 13, 1985.
Dave Hogan/Hulton Archive/Getty Images

"Live Aid turned our whole world upside down."

—JOHN DEACON

A United Nations blacklisting for boycott-busting did little to hamper the band's international activities. In January 1985 in Rio, Queen played the world's biggest-ever rock festival. The site, Barra da Tijuca, held 250,000 a night for ten concerts with Queen, George Benson, Rod Stewart, AC/DC, and Yes headlining two each.

To their astonishment, Queen sparked a fresh political flare-up on its first night, January 12. The set went swimmingly until the encores. While, in Europe, convivial hilarity had been the only reaction to Mercury wearing a wig and falsies for "I Want To Break Free," Rio, on the other hand, turned nasty and threw stones. Realizing it was something to do with the costume, Mercury ran to the side of the stage, whipped it off, and dashed back

LIVE AID

the Global Jukebox

WEMBLEY STADIUM LONDON · J.F.K. STADIUM PHILADELPHIA
JULY 13th 1985

WEMBLEY STADIUM LONDON	NIK KERSHAW	THE WHO	PHIL COLLINS	MADONNA	LIONEL RICHIE
ADAM ANT	PAUL McCARTNEY	PAUL YOUNG	CROSBY, STILLS AND NASH	PAT METHENY	DAVID RUFFIN
BOOMTOWN RATS	ALISON MOYET		DURAN DURAN	BILLY OCEAN	SANTANA
DAVID BOWIE	QUEEN		BOB DYLAN	OZZY OSBOURNE	SIMPLE MINDS
PHIL COLLINS	SADE	J.F.K. STADIUM PHILADELPHIA	FOUR TOPS	JIMMY PAGE	RICK SPRINGFIELD
ELVIS COSTELLO	SPANDAU BALLET	BRYAN ADAMS	HALL AND OATES	TEDDY PENDERGRASS	ROD STEWART
DIRE STRAITS	STATUS QUO	ASHFORD AND SIMPSON	THE HOOTERS	TOM PETTY AND THE	TEARS FOR FEARS
BRYAN FERRY	STYLE COUNCIL	JOAN BAEZ	MICK JAGGER	HEARTBREAKERS	THOMPSON TWINS
ELTON JOHN	STING	BEACH BOYS	JUDAS PRIEST	ROBERT PLANT	TINA TURNER
HOWARD JONES	U2	BLACK SABBATH	EDDIE KENDRICK	POWER STATION	NEIL YOUNG
	ULTRAVOX	THE CARS	PATTI LABELLE	THE PRETENDERS	
	WHAM!	ERIC CLAPTON	KENNY LOGGINS	REO SPEEDWAGON	

Live Aid, Wembley Stadium, London, July 13, 1985. *Popperfoto/Getty Images*

for the next chorus. But afterward, according to Iron Maiden singer Bruce Dickinson, as quoted in Laura Jackson's *Queen: The Definitive Biography*, "[Freddie] broke down in tears, he just had no idea why the audience reacted like they did."

Mercury was still expressing bafflement the following day when he talked to *Record Mirror* (interviewer unknown): "I don't know why they got so excited about me dressing up as a woman. There are lots of transvestites here." Somebody eventually explained to Queen that in South America the hook-line title had established "I Want To Break Free" as an anti-dictatorship anthem—delivering it in drag looked like mockery of passionately held aspirations. Remaining apolitical was proving quite a challenge.

 "They were absolutely the best band on the day, whatever your personal preference. They played best, they had the best sound, they got the global jukebox idea exactly."

—Bob Geldof

With a couple of months off, Deacon bought a Porsche, crashed it, and lost his driving license, while Taylor, after a few relatively obscure excursions into producing other artists, scored a couple of hits with popular British actor Jimmy Nail's cover of Rose Royce's "Love Don't Live Here Anymore" (U.K. No. 3 that April) and ex-Undertones singer Feargal Sharkey's "Loving You" (No. 23, June).

Break Free

Meanwhile, Mercury was going through some painful reflections about stardom and his personal life. "It was awe-inspiring and mind-boggling to be up there [in Rio] with all those people in the palm of your hand," he told an uncredited interviewer. "But the other side of the coin is that I must have been the loneliest person there. . . . I don't want people to think, 'Poor old Freddie,' because I can deal with it. But I'm so powerful on stage that I seem to have created a monster. . . . No one loves the real me inside. They're all in love with my stardom." He went on to talk about his relationship with his ex-girlfriend Mary Austin—"I don't feel jealous of her lovers. . . . We look after each other and that's a wonderful form of love"—and how he'd already left "the vast bulk" of his estate to her (with lesser bequests to his cats and his parents).

Despite his dismissal of Paul Gambaccini's AIDS alarm bell, it seemed that, as he approached forty, Mercury was considering some lifestyle adjustments. Perhaps not surprising, then, that when he got talking to Jim Hutton, then a barber at the Savoy Hotel, he began his most durable, as well as his final, gay relationship (even though he offended Hutton with his rather coarse chat-up opener, "How big's your dick?"). They got together at London club Heaven on March 23, 1985—Hutton's memoir, *Mercury And Me*, is certain about the date.

While Queen toured New Zealand and Australia during April, skirting a few anti-apartheid demonstrations en route, Mercury's solo material finally emerged. A one-off single called "Love Kills," recorded with Moroder for the *Metropolis* soundtrack, had reached the U.K. Top 10 the previous September, but in April the single "I Was Born To Love You" preceded his *Mr. Bad Guy* album. A combination of dance and romantic ballads—in a voice he'd deliberately made huskier by working through forty cigarettes a day, he said—it hit No. 6 in the U.K. Its failure to chart in America seemed predictable, given that Mercury called it "an extension of *Hot Space*."

But a sense of same-old same-old still hung about Queen. They needed new impetus. They had no idea it would come from Bob Geldof. He first called them in Australia. He asked for Spike Edney, who had done a stint with Geldof's Boomtown Rats, and requested he sound out the band about playing this huge concert for Ethiopia he was trying to organize. Queen said it sounded "pie in the sky." Geldof kept on chasing. He finally nailed them when one of his legendarily rude rants, addressed to Queen's manager Jim Beach, closed with, "Tell the old faggot it's gonna be the biggest thing that ever happened!"

Mercury liked his style and so did May, who recalled in 1991, "Geldof said there isn't a penny of this going anywhere else but to the people who need it and we were convinced. Exceptional guy. Doesn't take no for an answer from anyone. Passion such as that has to be rewarded."

Being Queen, they wanted to ensure they didn't go unrewarded either. In his Mercury biography *The Show Must Go On*, Rick Sky recalled Taylor saying the night before the gig, "It's a wonderful cause . . . but make no mistake—we're doing it for our own glory as well."

Although unpaid, like every other act, and with only a twenty-minute spot to fill, Queen hired the Shaw Theatre, London, for the typical three days of rehearsals they would have undertaken before a full tour. "We put together a show that made sense," said May. "Geldof said to us, 'It's a jukebox, play the hits.' So that's what we did, potted versions of the hits. It was a challenge because that was the first time we'd done a gig without our own lights and sound gear. We were naked. [We had] none of the props we thought we needed. It was a test."

On July 13, 1985, some minutes after 6 p.m. U.K. time, and at the very moment when U.S. TV switched to the international feed, Queen strode out in front of the seventy-five thousand at Wembley Stadium. A gently smiling Mercury, workmanlike in singlet, jeans, and boxing boots, plonked himself on the piano stool and caressed the opening notes of "Bohemian Rhapsody" to begin twenty minutes fifty-six seconds of what many still believe to have been the most powerful, concise, not to mention globe-bestriding rock set ever played: "Bohemian Rhapsody," "Radio Ga Ga," "Hammer To Fall," "Crazy Little Thing Called Love," "We Will Rock You," and "We Are The Champions." Mercury even had time for forty-five seconds of "ayoayo" call and response with the crowd.

Back home in Feltham, Middlesex, Bomi Bulsara turned from the TV to his wife, Jer, and said, "Our boy's done it" (Tim Teeman interview with Mrs. Bulsara, *The Times*, 2006). Backstage, Elton John ran to Queen's dressing room and yelled

THE THEME FROM BIGGLES · THE MOVIE

NO TURNING BACK

PERFORMED BY
THE IMMORTALS
FEATURING
ROBERT AHWAI · JOHN DEACON · LENNY ZAKATEK

MCAT 1057

that the band had stolen the show. Geldof's been saying it to anyone who asked ever since. Nobody disagreed.

Why? Taylor raised a sneaky technical point, talking to *Mojo*'s David Thomas in 1999: "We sent our brilliant engineer to check the system so he set all the limiters for us. We were louder than anyone else at Live Aid." But May, in 1991, gave all credit to their frontman: "Freddie is the kind of person who rises to the occasion. The rest of us played OK, but Freddie took it to another level. It wasn't just Queen fans. He connected with everyone."

Even stolid Deacon fell into raptures, talking to the *Daily Star*: "Live Aid turned our world upside down. Before, we'd promised ourselves a good long rest—no touring, no work, no band. Queen was rejuvenated by that wonderful day. We'd all been getting a bit tired. Jaded. Now we're bursting with enthusiasm and ideas." (Incidentally, when the band formally met Prince Charles and Princess Diana at Live Aid, Deacon had fielded a substitute, his roadie Spider, because he was "too nervous.")

At first, as their catalog sales soared in the aftermath of the global telecast, this fresh vigor lacked a collective purpose. Mercury immersed himself in Munich again, May tinkered with his solo album, while Taylor tried more production work and, with Deacon, played on a couple of Elton John tracks.

Then Australian movie director Russell Mulcahy pulled them together, asking whether they would record some music for the soundtrack for his *Highlander* movie about an immortal hero played by Christophe Lambert. The invitation spurred them into a series of *Highlander*-themed songs, four of which made it to Queen's next album: "Gimme The Prize," "Don't Lose Your Head," "Princes Of The Universe," and "Who Wants To Live Forever" (which May came up with while driving home from watching some rushes in January 1986). With this basis for a new Queen album—which they worked on in London and Munich from September 1985 to April 1986—Taylor again came up with a song they all immediately wanted to release as a single: "One Vision" hit No. 7 in the U.K. and 61 in America.

But even Live Aid couldn't make everyone love them. "One Vision" triggered some resentment that its fist-pumping pleas for "one god" and "one worldwide vision" somehow exploited the message of Live Aid. Nothing much to do with it, said Taylor; he'd drawn inspiration from way back, namely Martin Luther King Jr.'s 1963 speech from the steps of the Lincoln Memorial in Washington, D.C., hence the line "I had a dream."

The niggles continued, though. As part of their appeal to be removed from the UN blacklist, they had to make a public promise not to play in apartheid South Africa again. And with Mercury moving back from Munich to live full-time at Garden Lodge, the tabloids began to publish the first rumors that he had tested positive for HIV. He hadn't, but as Deacon sighed to *The Hit*'s Martin Townsend, "If you say no, then it becomes 'So and so denies, etc.'—I mean, they can twist it any way they want. . . ." Still, at the premiere of his friend Dave Clark's musical *Time*, Mercury was uninhibited enough in the public gaze to take over an usherette's ice cream tray at the intermission and walk around throwing her wares to, or at, anyone who called out.

Queen felt rather good. The band's long spell of internal struggle and strife seemed to have faded away. In March, the title track "A Kind Of Magic" hit U.K. No. 3 and topped the chart in thirty-five countries (not America, of course, where it faded at No. 42). The album, released in June, displayed the band's familiar hard-rock-to-disco scope but added the grand yet touching orchestrations of "Who Wants To Live Forever" and the fetching Supremes pastiche, "Pain Is So Close To Pleasure" (co-written by Mercury and Deacon).

The summer looked promising: a sold-out European tour coming up, *A Kind Of Magic* hitting No. 1 at home, and Wembley Stadium sold out on their own—twice over. ♛

Break Free

191

The Works
by Stephen Dalton

Queen's eleventh studio album remains an unsurpassed peak among the band's 1980s releases, creatively if not commercially. Made in the aftermath of their ill-fated disco-funk experiment *Hot Space* and a change of record label, *The Works* heralded a partial return to the heavy-rock sound of classic Queen. But it also offered a rich and eclectic musical mix, prominently showcasing the synthesizers and drum machines that came to define the band's later, more pop-friendly sound.

It may have failed to reverse Queen's declining U.S. profile, but *The Works* became a chart-topping success across Europe and beyond. Remarkably, all nine album tracks were released as singles or B-sides. Polished and emphatically modern in its sound and packaging, this was the record with which these revitalized 1970s veterans went head to head with the new generation of post-punk superstars, including U2, The Police, and Duran Duran.

A key theme of *The Works* is the battle between man and machine, soul and science. This subtext is mirrored musically in the mix of traditional guitar numbers with synthesizer-led songs, and also made lyrically explicit in the album's centerpiece track, "Machines (Back To Humans)." Deploying the jargon of home computing, fresh at the time but somewhat quaint today, the song's narrator rails against an increasingly mechanized world: "When the machines take over/It ain't no place for rock 'n' roll."

But the finest expression of this man-machine theme on *The Works* is unquestionably "Radio Ga Ga," drummer Roger Taylor's misty-eyed eulogy for the bygone wireless age. Rumbling along on a solid chassis of preprogrammed beats and throbbing synthesizers, this heavily electronic track is the closest that Queen ever came to the gleaming retro-futurism of Kraftwerk. But there is nothing robotic about Freddie Mercury's soaring, heart-bursting vocal or Brian May's wistful, vapor-trail guitar licks.

Taylor wrote "Radio Ga Ga" as a critical commentary on the growing dominance of MTV and video-led pop culture—a rich irony, given that Queen were early pioneers of the rock promo. And even more ironic considering the band's lavish

clip for this single, which incorporated segments of Fritz's Lang's 1927 science-fiction classic *Metropolis*, helped turn the song into a worldwide smash.

Bass guitarist John Deacon's sole songwriting contribution to the album, "I Want To Break Free," became another international hit. Built around an infectiously simple, stuttering rhythmic refrain, Deacon's escapist fantasy is graced with an octave-vaulting performance from Mercury and a striking synthesizer solo, which May later adapted for guitar to play live.

The memorable video for "I Want To Break Free," featuring all four bandmembers in drag, was intended as a parody of the famously drab British TV soap opera *Coronation Street*, but the sight of Freddie Mercury as a butch desperate housewife, years before his sexuality became full public knowledge, did not play well with MTV or Queen's more conservative fans. Indeed, this mildly risqué clip was later blamed for the album's lukewarm U.S. reception.

All the same, fans of Queen's muscular, adrenaline-pumped guitar sound were not short-changed by *The Works*. May's stomping "Tear It Up" is a ballsy blues-rock crowd-pleaser—routine ingredients, but it still gets the pulse racing. His only other solo composition on the album, "Hammer To Fall," is a full-fledged powerhouse anthem packed with sky-punching, sing-along lyrics. Fantastic stuff.

Equally impressive, Mercury's "It's A Hard Life" is a roaringly romantic power ballad reflecting on the strains and pains of long-term relationships. Ablaze with fiery guitar riffs and operatic orchestration, both of these mighty mini-epics can stand alongside "Bohemian Rhapsody" or "We Are The Champions" in the pantheon of all-time Queen classics.

All squeezed into a lean thirty-seven minutes, even the lesser tracks on *The Works* never feel surplus to requirements. Mercury's "Man On The Prowl" marks another of the singer's piano-driven pastiches of vintage 1950s rock 'n' roll, while "Keep Passing The Open Windows" is a wry number originally written for an aborted soundtrack to the movie version of John Irving's *Hotel New Hampshire*. Both are pleasant enough.

The soul-searching ballad "Is This The World We Created?" the only joint credit for Mercury and May, acts as a kind of bittersweet coda to this compact, hit-packed album. After *The Works*, Queen's final act became a sad catalog of creeping sickness and slow decline. But in 1984, with a newly modernized pop-rock sound and the triumph of Live Aid looming, they seemed almost invincible. ⚜

Korea, 1984.

b/w "Tear It Up," U.S., 1984 (withdrawn sleeve).
Courtesy Ferdinando Frega, Queenmuseum.com

A Kind Of Magic
by Sylvie Simmons

Sixty-three weeks on the U.K. chart and a string of hit singles— not bad at all for an album that started out as a hodgepodge of songs written for two different movie soundtracks and a couple of one-off tracks. Or, for that matter, for an album by a band that, according to the press, was breaking up—allegations that Freddie Mercury countered during Queen's July 1986 Wembley Stadium concert, a month after the album's release, by pointing at his butt.

Whatever might have been going on behind the scenes, it certainly seemed like the fairy dust that had hung over Queen's triumphant Live Aid appearance was still doing its job. Then again, it didn't hurt that Queen came up with so many memorable new songs for the album, including "One Vision," "Who Wants To Live Forever," and "Friends Will Be Friends."

It was their experience playing Live Aid in July 1985 that lured bandmembers from their various side projects and back into the studio to record a new song before the year was out. "One Vision," a rousing hard-rock anthem with the kind of Utopian lyrics you'd expect Bob Geldof's charity extravaganza to inspire. There are some daft lyrics too, about clams and fried chicken, and a dystopian, death metal–style vocal intro, but all in all it's stirring stuff, archetypically Queen. (A bit of a conundrum, then, that it should end up on the soundtrack to *Iron Eagle*, a Hollywood action movie about a hot-shot teenage fighter pilot—nothing to do whatsoever with feeding the world.)

Released as a single in November 1985, "One Vision" became the first hit from the album before there even *was* an album. In fact bandmembers were busy writing songs for *Highlander*, a movie about an immortal Scottish warrior who time-travels from the Middle Ages to swordfight in modern-day New York. Their work on the soundtrack was at the personal request of director Russell Mulcahy, a Queen fan. The band ended up writing everything, bar the orchestral score.

Six of the *Highlander* songs landed on *A Kind Of Magic*: Roger Taylor's title track, a mix of brooding synth rock and flamboyant pop, and "Don't Lose Your Head," with backing vocals by singer-songwriter Joan Armatrading; Brian May's

dark, full-on, heavy-metal "Gimme The Prize (Kurgan's Theme)" (Kurgan being the movie's baddie) and, at the other extreme, the haunting ballad, "Who Wants To Live Forever"; John Deacon's down-tempo, orchestral-pop "One Year Of Love"; and Freddie Mercury's dense, dramatic heavy rocker "Princes Of The Universe."

Also included were two non-soundtrack songs. "Friends Will Be Friends" is the kind of rousing piano anthem Queen could do in their sleep. "Pain Is So Close To Pleasure," though, is highly atypical—so Motown-esque that Freddie sounds like he has a side job with The Supremes.

A Kind Of Magic shot to the top of the U.K. charts, Queen's first new No. 1 album since 1980's *The Game*. Why the band didn't simply release a *Highlander* soundtrack album and have done with it, you'll have to ask them. It could be that, after Live Aid, they felt they had nothing left to prove. So often disparaged by critics, Queen had proved that day that they could do whatever they wanted, however they wanted to do it, and have the world in the palms of their hands. ⚜

b/w "Blurred Vision," Australia, 1985.

"Extended Version" b/w "Friends Will Be Friends" and "Gimme The Prize (Kurgan's Theme)," 1986.

From the film *Highlander*: b/w "A Dozen Red Roses For My Darling," 1986.

Tour Dates

The Works

24.08.1984	Forest National	Brussels, BEL
28–29.08.1984	RDS Simmons Hall	Dublin, IRL
31.08.1984	National Exhibition Centre	Birmingham, GBR
01–02.09.1984	National Exhibition Centre	Birmingham, GBR
04–05.09.1984	Wembley Arena	London, GBR
07–08.09.1984	Wembley Arena	London, GBR
11.09.1984	Westfallenhalle	Dortmund, FRG
14–15.09.1984	Sportspalace	Milan, ITA
16.09.1984	Olympiahalle	Munich, FRG
18.09.1984	Palais Omnisports de Bercy	Paris, FRA
20.09.1984	Groenoordhallen	Leiden, NLD
21.09.1984	Forest National	Brussels, BEL
22.09.1984	Europahalle	Hanover, FRG
24.09.1984	Deutschlandhalle	Berlin, FRG
26.09.1984	Festhalle	Frankfurt, FRG
27.09.1984	Schleyerhalle	Stuttgart, FRG
29–30.09.1984	Stadthalle	Vienna, AUT
05–07.10.1984	Super Bowl	Sun City, RSA
12–14.10.1984	Super Bowl	Sun City, RSA
18–20.10.1984	Super Bowl	Sun City, RSA
11.01.1985	Barra da Tijuca (Rock in Rio)	Rio de Janeiro, BRA
18.01.1985	Barra da Tijuca (Rock in Rio)	Rio de Janeiro, BRA
13.04.1985	Mount Smart Stadium	Auckland, NZL
16–17.04.1985	Sports & Entertainments Centre	Melbourne, AUS
19–20.04.1985	Sports & Entertainments Centre	Melbourne, AUS
25–26.04.1985	Entertainments Centre	Sydney, AUS
28–29.04.1985	Entertainments Centre	Sydney, AUS
08–09.05.1985	Nippon Budokan	Tokyo, JPN
11.05.1985	Yoyogi Taiikukan	Tokyo, JPN
13.05.1985	Aichi Auditorium	Nagoya, JPN
15.05.1985	Castle Hall	Osaka, JPN
13.07.1985	Wembley Stadium (Live Aid)	London, GBR

Tour dates and tickets courtesy Martin Skala, QueenConcerts.com

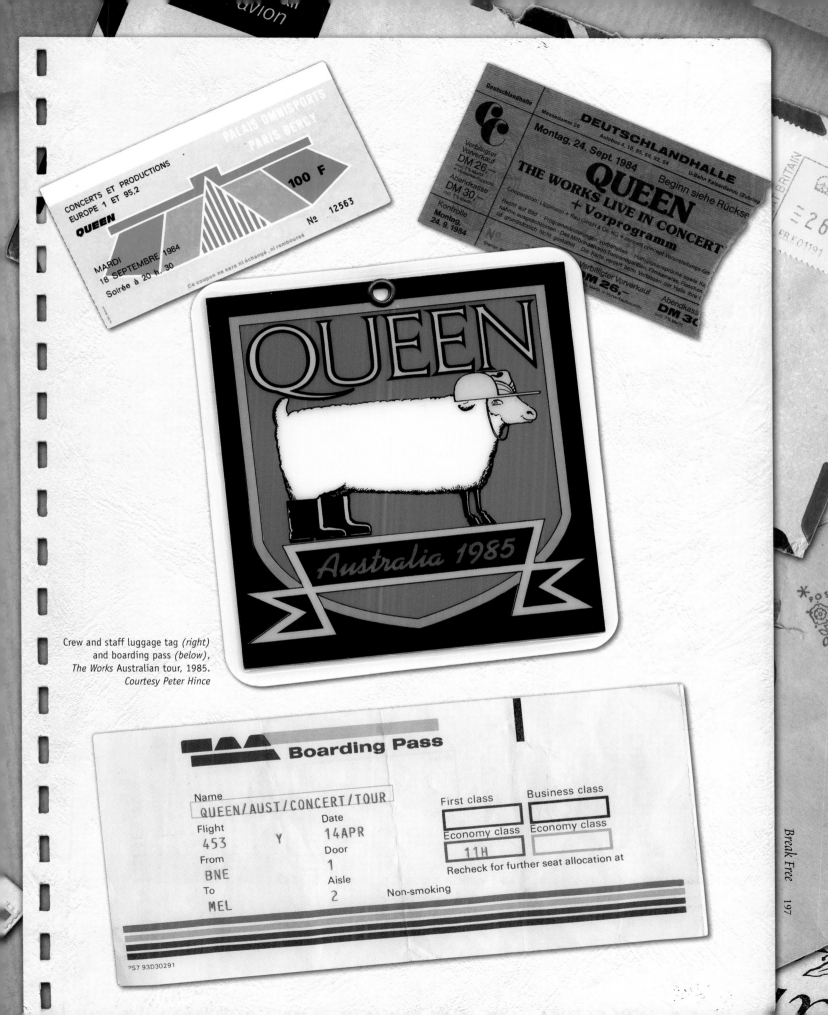

CONCERTS ET PRODUCTIONS
EUROPE 1 ET 95,2

QUEEN

100 F

№ 12563

MARDI
18 SEPTEMBRE 1984
Soirée à 20 h. 30

Ce coupon ne sera ni échangé, ni remboursé

PALAIS OMNISPORTS
PARIS BERCY

Deutschlandhalle
Messedamm 26

DEUTSCHLANDHALLE
Autobus 4, 10, 85, 89, 92, 94
Montag, 24. Sept. 1984
Verbilligter Vorverkauf
DM 26,–
U-Bahn Kaiserdamm (Zubring)
Abendkasse
DM 30,–
Beginn siehe Rücks

THE WORKS LIVE IN CONCERT
QUEEN
+ Vorprogramm

Kontrolle
Montag,
24. 9. 1984

Verbilligter Vorverkauf DM 26,–

Abendkass
DM 30

Crew and staff luggage tag *(right)*
and boarding pass *(below)*,
The Works Australian tour, 1985.
Courtesy Peter Hince

Boarding Pass

Name
QUEEN/AUST/CONCERT/TOUR

Flight
453   Y

From
BNE

To
MEL

Date
14APR

Door
1

Aisle
2

First class   Business class

Economy class   Economy class
11H

Recheck for further seat allocation at

Non-smoking

PS7 93D30291

9 WANT IT ALL

AT TIMES, QUEEN'S twenty-six-date European tour of summer 1986 took on the trappings of a triumphal progress—post–Live Aid, with the bandmembers in their late thirties at a slightly surprising career pinnacle.

Mercury, typically, captured the mood and sent it up with a gesture of absurd grandeur. If Queen were king, he'd dress accordingly. His partner, Jim Hutton, recalls in his *Mercury And Me* memoir that it was at their Paris hotel suite on June 14 when costume designer Diana Moseley delivered "Freddie's campiest costume, a deep red cloak trimmed in fake ermine and a jeweled crown fit for royalty. It was extraordinary to watch him as he threw the cloak over his white toweling robe, put on his crown, and strutted around. . . ."

He wore them only at the start of the encores, but the tour really did get a bit Cleopatra-esque when Queen traveled the 135 miles from Vienna to Budapest by hydrofoil on the river Danube and disembarked straight into a British embassy garden party held in their honor (at the Népstadion on July 27 they played "the first stadium rock gig behind the Iron Curtain," EMI claimed). And, of course, Queen maintained their usual air of a peripatetic medieval court. Dwarves, drag acts, and female attendants—naked, bar "artistic" body paint—adorned the party after a second night at Wembley Stadium on July 12.

A fun fair with mud wrestlers and strippers entertained the backstage throng at Knebworth on August 9—an outdoor festival in Hertfordshire, north of London, where Queen's biggest-ever paying audience (officially 120,000, often guesstimated at 200,000) saw what proved to be their very last gig anywhere.

Then, despite all the pomp and profit and ongoing conspicuous absence of American dates, Queen promptly decided to disband for another year.

Courtesy Ferdinando Frega, Queenmuseum.com

This image was shot spontaneously in Peter Hince's London studio one evening in February 1987. Freddie called Peter, saying he wanted to do a "fun" photo. This is the only posed studio image of Freddie with his robes and crown outfit. © *Peter Hince*

Magic tour, Råsunda Fotbollstadion, Stockholm, June 7, 1986.
Dave Hogan/Hulton Archive/Getty Images

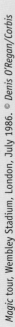

Magic tour, Wembley Stadium, London, July 1986. © Denis O'Regan/Corbis

Magic tour, Wembley Stadium, London, July 1986. © Tony Mottram/Retna UK

Soundcheck, *Magic* tour, Népstadion, Budapest, July 27, 1986.
© Denis O'Regan/Corbis

Courtesy Ferdinando Frega, Queenmuseum.com

Courtesy Peter Hince

Unused ticket, front and rear, Népstadion, Budapest, July 27, 1986, *Magic* European tour.

"They wouldn't let us into Russia; they thought
we'd corrupt the youth or something.'"

—Freddie Mercury, quoted by David Quantick,
New Musical Express, 09.08.1986

HARVEY GOLDSMITH ENTERTAINMENTS PROUDLY PRESENT

QUEEN

KNEBWORTH PARK 9TH AUGUST 1986
INFORMATION SHEET
WELCOME TO KNEBWORTH PARK – WE HOPE YOU ENJOY YOUR DAY.

Stockholm Leiden Paris Brussells Mannhiem Berlin Munich Zurich Dublin London

QUEEN
EUROPEAN TOUR 86

Marbella Barcelona Madrid Budapest Cannes Cologne Vienna

Newcastle Manchester

Window sticker.

Courtesy Ferdinando Frega, Queenmuseum.com

Harvey Goldsmith proudly presents

QUEEN
Status Quo
BIG COUNTRY **H** BELOUIS SOME

HOSPITALITY
SATURDAY 9th AUGUST 1986
KNEBWORTH PARK
NO BACKSTAGE ACCESS
NOT TRANSFERABLE MUST BE STUCK ON

THE KNEBWORTH FAYRE
"A NIGHT OF SUMMER MAGIC"
QUEEN
Status Quo
BIG COUNTRY
SAT 9th AUGUST 1986

Beneath the crown, of course, Mercury had his own troubles and ambitions. He wanted to make another solo album. Peter Freestone's *Mercury* suggests this was partly about unbridled self-expression, partly that band shouting matches took an increasing toll on him: "It was because of the prospect of arguments and disharmony that on occasion Freddie would refuse to go to the studio."

Further, as he continued his deliberate shift in the direction of a quieter life, he naturally shared every '80s gay man's worry about AIDS while trying to deal with the extra burden of protecting his private life from voracious media scrutiny. It proved an unwinnable battle. For instance, on Sunday, October 12, Mercury and Hutton returned from a shopping holiday in Tokyo to find the Sunday tabloid *The News Of The*

World running a story headlined "Queen Star Freddie In AIDS Shock." It claimed he'd been tested and found HIV-negative. From all subsequent accounts, it seems certain he'd still not taken the test. Confronted by a reporter at Heathrow Airport he yelled, "Do I look like I'm dying from AIDS?. . . Now go away and leave me alone." The following day, the *Sun* front page blared, "Do I Look Like I'm Dying From AIDS? Fumes Freddie."

During Queen's break, Taylor yearned to step out from behind the drums and lead his own group, so he set about finding the right musicians. At this point, Deacon and May were the band's most fragile members, mentally and emotionally. Although Deacon never spoke about his problems in interviews, the Jacky Gunn and Jim Jenkins

Stick-on passes, *Magic* tour, 1986. *Courtesy Ferdinando Frega, Queenmuseum.com*

Crew and staff laminate and luggage tag, *Magic* European tour, 1986. *Courtesy Peter Hince*

official band biography, *Queen: As It Began*, reports him "verging on a nervous breakdown" and "considering separation" from wife Veronica.

Meanwhile, the uproar in May's life had just reached the tabloids. During the summer, at the London premiere of the Bette Midler/Nick Nolte comedy *Down And Out In Beverly Hills*, he met Anita Dobson, an actress then starring in the U.K.'s most popular TV soap, *EastEnders*. He invited her to see Queen at Wembley, and soon he was writing and producing songs for her (she'd already had a Top 10 hit). A member of the support band on the European tour told Laura Jackson in *Queen: The Definitive Biography* that he found

Courtesy Ferdinando Frega, Queenmuseum.com

May in turmoil—about the apartheid issue, still (after a demonstration outside a Queen show at Stockholm's Råsunda Fotbollstadion on June 7), and about his marriage.

"After we did Wembley, that was the beginning of a major crisis for me," May said in 1991. He offered more insight into his state of mind, speaking to David Thomas of *Mojo* in 1999: "I never understand how I was able to take no drugs and not drink that much and yet become totally unstable. I was needy beyond belief. A certain amount of your neediness is satisfied by the party lifestyle. But you have a terrible hole inside you which needs to be one-on-one with everyone. And that's a need which can never be fulfilled. To be truthful, I was always screwed up about sex because I got married at totally the wrong time, at the beginning of all this. In the midst of all this I'm trying to be a good husband and a good father to my kids. . . . So that really excluded me from being wildly promiscuous. But emotionally I became utterly out of control, needy for that one-to-one reinforcement, feelings of love and discovery, and that's what I became addicted to I think."

He found a little light relief in playing and recording with spoof heavy metal band Bad News. But life was hardly simplified when his wife, Chrissy, gave birth to their third child, Emily, on February 17, 1987.

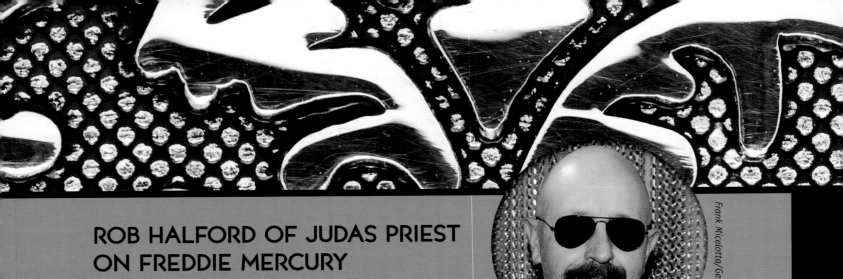

ROB HALFORD OF JUDAS PRIEST ON FREDDIE MERCURY

"Could Be Very Sweet And Demure . . . Then Rip Your Head Off"

As told to Gary Graff

LET ME START OFF BY SAYING that I have multiple iPods, and I have one iPod that is full of Queen. Actually it's got Queen and [Judas] Priest—one Nano iPod and all that's on it is everything by Queen and everything by Priest.

I was there when Queen first started to create its rumblings. I knew them when they were called Smile, before they changed the name to Queen. There was a very famous DJ called Alan Freeman who's not with us any longer, but he was just a tremendous guy with an ear for great rock music and all kinds of exciting things on the cutting edge. I remember hearing some of the very early tracks from the first Queen records and instantly getting the jolt of a fresh idea, of a new approach, of some great songs. So I eagerly awaited the release of the first Queen album and went to my record store and picked up the vinyl and just took it home and played it constantly over and over and over again.

The music and the production, the engineering, everything was just so spectacular and exciting. To hear that coming out of the speakers at that point was a great thrill. From that moment on I was a huge Queen fan and collected everything that the band produced—vinyl, CD, some iTunes now, DVDs, video pieces, and so on and so forth.

And the man that led it for me—with myself being a singer— was Freddie. He had this incredibly versatile, extraordinary voice that could be very sweet and demure and laidback with certain songs, and then he could just rip your head off with a song like "Ogre Battle." There are very few singers capable of covering that amount of territory and being convincing. It's easy to jump from style to style in terms of mimicry and imitation, but it's very difficult to do it with such a feeling of conviction and honesty. You listen to him singing "The Great Pretender" and you believe

that's what he was. Or "Crazy Little Thing Called Love" with the Elvis vibe, you believed that. When he performed he put his heart and soul into it, and you really believed what he was singing.

And you've only got to listen to the stuff he did with Montserrat [Caballé], the Spanish opera singer—their "Barcelona" really let Freddie do his complete classical opera interpretation. He loved classical work and classical singers. That was part of his mindset, and he brought it into the rock and pop stuff he did. "Mama, just killed a man. . . ." You felt like you were hearing somebody singing in desperation. That idea obviously came from some of the great classical operas.

Coupled with his voice was his tremendous stage persona—one of the most tremendous frontmen to walk on stage with a mic. Everybody in Queen was spectacular to watch in concert, but Freddie was "the man" from the moment he walked out and started to perform. Your eyes never left him because he was such a charismatic performer. And you could always sense in the music that he had a lot of fun . . . just sitting down at the piano. There was this sense of who knew where things would take him on any given day of writing? Anything was possible.

That really goes for Queen as a whole. They had the versatility and this attitude that they were not going to be led by anything other than their own instinct and their desire—and that could be anything. . . . That was exciting for me as a musician because I don't like repetition. I love to be entertained, and I love to see what a band can produce, musically. And that was the case with Queen. They became, and for a lot of us still are, one of the most unique acts in the history of rock 'n' roll. ⚜

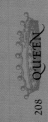

Magic tour, 1986. *Dave Hogan/Hulton Archive/Getty Images*

While Taylor and Deacon wintered at their Los Angeles homes, Mercury started solo work with his keyboard-maestro/co-producer friend Mike Moran. They soon recorded a period pastiche cover of The Platters' "The Great Pretender" (a U.S. No. 1 in 1955). Released on February 23, 1987, it hit No. 4 in the U.K. However, it was the B-side, "Exercises In Free Love," which led Mercury in an unexpected yet delightful direction. Casually thrown together in vaguely classical vein, it opened the door to his musical relationship with the great operatic soprano Montserrat Caballé.

The improbable connection arose from genuine enthusiasm. Bowled over when Peter Freestone took him to hear her with Pavarotti in *Un Ballo In Maschera* at the Royal Opera House in May 1983, Mercury took to mentioning her occasionally in interviews. He did so on Spanish television when Queen played Barcelona, Madrid, and Marbella in summer 1986. Queen's Spanish promoter, Pino Sagliocco, who was also staging some events around Barcelona's bid for the 1992 Olympics, spotted an opportunity and contacted Caballé's management who talked to Queen's manager Jim Beach. In March, Mercury and Moran found themselves lunching with the diva at the Barcelona Ritz.

Moran, writing in *More Of The Real Life . . . Freddie Mercury*, said Caballé's robust humour encouraged them to play her a tape of "Exercises In Free Love," wherein Mercury sang falsetto. A decisive dialogue ensued. "You seeng like mezzo soprano, no?"

"Thank you, dear."

"Eet eez you?"

QUEEN

"It is me."

"Wonderful, I shall give it a world premiere in three weeks time at Covent Garden . . . and [whacking Moran on the shoulder] you shall play!" She added that they should make an album together. Mercury covered his astonishment with a characteristic "Oh why not, my dear?"

True to her word, Caballé delivered "Exercises In Free Love" to the Royal Opera House aficionados. Mercury invited her back to Garden Lodge for supper and more discussion, which turned into a sing-song around the piano (partly recorded and available on the *Freddie Mercury Solo* boxed set released in 2000). Moran recalled her bumming cigarettes and declaiming that "it was wonderful being with people for whom music was a very natural expression rather than a ritualised process."

For several months, solo album shelved perforce, Mercury and Moran devoted themselves to the tricky task of writing duets suitable to both voices and recording the music over which the rigidly scheduled Caballé, on the road or on flying visits to London, could record her parts. Meanwhile, in May, they sang live together at the Ku Club, Ibiza, to premiere the Mercury/Moran song "Barcelona" in celebration of the city securing the Olympics. Released that autumn, the single and album of the same name were huge in Spain and did well in the U.K., reaching Nos. 8 and 15, respectively, perhaps as some kind of eccentric counterpoint to the year of acid-house raves.

No doubt the Caballé divertissement helped sustain Mercury as he entered the darkest period of his life. Hutton's memoir says that, in early April 1987, while he was visiting family in Ireland, Mercury told him on the phone, "The doctors have just taken a big lump out of me." When Hutton got home the next day, Mercury said the biopsy results showed he had AIDS. At the time, this meant almost certain death in an uncertain number of years. Mercury told Hutton if he wanted to leave he'd understand. Hutton said he wouldn't, not ever. He didn't want to take the test himself but said they practiced safe sex from then on. He added, "That was the last time we referred directly to [Freddie's] AIDS condition."

Hutton understood that the only other people Mercury told immediately were Mary Austin and Jim Beach. But the visible signs of the illness soon led him into the duplicities of denial. His first long-term partner, David Minns, wrote in the oral history he co-edited, *More Of The Real Life . . . Freddie Mercury*, that when he was invited to a Caballé recording session, "I arrived only to see my former friend displaying the discoloured areas on his face which were the outward manifestations of one of the AIDS-related illnesses. He exclaimed: 'It's alright, dear! There's no need to look at me like that. I've just been drinking too much vodka and doing too much. . . . The doctors say I have a liver complaint.' Oh God, I thought."

His German friend Barbara Valentin told Laura Jackson that, before the Ku Club show with Caballé, she applied layers of makeup to hide these small, purple Kaposi's Sarcoma lesions. More painfully, though, he'd developed an open wound on his right leg and a large scabbed lesion on the ball of the foot, neither of which would ever heal.

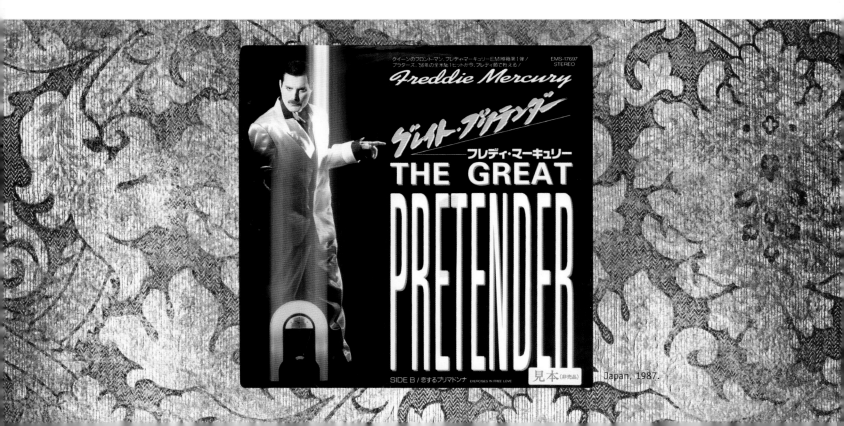

Japan, 1987.

"[W]e always rowed about money. A lot of terrible injustices take place over songwriting."

—BRIAN MAY, QUOTED BY
PHIL SUTCLIFFE, Q, 03.1991

Queen's year off closed with Deacon having apparently repaired himself to some degree and started writing Queen songs, May still caught in his internal maelstrom, and Taylor engaged with his new band project, The Cross, which led to his personal life turning temporarily upside down.

On a video set for a single, "Cowboys And Indians" (U.K. No. 74 for one week that October), he met and fell for a model called Debbie Leng— renowned for sucking sexily on a Cadbury's Flake chocolate bar in a TV ad. Subsequently, on January 25, 1988, he married his longtime girlfriend Dominique Beyrand at Chelsea Registry Office. A month later he left her to live with Leng. Taylor never spoke about these events, but it has been suggested this added up to "a civilized arrangement" for the benefit of the children.

When Queen returned to the studio in London, then Montreux, that January, May felt barely capable of contributing. "*The Miracle*, I don't know how I got through it," he told this writer in 1991. "I took a back seat on the writing, but I'm surprised how much guitar there is on it. I can remember whole days sitting there blank, I couldn't get up off the chair, I was in such a depression. But there were a few days when I was fighting it and I got up and played—which was the only good thing that happened to me then.

"My dad died at the same time [June 2, 1988], and my marriage broke up [that summer], so for a while I didn't *exist* as a person. I'd look at myself in the mirror and think, 'Oh, he looks all right, he's a rock star.' But inside there was almost nothing there. . . . I was . . . I can't describe how bad I was, it just all *went*. No amount of fame or money can insulate you from that sort of pain. . . . The group tends to be the most stable family that we've got. Oftentimes it saved me, I think. Life would be so awful that going into the studio was the only thing I could stand to do."

In fact, Mercury deliberately enabled the four bandmembers to get closer to one another when he suddenly proposed that the rule on songwriting credits he'd instigated while they were recording their first album (whoever writes the lyrics takes the publishing royalties) should be abandoned at last and all songs credited to "Queen" with the income shared equally. While he never spoke publicly about the issue, it seems reasonable to

surmise that his attitude had softened because of his illness. Regardless, agreement was swift and unanimous. In 1991, Taylor told Bob Coburn of the U.S.-based *Rockline* radio show, "It was just the best decision that we ever made. It removes all the ego things that get in the way of making decisions on merit."

May felt the same, though he also saw it as a small act of contrition from him and Mercury to the others. "I think Freddie and I squashed Roger and John in the beginning," he told me in 1991. "We were the major songwriters, and we didn't give them enough say. Now it's totally equal. I wish we'd done it earlier. It does mean a sacrifice, letting your baby go. But you get a better product because your name is on *every* track so you get more arguments . . . when someone brings in a song it gets torn apart and very critically looked at. It's survival of the fittest because it needs everyone to do their bit to finish a track, and if you're a bit iffy you won't go near it. If a song somehow never gets a guitar part put on, it's sort of a hint. . . . It also helps when you decide on singles, you're not partisan anymore; you're not saying, 'I want *my* song to be the single.'"

But still they stopped and started constantly as individual interests intervened. Deacon continued his family-travel therapy whenever he got the chance. Taylor's The Cross, a band of unknowns (bar Spike Edney on keyboards), toured the U.K. in February and Germany in April, promoting their debut album *Shove It*, which peaked at No. 58 in the U.K. May threw himself into a plethora of pan-generational studio sessions with artists including Living in a Box, Black Sabbath, Holly Johnson, Fuzzbox, Steve Hackett, and Lonnie Donegan (as well as Anita Dobson, whose album *Talking Of Love*, released in November, didn't chart). Mercury grandly concluded his Caballé activities—and his public performance career, it transpired—with an October show in Barcelona attended by King Juan Carlos and Queen Sofia to celebrate the passing of the Olympic flame from Seoul. He also sang, without comment, at a gala performance of the musical *Time* to raise funds for the Terence Higgins Trust HIV/AIDS campaign (*Time* was co-written by Mercury's friend Dave Clark, formerly of the famous Five). In January 1989, Mercury released his last solo single, "How Can I Go On?" ("Is anybody there to comfort me?/Lord . . . take care of me").

Nonetheless, Queen's *The Miracle* emerged on May 22, 1989—preceded by the single "I Want It All," a May-inspired anti-hymn to greed and general voracity—and rose to U.K. No. 1, U.S. No. 24. The album deployed surging Queen harmonies and May guitar swerves with power and discretion, while showing a familiar agility in genre-hopping from party rock to the sweet peace-and-love anthemics of the title track; highlights included the buzzing bass

and synthesizer grooves of "The Invisible Man," the Latin inclinations of "Rain Must Fall" and "My Baby Does Me," and the chest-beating "Was It All Worth It." They even let off steam by blasting the tabloids with "Scandal" ("They're gonna turn our lives into a freak show").

According to Hutton's memoir, just as *The Miracle* hit the shops, Mercury asked the band to start work on another album: "Queen were dazed by Freddie's eagerness to return to the stresses of the studio. . . . But they all said 'Yes' in unison." (Official website queenonline.com places the transition from *The Miracle* to *Innuendo* sessions even earlier, in January 1989—that is, with no interlude at all.)

Then, in Montreux, while they ate dinner at Le Bavaria restaurant, he told them why he didn't want to stop recording. Of course, they already knew it in their hearts. Hutton wrote, "Someone at the table was suffering from a cold and the conversation got round to the curse of illness. Freddie still looked fairly well, but he rolled up his right trouser leg and raised his leg to the table to let the others see the painful, open wound weeping on the side of the calf. 'You think you've got problems!' he told them. 'Well, look what I have to put up with.' Everyone was very shocked, but also very sympathetic." (Laura Jackson's band biography indicates this meeting took place in January 1991, but Hutton was an eyewitness.)

Talking to DJ Kevin Greening for a BBC Radio 1 documentary in 1995, May seemed to refer to the same occasion when he recalled Mercury saying, "You probably realize what my problem is, you know, my illness. Well that's it, and I don't want anything to be any different whatsoever. I don't want it to be known, I don't want to talk about it, I just want to get on and work until I can't work any more." Taylor added it was clear "Freddie felt that was the best way to keep his spirits up and he wanted to leave as much [music] as possible . . . we backed him up right to the hilt. *Innuendo* was made very much on borrowed time." In the same program, Mary Austin said that, in Mercury's last months, making music "fed the light inside. . . . Life wasn't just taking him to the grave."

Having been told the truth, the band had to shift from repeating Mercury's earlier evasions to telling deliberate untruths. "We were lying to everyone, even our own families," said May to David Thomas of *Mojo* in 1999. "Freddie used to say, 'I don't want people buying our records out of fucking sympathy.'"

Taylor described the process of making *Innuendo* to *Rockline* radio listeners in February 1991—without explaining that it was all geared to Mercury's health: "We'd go into the studio, work for about three weeks, and take two weeks off. [It] was really a happy album to make. . . . It sort of wrote itself. The material has depth and maturity to it."

Freestone's memoir confirmed Taylor's counterintuitive "happy album" comment: "Freddie really loved [it]. . . . Each time he brought a cassette of the day's work home he was incredibly excited . . . he would wake everyone up and make us listen. He was giving it his all. . . . If we were still worried that all this hard work was shortening his life, he made it very clear that he didn't care." (In other respects, though, Mercury took measures to extend his life, such as his sudden decision in October 1989 to end his forty-a-day smoking habit and insist on a smoke-free studio.)

Co-producer Dave Richards described one of the bursts of spontaneity generated by these emotional crosscurrents when, in 1995, he talked about the creation of the title track for a BBC Radio 1 documentary. It began with Mercury sitting beside him in the Montreux control room and the rest of the band playing in the concert hall next door, linked via audio and TV: "It was an improvisation-type song, set up like a live performance, and they got into a nice rhythm and groove, and some chords, and then Freddie said, 'Oh, I like that,' and rushed downstairs to the concert hall and started singing along with it. . . . It just happened. It was wonderful."

Locked into Mercury's cycle of work, exhaustion, and recovery, for more than a year the band barely looked up, apart from Taylor's use of Queen downtime to record a second album with The Cross and May's small-time venture into writing music for fringe theatre company Red & Gold's production of *Macbeth* (performed in November 1990). Meanwhile, intermittently back at Garden Lodge, Mercury gradually told a few family members and close friends what ailed him; in 2000, in the first interview his sister Kashmira Cooke and her husband, Roger, had ever given, Roger told the *Mail On Sunday* that when they visited on August 18, 1990, "Freddie said suddenly, 'What you have to understand, my dear Kash, is that what I have is terminal. I'm going to die.' After that, we talked no more about it."

But business had to be taken care of. Long since informed by Mercury that he had AIDS, Beach negotiated Queen's purchase of their entire back catalog in America from Capitol, who had disappointed the band. He then used that property as a substantial lure for a new U.S.

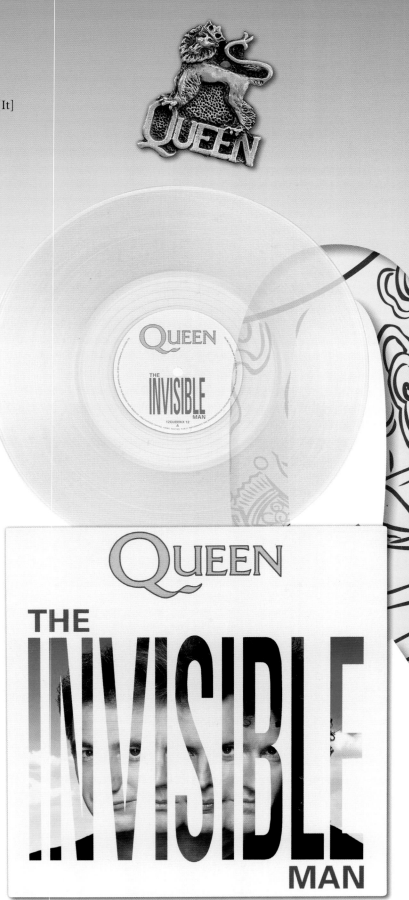

"12" Version" b/w "Single Version" and "Hijack My Heart," 1989.

"12" Version" b/w "7" Version" and "My Life Has Been Saved," 1989.

Limited edition hologram pack, b/w "Stone Cold Crazy," U.K., 1989.

Promo only, Japan, 1989.

"I just thought, 'Interesting, but nobody will ever buy it because it's crap.' . . . [Our record company is] sorting it out. . . . We don't want to get involved in litigation with other artists ourselves, that doesn't seem very cool really. Anyway, now I think it's quite a good bit of work in its way.'"

—Brian May on Vanilla Ice's sampling of "Under Pressure"

'Headlong,'" said May, who originated the song. "Fred, in particular, if there's too much guitar in the mix he gets very impatient. We compromised in the end, but it's difficult."

As they finished the album by November 1990, it emerged that white rapper Vanilla Ice had, without permission or payment, based his U.S. and U.K. smash hit "Ice Ice Baby" on samples from Queen and David Bowie's "Under Pressure." At first May considered the track "crap." After money had changed hands, he wryly described it as "quite a good bit of work in a way."

In January 1991, harking back to the boldness of "Bohemian Rhapsody," Queen released the 6:30 multipart, choired-up, guitar-orchestrated, flamenco-interluded extravaganza "Innuendo" in the U.K. It hit No. 1 immediately. In America, Hollywood went with the more orthodox rocker "Headlong," and nothing happened.

Despite the creeping pace of its creation, *Innuendo*, out in February, struck no one as a valedictory. Bursting with energy and variety—even in the sleeve illustrations adapted from drawings by nineteenth-century French artist, Grandville, a Taylor discovery—it earned the comparisons with *A Night At The Opera*, which May and Taylor soon echoed in interviews (alongside necessary musings about whether Mercury might be persuaded to tour again). In particular, Mercury sang magnificently; who else could deliver with equal efficacy suave Noël Coward–ish wit ("I'm Going Slightly Mad"), Bon Scott's coarse roar ("The Hitman"), and a male Judy Garland's tightrope-teeter between showbiz melodramatics and real-life emotional depth ("The Show Must Go On")?

More and more, as his own illness and the AIDS epidemic bore down on him, Mercury's work and life and impending death became one. During fall 1990, his friend and cook at Garden Lodge, long-ago former lover Joe Fanelli, told Mercury he had AIDS (a few months later, Mercury bought Fanelli a house to offer him a measure of security). After that, Hutton finally took the test and learned he was HIV-positive. He didn't tell Mercury for another twelve months.

Mercury did what he could. With *Innuendo* finished, he led the band back to Montreux in January 1991 "to record some B-sides." He liked some of them so much he said Queen should hold them back "for the next album." At his side throughout, Peter Freestone later wrote, "Freddie must have realised by now that time was really short. . . . He was going from track to track which was basically what he did until the end of his life. While he had a voice, he would continue recording." ♕

record deal; no matter what the future might hold, a potentially lucrative past could be traded on. Soon he'd secured a deal and, it's said, a £10 million advance from brand-new Hollywood Records, a Disney subsidiary.

When the Brits (the U.K. equivalent of the Grammies) offered Queen an "outstanding contribution" career award in February 1990, they felt they had to acknowledge it graciously by collecting in person. Gamely, Mercury went along, even though he knew his gaunt appearance would attract another flurry of comment and TV exposure.

Taylor released his second album with The Cross, *Mad, Bad And Dangerous To Know*, on German label Electrola in March. Valiantly, they toured Germany in May. Then he returned to the stop-start progress on *Innuendo* in London and Montreux, a place whose Swiss order and calm Mercury used to detest but now valued profoundly.

With Taylor hard hit by his father Michael's death in late July and Deacon quiet as ever, May found himself able to step up to the challenge of keeping *Innuendo* on track. His relationship with Anita Dobson by then established—though always volatile—he had emerged from depressive near-inertia on *The Miracle* sessions. "You do get through in the end," he told me the following year. "I know who I am now. I'm productive again. In fact, the other three have all had a lot of stuff to deal with in the past year, and I was the one saying, 'OK, I'll hold the fort while you deal with it.' It was a big surprise to me that I could do that."

Not much changed in the studio. Musical intensity overruled any tendency to pussyfoot around Mercury's illness—just as the singer had wanted. "We had a big fight over

216

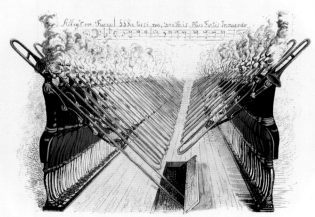

QUEEN

INNUENDO
(EXPLOSIVE VERSION)

QUEEN

NEW ALBUM & SINGLE
Jan.30.1991 In Store

驚くべき完成度、熱すぎるロック・スピリットに支えられた
通算14作目のスタジオ・アルバム。

F.MERCURY   B.MAY   R.TAYLOR   J.DEACON

INNUENDO • I'M GOING SLIGHTLY MAD • HEADLONG • I CAN'T LIVE WITH YOU •
DON'T TRY SO HARD • RIDE THE WILD WIND • ALL GOD'S PEOPLE •
THESE ARE THE DAYS OF OUR LIVES • DELILAH • THE HITMAN •
BIJOU • THE SHOW MUST GO ON

TOCP-6480 ¥2,620 (tax incl.)

3-Track CD Jan. 30.1991 In Store

① INNUENDO ② UNDER PRESSURE ③ BIJOU
(EXPLOSIVE VERSION)   (with David Bowie)   TOCP-6571 ¥1200 (tax incl.)

INNUENDO

EMI TOSHIBA EMI

The Miracle
by Daniel Nester

ORIGINALLY ENTITLED THE INVISIBLE MEN but changed to *The Miracle* three weeks before its release in June 1989, Queen's thirteenth studio album features a first for the band: collective songwriting credit. The band had done it before—"Under Pressure" is credited to "Queen and David Bowie"—but this time it was a "pre-agreed thing" before going into the studio, Roger Taylor explained in a BBC Radio 1 interview shortly before the album's release.

"It's a major decision, in fact," Brian explained. "Doesn't sound like a big thing, but it makes a big difference in the studio. You have a tendency to get very possessive about your own songs if your name's in it somehow. We decided to chuck everything into the pool and say everything's written by Queen."

The end result largely sounds like an album written by committee, with some notable exceptions. It might be asking too much of any band that has taken a two-year hiatus, during which its members took part in a dizzying array of solo activities, to find any common musical ground—one had recorded an album with opera diva Montserrat Caballé (Freddie); another produced an album by *EastEnders* star and future second wife Anita Dobson and jammed with Black Sabbath, Bad News, and Def Leppard (Brian); a third started his own rock band called The Cross with himself as lead singer (Roger); and the fourth directed two comedy videos by Morris Minor & the Majors when not off skiing with his family (John). Perhaps the most charitable way to look at *The Miracle* is that it is indeed miraculous the album was made at all, let alone remains slightly relevant and listenable twenty years later.

With its cheesy electronic drums and a choir of Freddies, "Party" opens the album as if we've pressed play on *Mr. Bad Guy II*—not a good sign. In *Queen: Complete Works*, Georg Purvis describes "Party" as "perhaps one of the worst tracks ever record by Queen." This overstates the matter a bit: if hopes weren't so focused on Queen regaining rock god status, "Party" and the track that abruptly follows it, "Khashoggi's Ship," might be viewed as updates of the usual

Queen album filler like "Bring Back That Leroy Brown" from *Sheer Heart Attack*. Both "Party" and "Khashoggi's Ship" have merit if for nothing else than Brian May's blazing Red Special work—power chords and trill fills, harmonic effects he'd picked up in the post-*Magic* tour gap years—which cut through an otherwise Europop production.

The Miracle's group songwriting credits also spawned a cottage industry among fans to identify who wrote which song. The title track, an ambitious five-minute patchwork arrangement, multiple movements, and two endings, is widely attributed to Freddie with help from others. Just who is to blame for the jejune lyrics' shout-outs to "Captain Cook and Cain and Abel, Jimi Hendrix to the Tower of Babel" and "Sunday mornings with a cup of tea" as miracles, as well as a call for "peace on Earth/an end to war," is anyone's guess. What's certain is "The Miracle" is the strangest song on an album full of strange songs, from a band whose stock-in-trade is to write strange songs.

Even the novice Queenspotter can tell "I Want It All," the LP's lead-off single and the album's strongest track, is Brian May's baby. Presented fully formed to the band during sessions, the track's rock-oriented production alone—live-sounding drums, a bass that doesn't sound fart-like—qualifies it as a stand-out. "I Want It All" enters the band's best-of songbook because it's Queen doing what Queen does best: taking some outside genre, in this case a cowboy song—my guess would be Brian channelling Hank Marvin and the Shadows' version of "(Ghost) Riders In The Sky"—and rocking it out. Rock critics have perennially pooh-poohed the band's approach as insincere pastiche; the Queen faithful see it as smart, headbanging fun.

"The Invisible Man," the album's third single, draws from the Roger Taylor arsenal of songwriting: jumpy riffs, no key change, and a topical lyric. With a synth bass line and one of Brian May's most face-melting solos in his career, "The Invisible Man" could have served as the template for *Hot Space* songs had Brian been allowed to play more. It's hard to place the exuberant "Breakthru," the album's second single—complete with "Don't Stop Me Now"–ish, jazz-hands chorus and key change—as coming from Roger's demo tapes. The song, as it turns out, is at least two songs in one: the a capella intro comes from another song, an unreleased Freddie ballad called "A New Life Is Born," that was grafted onto the track.

"Rain Must Fall" and "My Baby Does Me," two trifles widely attributed to John Deacon, are again saved by Brian May's eclectic guitar work. In another era, without an overdependence on synthesizers and drum machines, many songs on *The Miracle* might have been redeemed by live musicianship. "Rain Must Fall," for example could have been an update of Deacon's "Who Needs You," a gem off of *News Of The World*. The group songwriting and grand compromises on *The Miracle* might have kept the band together, but it also seems to have prevented a cohesive sound from coming to the fore.

"Scandal," another Brian track, isn't nearly as marred by production and is a highlight of side two. (Not one of Roger's favorites, however: his commentary on *Greatest Video Hits 2* assesses both track and video as "going through the motions.") One can't help but suspect "Was It All Worth It," the album's

closer, was either a premature goodbye or dry run for the true valedictory, "The Show Must Go On," on their the next album, the band's swan song.

The band reportedly had thirty to forty songs to whittle down to the album's final ten. Two—"Chinese Torture," a Brian May sweep-picking harmonics-effect showpiece that lives up to its name, and "Hang On In There"—were offered as CD bonus tracks. Another three were released as B-sides, essentially doubling the number of non-album tracks in the band's career: jazzy Freddie fantasia "Stealin'" backs "Breakthru"; "Hijack My Heart," an excellent Roger vocal track, backs "The Invisible Man"; and "My Life Has Been Saved," an excellent John-penned track, backs "Scandal." Inclusion of any or all five of these tracks in the album proper would have made for a vast improvement.

Bootlegs abound of several other unreleased tracks, among them "Dog With A Bone," a mid-tempo rocker; an early version of "Too Much Love Will Kill You," which would appear on Brian's first solo album then *Made In Heaven*; "I Guess We're Falling Out," a half-finished Brian May track; and "Face It Alone," the rarest of the bootlegs and also the most promising, a ballad with Freddie and Brian following a melody line in various directions.

In the final analysis, if we're to rate *The Miracle*, an interesting exercise might be to compare it alongside other bands' thirteenth albums. The Beatles never hit thirteen—*Let It Be*, the band's swan song, is number twelve. The Who's notoriously meager studio output holds at eleven with *Endless Wire*. There's Genesis' *Invisible Touch*, Aerosmith's *Just Push Play*, Deep Purple's *Slaves and Masters*, Kiss' *Asylum*, and Judas Priest's *Jugulator*. The list of mediocrity goes on.

But if we're to be truly fair, we might look to those bands that retained the same line-up over their careers—no Mach 1 and Mach 2 line-ups, no tribute band lead singers. For that sort of comparability we're left with Queen's *The Miracle* and Rush's *Presto*, also from 1989. *Presto* is a synth-heavy affair. The band sits poised to go back to its rock roots, but the band's experimental side isn't quite there yet.

Sound familiar? This might be just the sort of charitable review we could give *The Miracle*. Especially considering the follow-up album would be their last and one of their best. ⚜

Innuendo

by Melissa Blease

QUEEN'S 1991 ALBUM INNUENDO—the last to feature entirely new material and the final studio project to be recorded before Freddie Mercury's death—is an elaborate tapestry that weaves both bold flourishes and sublime, subtle nuances together into a richly decorated masterpiece.

Bookended by two classic but stylistically disparate anthems, a dozen strikingly individual songs chart a course that many believe mapped the emotions of those at the helm. If this is the case, what must have been an inordinately harrowing experience produced a surprisingly upbeat album that offered one of the most charismatic characters in rock a fitting finale. But even if you ignore such a context, Innuendo—from the rumbling beats at the start of the extraordinary, baroque title track to the defiantly audacious anthem "The Show Must Go On"—is a bold, uplifting adventure, with the many experimental twists and turns along the way underpinned by the band's trademark style from start to finish.

The thrilling guitar breaks, catchy refrains and raspy vocals on "Headlong," the grungy "Hitman," and the fast-paced rhythms that infuse the otherwise moody slow-burner "Ride The Wild Wind" with energy evoke similar former glories on a pomp-rock theme. The iridescent sheen of glamour that lightly coats every song sparkles most brightly on three intelligent lullabies: the emotive "I Can't Live Without You," the heartbreakingly tender "Don't Try So Hard," and the dreamy, ephemeral "Bijou" all showcase both Mercury's inimitable vocal range and his fellow bandmembers' ability to instinctively gauge when to allow their frontman his moment in the spotlight. Elsewhere, a life-affirming blast of rock gospel set against an operatic backdrop in "All God's People" brings a spirited thrust to the proceedings somewhere around the middle of this gloriously eclectic trip. So far, so very good.

It would be easy to single out the powerfully emotional "The Show Must Go On" as the album's defining aria; indeed, it's an edifying, unforgettable tour de force. But two other tracks stand out above the rest. The layer of vaguely sinister, dark undertones that ripple menacingly beneath the superficially camp, eccentric surface of "I'm Going Slightly Mad" lift the song from mere novelty status into more insightful realms, turning it into an idiosyncratic paean to the bleak, disturbing feelings of desolation, alienation, and sheer derangement experienced when contemplating the imminent arrival of the Grim Reaper. The surreal accompanying video featured Brian May dressed as a penguin, John Deacon as a court jester, Roger Taylor with a kettle on his head, and Mercury—his manic grin beaming out from underneath a mask of melting greasepaint—wearing a formal dinner suit and balancing a bunch of bananas on top of a wild, wild wig. Combining elements of the visual extravaganzas that promoted both "Bohemian Rhapsody" in 1975 and "I Want To Break Free" almost a decade later, it was as bizarre—and, in parts, hilarious—as it was shockingly moving, exemplifying the time-honored bravery of a pioneering rock band playing games with their audience and taking a gamble against odds that, this time around, were most definitely not stacked in their favor.

Meanwhile, "These Are the Days of Our Lives" offers a very different perspective on a similar, defining theme. On one level, this contemplative, wistful ballad—penned by drummer Roger Taylor but, like the rest of the album, credited to the band as a whole—is an overly sweet, sentimental ditty, lacking depth or focus and not very typically Queen. But here, it stands alone as an enduring tribute to a man who turned his whole life into a performance. Listen carefully to Mercury's final, breathless whispers at the end of the song, and you can rest assured that, underneath the crown, the furs, and the brazen, largely untrammelled ego, there was a humble man who appreciated those around him for supporting the spectacle of his roller coaster existence as much as he enjoyed creating it. ⚜

Tour Dates

Magic

07.06.1986	Råsunda Fotbollstadion	Stockholm, SWE
11–12.06.1986	Groenoordhallen	Leiden, NLD
14.06.1986	Hippodrome de Vincennes	Paris, FRA
17.06.1986	Forest National	Brussels, BEL
19.06.1986	Groenoordhallen	Leiden, NLD
21.06.1986	Maimarktgelände	Mannheim, FRG
26.06.1986	Waldbuhne	Berlin, FRG
28–29.06.1986	Olympiahalle	Munich, FRG
01–02.07.1986	Hallenstadion	Zurich, CHE
05.07.1986	Slane Castle	Slane, County Meath, IRL
09.07.1986	St. James Park	Newcastle, GBR
11–12.07.1986[1,4]	Wembley Stadium	London, GBR
16.07.1986	Maine Road	Manchester, GBR
19.07.1986	Müngersdorfer Stadion	Cologne, FRG
21–22.07.1986	Stadthalle	Vienna, AUT
27.07.1986[2]	Népstadion	Budapest, HUN
30.07.1986	Amphitheatre	Frejus, FRA
01.08.1986	Mini Estadi	Barcelona, ESP
03.08.1986	Rayo Vallecano	Madrid, ESP
05.08.1986	Estádio Municipal	Marbella, ESP
09.08.1986[3]	Knebworth Park	Stevenage, GBR

Notes

1–3. Provided the material for Live Magic.

4. The July 12 show appears in its entirety on the *Live At Wembley 1986* double-CD and the *Live At Wembley Stadium* DVD.

Tour dates and tickets courtesy Martin Skala, QueenConcerts.com

"I used to think we'd last five years, but it's got to the point where we're all actually too old to break up. Can you imagine forming a new band at 40? Be a bit silly, wouldn't it?'"

—Freddie Mercury

10 GOODBYE EVERYBODY— I'VE GOT TO GO

quiet, the lake and the mountains—he went home to recover via rest and treatment, which included blood transfusions and the drugs then available, such as AZT, which were intended to slow the disease's progress (a Hickman line, an intravenous tube installed semipermanently under the skin, enabled Garden Lodge residents and dedicated caregivers personal assistant Peter Freestone, cook Joe Fanelli, or partner and gardener Jim Hutton to administer drugs without need of a nurse).

While Mercury recuperated at home, Freestone began to notice the singer drifting apart from many of his close relationships. In his *Mercury* memoir, he attributed it to a kind yet self-protective intention: "He didn't want to put people he loved through the pain of watching him die and being unable to do anything about it. . . . These people also reminded him of what his life used to be like, a life which he could no longer enjoy. . . . Freddie, in the event, had the willpower to do as he was told by his doctors. No smoking, no drinking and certainly no recreational diversions." During these months, though, Freestone also noted Mercury taking a similar approach with work friends like Mike Moran, his partner on the Montserrat Caballé project; he'd talk to them on the phone, but if they suggested visiting he'd say, "No, you don't want to see me today, dear. I'm not looking very good."

During Mercury's recovery periods, the others kept busy in their own way. Deacon invariably returned to domestic comfort, in March, just as Debbie Leng gave birth to their first child, Rufus Tiger; Taylor set about a third album with the Cross—*Blue Rock* came out that September, again only in Germany. Still feeling able to take on the heavy lifting, May did an early-summer promotional tour for *Innuendo* in America and Canada. Otherwise, he occupied himself with solo recording (first heard in July via his song "Driven By You," advertising U.K. Ford in a TV ad) and putting together the Guitar Expo rock night at a cultural festival in Seville, Spain, on October 19. He assembled a cast including Joe Walsh, Joe Satriani, Extreme's Nuno Bettancourt, and, among other vocalists, Paul Rodgers; not insignificantly for the longer term, the former Free and Bad Company frontman thanked May for getting him "back in the public eye."

Meanwhile, in late May, when the guitarist returned to Montreux from his North American trip, the other three had already completed their parts in the last video Mercury managed to shoot, "These Are The Days Of Our Lives," with his knowing farewell look straight at the camera and twinkling murmur of "I still love you."

Mercury had just bought a (maybe) £350,000 penthouse apartment overlooking Lake Geneva to accommodate his Montreux sojourns more privately. He was so obviously pleased with it that, on September 5, his forty-fifth birthday,

WHILE FREDDIE MERCURY FOUGHT FOR HIS LIFE and *Innuendo* topped the U.K. chart (and in America reached only No. 30), Brian May had a piece of the No. 1 single "The Stonk" by Hale & Pace & the Stonkers (he co-wrote and co-produced it with two British comedians for children's charity Comic Relief). At much the same time, after the Gulf War ended on February 28, 1991, the Hollywood label released a single, free and exclusive to the U.S. Armed Forces, which intercut "We Are The Champions" with President George Bush's victory speech.

The band may never have known about this last oddity. They remained engrossed in the sporadic creativity of Mercury's dwindling months—which still included video shoots. For "I'm Going Slightly Mad," probably shot on February 14, Mercury storyboarded May as a penguin, Deacon as a jester, and Taylor as a character who walked around with a boiling kettle on his head. Mercury himself played a Lord Byronic figure, wearing a bunch of bananas for a hat. Natural hilarity was muted, though, because Mercury looked haggard and could barely stand (for the pain in his legs he took dihydrocodeine regularly and, later, diamorphine). He had a bed on the set and would lie down between takes. And after all that, the single did no better than No. 22 in the U.K.

Between short, intensive spells of work—virtually all in Montreux now, since Mercury had come to love the peace and

> *"I'm in awe of Queen as a band, just from the way they morphed from pretty much a direct hard rock band into a massively effective progressive rock band and the way they married classical into hard rock … and the way they kept pushing the envelope. 'Bohemian Rhapsody,' to me, took rock to another level. And Queen was mega-versatile—songs like 'Crazy Little Thing Called Love' that were practically 1950s to songs like 'Killer Queen' and 'Tie Your Mother Down' that were out-and-out rockers. Just watching that band morph and change directions over the years was just amazing.'"*
>
> —PAUL O'NEILL, TRANS SIBERIAN ORCHESTRA

Freestone, Fanelli, and Hutton produced a birthday cake in the shape of the building (created by Jane Asher, Paul McCartney's girlfriend in the '60s, later an actress and celebrity cook).

In the end, he probably used the apartment only three times, as Queen, pursuing his instructions to throw every song they had at him while he could still sing, recorded what were effectively demos—with special attention given to the vocal track—in May, June, August, October, and November. "We became closer," Taylor told Adam Jones of *Rhythm* magazine in 2002. "He wanted to occupy his mind and his days. So we spent long, cloistered periods just backing him up and forming a protective wall. It was actually a good time in a way, because we felt very close—the closest we've ever been."

For all his resilience, just after his birthday Mercury began preparations for his departure. He asked his doctors—Gordon Atkinson and AIDS specialist Graham Moyle—to Garden Lodge for a thank you dinner. On September 17, he wrote a new will.

During Queen's later Montreux sessions, as Taylor recalled for *Rhythm* in 2002, "Freddie was doing all his singing in the control room because he couldn't walk into the studio." He refused to use crutches or sticks. But he did rise to the challenge on his very last recorded vocal, "Mother Love" (later released on *Made In Heaven*). In BBC Radio 1's 1995 Queen documentary, May said, "At some point Fred said 'No, no, no, this isn't good enough, I have to go higher here, I have to put more into this, I have to get more power in.' So he downs a couple of vodkas, stands up, and goes for it. And you can hear the middle eight of 'Mother Love' just soars to incredible heights . . . and this is a man who can't really stand any more without incredible pain and is very weak, has no flesh on his bones, and you can hear the power, the *will* that he's still got."

However, Mercury had clearly taken his own measure of the willpower remaining in his once prodigious reserves. In *Mercury And Me*, Hutton writes, "It was during that visit [to Montreux] that he made the important decision to come off his medication and die. . . . The fight against his disease was over; he was ready to slip away without any further struggle." After returning from Montreux on November 9, he took only painkillers. Freestone's memoir adds, "He had never let the disease totally dictate his life and when he felt his control slipping, he made a conscious decision to re-take it. Ultimate control. . . . The doctors had told each of us that we had to enable him to let go, that in order to make it easier for people to die, they had to be told that it was OK by those they were about to leave behind."

As he gradually declined over the next two weeks—and journalists gathered at his gate—Mercury bade (probably unspoken) farewells to his parents, the band and their partners, and a few good friends like Elton John. Regular visitors to Garden Lodge remained Mary Austin, Dave Clark, and Jim Beach—by then not only Queen's manager but Mercury's executor.

On Friday, November 22, Mercury and Beach spent five hours together. One immediate outcome was that, the following day, Queen's publicist Roxy Meade read to the media assembled outside the house Mercury's statement that he had AIDS: "I felt it correct to keep this information private to date in order to protect the privacy of those around me. However, the time has now come for my friends and fans around the world to know the truth."

Over the following weeks, some gay rights and AIDS campaigners complained that Mercury had announced his illness too late to benefit the cause. But Roger Taylor supported him. "The last thing he wanted was to draw attention to any kind of weakness or frailty," the drummer told BBC Radio 1 in 1995. "He didn't want pity . . . and he was incredibly brave about the whole thing. Having said that, he didn't want to be usurped by going, popping off—'Look, I might pop off at any moment,' that's what he used to say—having not announced it, so I think it was absolutely right to do it at the time it was done."

Mercury died on Sunday evening, November 24, 1991.

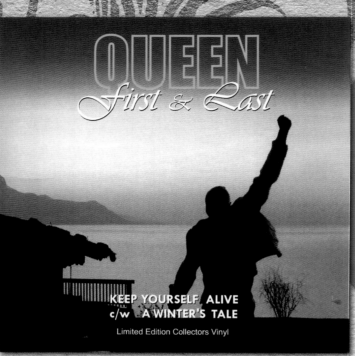
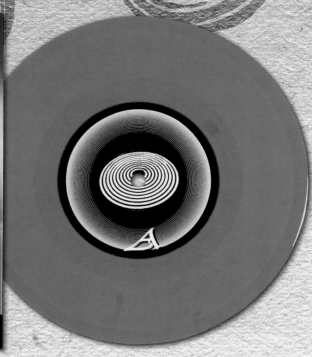

Limited-edition vinyl featuring Queen's first and last 7-inch releases. "First & Last" was released with four sleeves, each featuring one of Mick Rock's *Queen II*-era images on the back, as well as in red vinyl.

An announcement just after midnight said the cause of death was "broncho-pneumonia brought on by AIDS." The following morning, the band issued their statement: "We have lost the greatest and most beloved member of our family. We feel overwhelming grief that he has gone, sadness that he should be cut down at the height of his creativity, but above all great pride in the courageous way that he lived and died. . . . As soon as we are able we would like to celebrate his life in the style to which he was accustomed."

Incongruously, May's "Driven By You" single came out that Monday. He'd worried that some such ghastly coincidence might arise, but he checked with Mercury via Beach and received characteristic reassurance: "He must release it, what better publicity could you have?" He wasn't wrong: it reached U.K. No. 6.

For a few days, while Garden Lodge took delivery of so many flowers they covered the lawn, formal and religious process took over. Freestone, whose father managed a local undertaker's, made the practical arrangements. He registered the death; the certificate names the deceased as "Frederick Mercury, otherwise Frederick Bulsara," suggesting that even Freestone knew so little of his friend's Asian background that he was unaware of his given first name, Farrokh. Mercury's parents arranged the Zoroastrian religious observances in the ancient Avestan language (a relation of Vedic Sanskrit).

On Wednesday the 27th, at John Nodes & Son, the undertaker's in Ladbroke Grove, the family and two priests gathered early in the morning for the first stages of the service.

Then they drove to West London Crematorium, Harrow Road, joining about thirty other mourners, including the band, Hutton, Freestone, Fanelli, Mary Austin, Dave Clark, and Elton John. Police confined photographers and reporters behind barriers on the other side of the road. The service began with a tape of Aretha Franklin, Mercury's second-favorite vocalist, singing a gospel medley—"Precious Lord (Take My Hand)" and "You've Got A Friend"—and closed with his absolute favorite, Montserrat Caballé, and a recording of "D'Amor Sull'Ali Rosee" ("On The Rosy Wings Of Love") from Verdi's *Il Trovatore*.

Then everyone dispersed to go through their own experiences of mourning, its aftermath, and fallout.

Mercury had told Hutton, Freestone, and Fanelli they could stay at Garden Lodge as long as they wished. But he didn't write it in his will. They had to leave within a couple of months as the main beneficiary, Mary Austin, who was about to have her second child, prepared to move in (she got half of the £8.6 million estate, after bequests, plus future royalty income). But all three received bequests of £500,000. In subsequent years Hutton went home to Ireland, Freestone became a nurse, and Fanelli shortly died of AIDS. The will divided the other half of the remaining estate between Mercury's parents and his sister.

(continued on pg. 232)

"The older I got, the more I got into Queen, and I got into the harmonies, which were just unreal. . . . It was one of those things where you go, 'Man, I wish I would've started listening to this earlier.' I think Freddie Mercury was one of the best singers that ever lived. I think he would look around at a lot of this stuff today and laugh his ass off 'cause it would be so funny to him. Then again, he'd probably be a god to some of these people because he was such a great frontman, such a good singer, and just incredibly gifted man.'"

—COREY TAYLOR, SLIPKNOT

"Some of my favorite songs and some of the only songs that I know all the words to are Queen. . . My favorite's definitely 'We Are The Champions.' Something about that song is so powerful, and if they play it at a stadium or in a sports arena, everyone knows that song. It's so amazing when you can have a part of history like that, a song that the whole world knows. It's such a feat.'"

—Lance Bass, *NSYNC

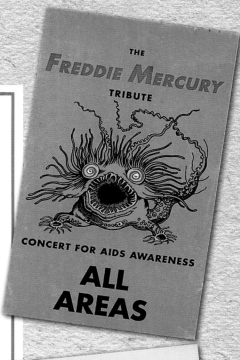

THE

FREDDIE MERCURY
TRIBUTE

SOLD OUT
THANK YOU ALL

CONCERT FOR AIDS AWARENESS
Profits to Aids Charities Worldwide

EASTER MONDAY APRIL 20th 1992
WEMBLEY STADIUM
Gates open 3.30pm   Show starts 6.00pm   Show finishes approx. 9.00pm

General Admission £25
A limited number of Reserved Seats at £30 and £35 available only by calling 081 862 0202

Personal callers welcome at Wembley Box Office and at Virgin Megastore Oxford St. & Marble Arch
also Allders of Croydon, Allders of Sutton, Bentalls of Kingston, and all branches of Keith Prowse

CREDIT CARD HOTLINES
Wembley Stadium 081 900 1234 / 071 240 7200 / 071 379 6131 / 071 836 4114
071 734 8932 / 071 580 3141

Limit of 6 tickets per person
(All tickets subject to booking fee except for personal callers at Wembley Box Office)
INFORMATION LINE (0891) 500 255 (calls charged at 36p cheap rate, 48p other times)

Concert produced by Queen and Harvey Goldsmith Entertainments   © 1992 Queen Productions Ltd.

THE

FREDDIE MERCURY
TRIBUTE

CONCERT FOR AIDS AWARENESS

STADIUM
ACCESS

Passes, Freddie Mercury Tribute Concert for AIDS Awareness, Wembley Stadium, London, April 20, 1992.

SLASH ON BRIAN MAY

BRIAN MAY IS A PHENOMENAL GUITAR PLAYER—one of a kind, actually, and one of my all-time favorite guitarists. Everybody's familiar with Brian, but at the same time I think he's extremely underrated because he's such a unique individual as far as his guitar style and his sound are concerned. He's just a brilliant player, and all of those intricate melody lines that he uses for a majority of the Queen material—it's really sort of technically amazing how he does it.

He's a very delicate player, for starters. In some cases you can definitely hear it, but in a lot of cases you wouldn't expect the sound you hear to be coming from somebody who's approaching the guitar with such a light touch. It sounds a lot more aggressive than the way he's physically playing with his hands. That comes from a combination of things that are unique to him. He plays with a coin, and that has a certain kind of attack that is definitely audible in the songs. And while Vox amps have been around forever, his use of the Vox has definitely given him an original sound that's unencumbered by a lot of technology. A lot of the stuff that's amazing that he does is encompassed by his own ears and how he puts harmonies together or phrases that he uses and notes that he uses.

Also, I've heard all kinds of stories and read all kinds of articles about his guitar. That guitar has such a unique sound that I think only Brian can pick it up and play it and make it sound like that. I don't think the guitar would sound like that for anybody else but him.

So that's a start. And then what you have on record, in the discography of Queen, is a brand of rock 'n' roll that is almost completely different than any other band because the chordings are so different and there's so many layers of melodies going on, so many different harmonies and counterpoint stuff. It's got a certain kind of . . . you want to say classical, but some of it is almost ragtime. It's just a completely unique choice of notes and melodies, almost a whole style of music unto itself. You put that all together and you've got somebody who is completely left-field as far as his contemporaries are concerned.

When I first started listening to Queen, I was actually drawn to their really hard rock stuff. That's how I started. I didn't start to recognize the other stuff until later. But even in his rock 'n' roll stuff, like "Tie Your Mother Down" or a great song called "Fight From The Inside" on *News Of The World*, he still has his own approach. He still hits all the right notes that make them rock, but it's done with a certain type of style that's hard to explain, but it's something he does very naturally.

A lot of people could be judgmental and say because Queen does all this multilayered stuff that it's a recording phenomenon. But they'll turn right around and do hard-hitting rock songs that are as good as or better than anybody else. Roger Taylor's "Fight From The Inside" is one of my favorite songs, and his "Sheer Heart Attack" is fucking awesome; I covered that in a band I was in when I was a kid. Brian's "Brighton Rock," that was fucking awesome, too, and "Stone Cold Crazy."

One of the biggest Queen songs of all time, "We Are The Champions," is very indicative of Brian's sound and style. It's something that everybody instantly recognizes. That real simple approach he's got in that song is an earmark for a lot of the Queen approach, that very melodic, kind of classical technique and sound and style. And that whole bit he does at the end of the song, which is really a simple one-guitar thing but it's played in such a way and with such great intonation and a certain timing to it that you have to stop for a second and go, "This guy's really great."

You just have to realize what a wide range of music Queen covers. Really great bands have a certain chemistry and they work well together. But not too many bands are as musically gifted as individuals like Queen is. I've never sat there over the years and analyzed who

"GENUINE, SINCERE, POLITE, AND PLEASANT"

As told to Gary Graff

wrote what, but I'd find out that Brian did a lot of stuff I wouldn't have expected he wrote, and John Deacon did this and Freddie did that, and a lot of my favorite Queen songs Roger actually sang. But they all come together and have this very unique musical direction. Stuff that seems to feature Freddie and the vocal harmonies, Brian will manage to keep the guitar sections as interesting as the vocals by having call-and-answer guitar harmonies that are very tied together with the vocals. He'll do one line that complements the track and maybe another one that

is underlying the whole thing, or adding nuances that are part of the intricacy of how the melody's tied together. It's the kind of stuff that makes you think of composers way back in the day sitting down and writing out huge classical compositions.

The cool thing is I've played with Brian a few times, and his playing is very indicative of his personality. He's one of the few guys you can meet who's so genuine and sincere and polite and pleasant to be around—a lot like his guitar playing. ⚜

Slash and Brian perform at the Freddie Mercury Tribute Concert For AIDS Awareness, Wembley Stadium, London, April 20, 1992.
Mick Hutson/Redferns Collection/Getty Images

(continued from pg. 226)

Some expressed surprise that Mercury left nothing to AIDS charities, but in line with his wishes, the immediate U.K. re-release of "Bohemian Rhapsody" backed with "These Are The Days Of Our Lives" produced £1 million for the benefit of then-struggling AIDS charity the Terrence Higgins Trust. In America, "Bohemian Rhapsody," coincidentally boosted by the *Wayne's World* movie phenomenon, reached No. 2 in May 1992 and raised $300,000 for the Magic Johnson AIDS Foundation.

Then, picking up a "special award" for Mercury at the Brits in February, May and Taylor announced A Concert for Life, both a Live Aid–style Wembley Stadium celebration of Mercury and a fundraiser for the newly created Mercury Phoenix Trust to finance AIDS projects in the U.K. and around the world (trustees May, Taylor, Beach, and Austin, with Deacon opting out for reasons unreported). Before any of the bill had been announced all seventy-two thousand tickets sold out in six hours.

Queen committed themselves to securing artists suitable to the occasion in terms of status and association with Mercury. Taylor told *Mojo*'s David Thomas in 1999, "I threw all my energy and my persuasive telephonic powers into it. That was good for about three months and it kept my mind off what I was going to do."

With Gerry Stickells hammering out the details as ever, by April 20 Queen had a potent list of names together and had even rehearsed with those who were going to sing as substitutes for Mercury—a difficult business for all comers.

That afternoon, May's opening announcement promised Mercury "the biggest send-off in history" and Taylor set out the objectives: "Today is for Freddie, it's for you, it's to tell everybody around the world that AIDS affects us all. That's what these red ribbons are about. And you can cry as much as you like." Deacon drew the short-straw punch line, "The show must go on."

Said show had highs (George Michael's bravura "Somebody To Love"). It had lows (Robert Plant valiantly losing his battle with "Innuendo"). It had controversies (gay Elton John dueting with Axl Rose despite his homophobic "One In A Million" lyrics). It had embarrassments for those who blush at anything a little off the wall (Elizabeth Taylor's speech, David Bowie kneeling to recite "The Lord's Prayer"). It achieved practical results: glimmerings of AIDS awareness conveyed to an alleged one billion TV viewers in more than seventy countries; a flying start for the Mercury Phoenix Trust (which, by February 2009, reported £8 million granted to six hundred AIDS organizations globally).

And it served an emotional purpose for masses of fans and for Queen themselves. In 2002, Taylor told *Rhythm* magazine,

"It helped me at the time . . . it took away a bit of the pain." Speaking to VH1 in 1997, May remembered how Def Leppard singer Joe Elliott showed him that this was a fitting farewell both to his friend and, probably, his own life as a megastar: "He grabbed my sleeve as we were going offstage at the end and said, 'Brian, you have to stop and just look at this and think what it is, because you're never gonna see anything like this again.' And he was right. . . ." (At the time, but subsequently disproved, it turns out.)

Still, they made no official declaration that the band was over. In a radio interview, Mercury had once hypothesized that "If I suddenly left . . . they would just replace me," but he added, eyebrow audibly raised, "Not easy to replace me, huh?" Over the next few months the other three variously called the very idea "impossible" and "wrong" because it would mean "*pretending* to be Queen."

Essentially, for the next year or so Deacon and Taylor took a break. The drummer pondered his future—"Not sure if I even wanted to be involved in music any more"—and the bassist virtually started his retirement right there (his sixth child, Cameron, arrived on November 7, 1993). But May at last seriously set about launching his solo career. In September 1992, his second single, "Too Much Love Will Kill You," which he'd sung at A Concert for Life, reached No. 5 in the U.K., and the following month his album *Back To The Light* hit No. 6 (but only 159 in the States). Next, unpredictably, in November he gathered up the new Brian May Band—featuring Spike Edney on keyboards, Chicagoan Jamie Moses on second guitar, plus a veteran hard rock rhythm section in Cozy Powell on drums and Neil Murray on bass—and flew to South America (Argentina, Chile, Uruguay, and Brazil) to develop their teamwork.

Over the following months he gigged hard, supporting Joe Cocker at the Vélez Sarsfield Stadium in Buenos Aires, headlining a club in Rio de Janeiro, and supporting Guns N' Roses on an American tour. On he went, quietly appreciated by the band for gestures like always refusing limos and travelling in the communal van. Pausing only for occasional interesting sessions (with Dweezil Zappa and Paul Rodgers, for instance), from May 22 to December 17 he played one-offs in Israel, Turkey, and Greece, toured the U.K. and Europe (partly supporting Guns N' Roses), North America again, Japan, and Europe again, concluding with the band's eighty-ninth date of the year, Oporto, Portugal.

By the time May slowed down, Taylor had a new solo album on the go. He reintroduced himself with a startlingly aggressive political single, "Nazis" in May 1994. Thinking "at my stage of life I might as well write about something I believe," he told

Radio 1 that a TV program about Holocaust denial had lit his fuse: "I just thought that's the most outrageous, stupid, and dangerous belief." "Nazis" reached No. 22 in the U.K., as did his album *Happiness* that September (out on Parlophone in America, it didn't chart).

And all the while, Queen's past loomed over them as live, re-released, and compiled material kept on selling—notably the *Five Live* EP featuring George Michael with Queen from A Concert for Life (U.K. No. 1 in May 1993,). But they all knew there was unfinished business.

By spring 1994, Taylor and Deacon had started work on Mercury's valiant last recordings from Montreux. In his Radio 1 interview about "Nazis," Taylor said: "I've seen quite a lot of John and a little bit of Brian. And we have started work on finishing some stuff that we started with Freddie. In due course I think that will appear as a complete album. He was working right up to the end with the full intention of those works coming to fruition. So it's almost a duty to finish them." Listening to those recordings felt "odd" at first, Taylor said, "with Fred just a disembodied voice in the headphones."

Looking back in 1999, he told *Mojo*'s David Thomas: "It took a couple of weeks to get over the sound of Freddie. The worst thing was the little spoken ad libs in between the takes, that was weird. But after a while you know every breath and they cease to be so poignant, it's all just part of the material."

May seemed hesitant. But then, as he admitted to *Q* magazine in 1998, he suddenly realized he was getting left out—and promptly took charge: "After Freddie died, my way of dealing with it was to go back out on tour. But Roger and John became very impatient with me and started working on the tapes. I didn't want this stuff to go out without my involvement so I took the tapes off them, felt that they'd done it wrong and spent months putting it all back together. Doing *Made In Heaven* was like assembling a jigsaw puzzle. . . . Because the others had begun without me, it started off in a fairly stressful way. It became an enormous task and it took literally two years out of my life, sitting in front of a computer trying to make the most out of the scraps that we had of Freddie's vocal, or arranging and producing and performing to fill in the gaps."

"*Made In Heaven* was hard work," Taylor agreed, speaking to *Rhythm* in 2002. "I think it's a very strong album—certainly

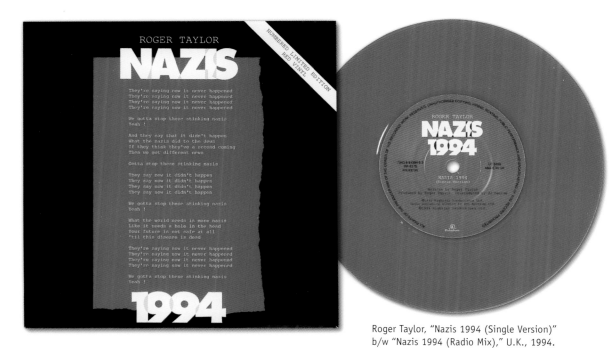

Roger Taylor, "Nazis 1994 (Single Version)" b/w "Nazis 1994 (Radio Mix)," U.K., 1994.

the most emotional album. When you look back . . . you go around pretending that it's not that bad; it was five years [after Freddie died] before any of us really realised the tremendous effect it had."

But at least they'd had twenty years of extreme experience with Mercury: tempests of diva temperament alternated with, if not exactly balanced by, summer breezes of genuine kindness and adroit diplomacy. As Mercury explained in an archive interview on Radio 1's 1995 Queen documentary, essentially he believed in creative conflict: "A Queen album is made up of that anyway. You have to fight. That's the best way. With me, if it was made too easy, I would come up with . . . lesser material. I like to fight, and I make everyone else fight as well. Then you get the crème de la crème, the cream of the crop." In his memoir, Freestone assessed Mercury's approach as instinctive yet also cynically pragmatic on occasions: "Freddie needed conflict and confrontation as a vital catalyst . . . he knew the value of a tantrum . . . if he could make people worried that he was going to walk out on a project."

So the three went at the album and each other, in memory of "precious" times and their flouncy friend's ultimate toughness. As May told Radio 1, "I never saw him lay down, put his head in his hands, and let it all get on top of him, never ever."

Released in November 1995, *Made In Heaven* reached No. 1 in the U.K. and No. 58 in America, and did very well around the world. It justified the trio of survivors' struggles with an improbable display of high-octane Queen-ness. While they built from fragments (and older songs and tracks) on occasions, even from the shadow of death Mercury sings with undiminished power and scope, giving everything to one agonized song about himself, "Mother Love" ("I don't want pity, just a safe place to hide") and another by and about his friend the guitarist, "Too Much Love Will Kill You" ("Torn between the lover/And the love you leave behind").

Mercury's conflict theory was on May's mind when he took part in that Radio 1 documentary just after *Made In Heaven*'s release: "This last album is . . . one of the most ridiculously painful experiences creatively I've ever had, but I'm sure the quality's good partly because we did have those arguments. Whether it's healthy for life or not is another matter. I don't think so. And having had twenty years of this very volatile democracy, I don't feel I need it in my life any more. I've done it for this album because I thought it was very important to get those last pieces of Freddie out there. If it hadn't been for that, I wouldn't have wanted to do it, I would have valued my life more than the process." ♔

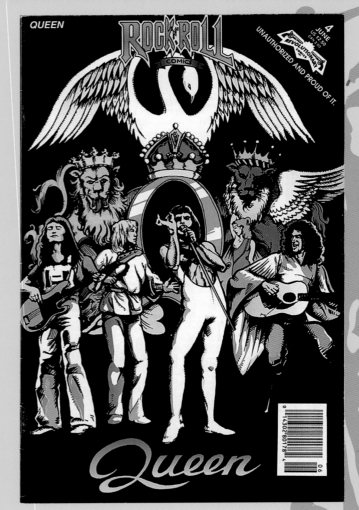

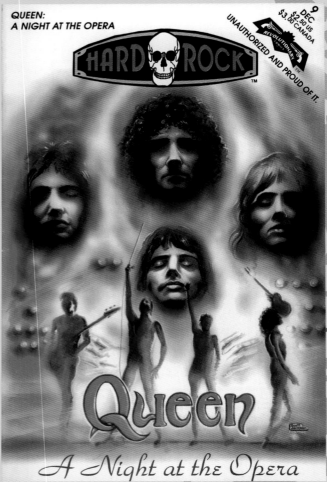

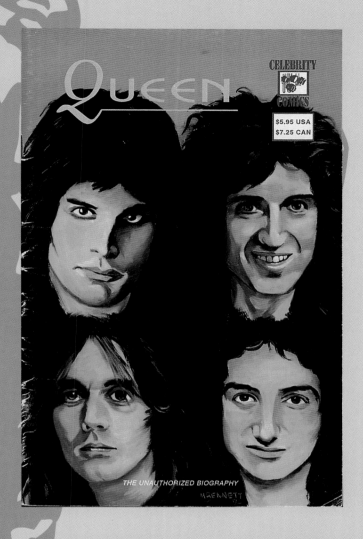

Unofficial Queen comics: *Rock 'N' Roll Comics*, © Revolutionary Comics, 1992 *(opposite top)*, *Hard Rock*, © Revolutionary Comics, 1992 *(opposite bottom)*, and *Rock 'N' Roll Comics*, ©Revolutionary Comics, 1993 *(right)*. All courtesy Jay Allen Sanford. *Queen: The Unauthorized Biography*, © Personality Comics, 1992 *(above)*.

QUEEN

TOO MUCH LOVE WILL KILL YOU

b/w "We Will Rock You" and "We Are The Champions," 1996.

Made in Heaven

by Sylvie Simmons

1995.

THE PICTURE ON THE SLEEVE of Queen's fifteenth studio album couldn't be much more metaphorical: a shadowy shot of Freddie Mercury in familiar pose, legs apart, right arm punching the air in triumph, only he's turned his back on us and is looking into the distance at a peaceful, idyllic vista—a lake under a sky washed with the faint blood of sunset.

In November 1995, when *Made In Heaven* was released, Queen's flamboyant frontman had been dead for four years—the photo is of a statue. None of which would be enough to stop Mercury from working the crowd—or, given the circumstances under which the album was made, of working the emotions.

In 1991, with *Innuendo* topping the U.K. charts and widely hailed as their best album since the 1970s, Queen should have been on a high, were it not for their singer's rapidly deteriorating health. Freddie knew he was dying; they did too. They also knew they wanted to make a final album. There wasn't a lot of time to write new songs, though Mercury finished one in its entirety, the ballad "A Winter's Tale," and co-wrote another emotive ballad with Brian May, "Mother Love." He also sang songs that were already written, like "Too Much Love," from a Brian May solo album, John Deacon's "My Life Has Been Saved," and "Heaven For Everyone," which Roger Taylor had written for his side band The Cross. Yes, there's definitely a theme of pain and reflection, just as there was with the songs Johnny Cash covered toward the end of his life. And, like Cash, Mercury made the songs his own.

Returning the favor, Queen covered two songs from Mercury's 1985 solo debut *Mr. Bad Guy*, giving the full-on, heavy, pomp-rock treatment to "I Was Born To Love You" and adding the trademark Queen sound to "Made In Heaven." Choosing one of Freddie's solo songs for the title track and one of his most breathlessly over-the-top creations at that—part poignant Puccini aria, part passionate hymn—was no accident. Because although this album is all about Queen—the band, the production, the painstaking team effort that pieced together all the various odds and ends into a seamless hole (the *Hot Space*–ish "You Don't

Fool Me" is a prime example of an epic song conjured from a bunch of different snippets Mercury sang on)—it is also all about Freddie.

When Mercury died, Queen's official statement said that, as soon as bandmembers felt able, they would "celebrate his life in the style to which he was accustomed," and that's what they tried to do here. Which is why, among the perfectly understandable introspective songs, there are still moments of life-affirming, show-must-go-on, Freddie Mercury grandeur.

Just listen to "Mother Love"—it's hard not to get a lump in your throat when Mercury sings lines like "I've walked too long in this lonely lane/My heart is heavy and my hope is gone" or when May steps in as vocalist on the last verse. But suddenly, in the fade-out, here's Freddie, back in his full glory, instructing the crowd at a 1986 Wembley Stadium concert in operatic vocal exercises. You can just picture him, standing at the microphone, legs astride, hand in a fist, triumphantly punching the air. ⚜

11 CARRY ON, CARRY ON

So BEGAN A LONG PERIOD OF UNCERTAINTY for May, Taylor, and Deacon regarding their musical and, to varying degrees, their personal identities. They didn't know whether or not they would play together again, still mourned for Mercury, had no plans. But in the world's eyes they were Queen, commercially and ceremonially.

Reminders constantly arose. For months the *Made In Heaven* singles drifted in and out of radio playlists and the U.K. charts (none of them made much impression in America). The *Ultimate Queen* twenty-CD box set emerged late in 1995 and a CD-ROM computer game, *Queen: The Eye*, soundtracked by their music, twelve months later. At the Brits in February 1996, Taylor presented the new Freddie Mercury Award for music-related charity work to the War Child campaign for the welfare of children in war zones. And so on.

More personally, family, friends, and fans had been discussing the possibility of a Mercury memorial. After rejection in London, the proposal found a welcome in Montreux. The municipal commune agreed that eminent Czech sculptor Irena Sedlecká's dynamic, life-size bronze—already seen in silhouette on the cover of *Made In Heaven*—should be installed beside his (latterly) beloved Lake Geneva. Unveiling it on November 25, 1996, in the presence of, among others, Jer and Bomi Bulsara and Montserrat Caballé, May thanked the township for offering Mercury "a kind of sanctuary." The base carried a dedication written by May: "Lover of life, singer of songs."

But the memorial did not mean closure. Another Queen year began, rewardingly, with the great French choreographer Maurice Béjart presenting *A Ballet For Life* (known as *Le Presbytère* in French), accompanied by six Mozart pieces and seventeen Queen songs—from 1974's "Brighton Rock" to 1995's "A Winter's Tale"—in memory of Mercury and

Stick-on guest pass, Arrowhead Pond, Anaheim, April 3, 2006.

Stick-on pass, Wembley Arena, London, November 8, 2008.

Olympiahalle, Munich, April 14, 2005. *Joerg Koch/AFP/Getty Images*

Argentinean dancer Jorge Donn, who also died of AIDS. This was no pop gimmick for Béjart, who wrote of his "love affair with the music by Queen. Invention, violence, humor, love: it's all there." May, Taylor, Deacon, and Elton John all attended the January 18, 1997, premiere at the Théâtre National de Chaillot, Paris, and joined the dancers onstage to play "The Show Must Go On." Afterward, in a VH1 interview, Taylor allowed that having "a few bits of Mozart thrown in" around the band's music was "quite a flattering mixture."

A 2007 photo silhouettes the statue of Freddie that was unveiled on the shore of Lake Leman, Montreux, November 25, 1996. *Fabrice Coffrini/AFP/Getty Images*

But in the same TV program, May showed his continuing emotional confusion about the future: "I've been trying to get Queen out of my system. I know that probably doesn't sound very nice, but in a way it's unhealthy to be just clinging to the past." Taylor spoke seriously too: "It's been five years since Freddie's death, and I think we don't feel quite so precious about it as we did. . . . I think maybe the future is open to us doing something again. . . . Elton said, 'You lot are like a fantastic racing car, sitting in the garage with no bloody driver,' which was a great analogy. We'll see."

Taylor and May then responded to EMI's request for a compilation by putting together *Queen Rocks* (*Rocks, Vol. 1* in the United States), released on November 3, a hard and heavy collection notable only for its lone quiet track, a new song mourning Mercury called "No One But You (Only The Good Die Young)." May wrote it for his ever ongoing second solo album and sent a demo to Taylor. When he eventually listened, as he told Radio KKLZ, Las Vegas, in December 1997, "I just thought, 'It sounds like a Queen song,' and 'Boy, do we need John here.'" They called Deacon and he joined them in recording both the track and a simple black-and-white performance video. A U.K. single in January 1998 reached No. 13. Of course, nobody knew it would be Deacon's last recording with the band (to date).

This coming together made the fragile May feel more separate again. In an April 1998, interview with Ian Fortnam (unpublished then, now at rocksbackpages.com) he said: "It reminded me that really I'm happier doing what I do now [recording with the Brian May Band]. I don't have to be Queen anymore. In some ways, although I have great sadness about it, it's a relief."

While Deacon largely withdrew from Queen (bar some business oversight) and public life generally, Taylor and May spent the next year on solo albums—and the odd meeting with Robert De Niro, who seemed "really into" an idea they had for a stage musical.

Working at his home studio in the Surrey countryside, May finished *Another World* in spring 1998. Almost immediately, on April 5, Brian May Band drummer Cozy Powell died in a car crash. Aged fifty, the formidable ex-member of Black Sabbath, Rainbow, and Whitesnake had been a good friend of May's since 1976. May reacted by hitting the road with his band, as he had done in the aftermath of Mercury's death, touring Europe, the U.K., Japan, and Australia, from June to November.

QUEEN ROCKS

New!
Special Heavy Vinyl
18 Classic Queen rock anthems
including their brand new single
No-One But You
(ONLY THE GOOD DIE YOUNG)
PLUS
We Will Rock You, One Vision,
Fat Bottomed Girls & I Want It All

The compilation Roger and Brian assembled for EMI in 1997.

13th QUEEN CONVENTION
QUEEN ROCKS !
PRESTATYN
7-8-9-10 MAY
1998

LIMITED
EDITION
NUMBERED
ORANGE
VINYL
8861237

roger taylor

PRESSURE ON

3991
LIMITED EDITION

roger taylor
PRESSURE ON

side one
1. PRESSURE ON

℗1998 The copyright in this sound recording
is owned by Nightjar Productions Ltd.
under exclusive licence to EMI Records Ltd.
©1998 Nightjar Productions Ltd.

After three years of sporadic work, Taylor finally completed his solo, *Electric Fire*, released that October and previewed, on September 24, by a live performance to the biggest internet audience up to that time, 595,000. Even so, the album reached only No. 53 on the U.K. chart and dropped out after one week—much like May's *Another World*, which hit No. 23 but disappeared after two weeks. While Taylor had come to insist he played solo for "fun" only, May admitted a degree of frustration to *Mojo*'s David Thomas in 1999: "I've done some damn good stuff and some of it warranted wider exposure."

The past tugged at them relentlessly, symbolized aptly when restoration of the Red Special guitar May built with his father revealed it was clogged with shards of metal shaved off the pre-decimalization (1971) sixpenny bits he'd always used instead of a plectrum.

> "I love Queen. The more you listen to Queen, the more you realize, especially if you're a musician, how much of a genius Freddie Mercury was, and Brian May and those guys are. Freddie Mercury was just an incredible talent. He was a piano player, singer, could play pretty much anything; and performance-wise he was outrageous. It's just the sensibility of the music that seems to be missing so much nowadays, and it just routes right back to the blues and R&B. You can hear those elements and traces throughout their songs, whether it's 'Crazy Little Thing Called Love' or 'Fat Bottomed Girls,' which to me is a country song. They're just timeless, timeless classics—which sounds like [the name of] a K-Tel record, but they really are timeless classics.'"
>
> —Kid Rock

In January 1999, they started looking at old Queen rarities and outtakes, probably for what eventually became the *Freddie Mercury Solo* ten-CD box (November 2000, called *Solo Collection* in America). In June, Queen even featured on a Royal Mail postage stamp and provoked traditionalist protests because of it. Whereas regulations decreed that only dead people and Royal Family members could have their own stamp, the stamp clearly depicted Taylor at the drums behind Mercury.

The very much undeceased drummer still hankered for the old band. At the end of his low-key U.K. solo tour in March and April 1999, Taylor told the *Daily Express*: "I spoke to Brian last week and he suggested we book a studio, write a song and

see what happens. I haven't spoken to John in ages, but Brian and I are hopeful he will do it."

However, around that time, May's volatile, on-off relationship with Anita Dobson blew apart (the tabloid version blamed an affair of his), and he slipped into another depression. Some months earlier, when Ian Fortnam interviewed him at his country home, May described the fundamental sense of isolation he often suffered: "It's an icy feeling which can grab your heart and say, 'Nobody loves me. . . . Here I am on my own.' Depression is a sort of illness which can get you, and I drift in and out of it."

The extended separation from Dobson may have been his lowest ebb. Looking back in 2002, he told the *Daily Mirror*'s Nina Myskow, "I thought my life was over. . . . Depression would clamp down like a fog. . . . I can remember looking up at planes and thinking, 'My God, somebody built that plane, somebody is flying it. . . . How can people be so in control of their lives?'"

He started to get a grip when he admitted to himself he needed specialist help. In late 1999 or early 2000, he checked into the Cottonwood clinic, near Tucson, Arizona, better known for its drug and drink rehabilitation. Despite that, it seems to have led to a turning point. "It was the beginning of a new life," he told Myskow. "Wipe the slate clean. . . . I'm not religious, but I thank God every day."

By April 2000, May and Dobson were reported holidaying in Seychelles—tabloid stories had him proposing there. They married on November 18 at Richmond Registry Office, Surrey. Taylor, who'd had his fifth child, Lola, that April, served as best man. Deacon didn't come. May later told Myskow that getting married had "strengthened our relationship beyond belief. Now I'm incredibly productive, very enthusiastic, very happy."

Musically, subsequent years found May and Taylor still dancing around the notion of Queen's rebirth. It depended on running into a singer able to handle all the implications of "standing in Freddie's shoes." Early in 2001 they thought it might have happened when they re-recorded "We Are The Champions" with Robbie Williams for the Chaucer-based movie *A Knight's Tale* (starring the late Heath Ledger).

May thought him such a strong candidate that, as he told an Oxford University student interviewer, the first time they met he looked Williams in the eye and said, "OK, you want the job then?" And Williams had always held Mercury in awe. Hope flared, then fizzled, and as May told Mick Wall for *Mojo*

Classic: Queen in 2005, "It never came to fruition, I don't really know why."

A low-key period ensued, interrupted by one major celebration when May, Taylor, and Mercury's mother, Jer—without Deacon—accepted Queen's Rock and Roll Hall of Fame induction at the Waldorf-Astoria, New York, on March 19.

Meanwhile, the Queen musical had gained momentum as soon as the putative plot moved away from band biography to future fantasy set in a land where rock 'n' roll was banned. May and Taylor involved themselves throughout, encouraged by co-producer De Niro's Hollywood oomph. When We Will

Rock You opened at the Dominion Theatre, London, on May 14, 2002, many critics hated it: "Shallow, stupid and totally vacuous" (The Daily Mail) and "Guaranteed to bore you rigid" (The Daily Telegraph). But ticket sales soared. Over the following months and beyond, May and Taylor (by then trying to get over the breakup of his long relationship with Debbie Leng) attended further premieres in the United States, Spain, Germany, Russia, Australia, South Africa, and many other countries as the show became a worldwide smash, much like Abba's Mamma Mia. Everywhere they went they played at cast parties to show their support—and maintain Queenly quality.

Taylor delighted in the show's success as "an adult panto," and, in London, May would make surprise visits, bursting up through a stage trapdoor mid–"Bohemian Rhapsody" to take the guitar solo live.

Elder statesmanship on the periphery of rock 'n' roll beckoned as ceremonial duties proliferated: joining the U.S. Songwriters' Hall of Fame and the Hollywood Walk of Fame. Even May soloing "God Save The Queen" on the roof of Buckingham Palace to celebrate Queen Elizabeth II's fiftieth anniversary as monarch on June 4, 2002, looked a strange combination of rock thrill and establishment embrace.

More meaningful, though, was their role in organizing, and their appearance at, the first concert for Nelson Mandela's 46664 AIDS awareness campaign and charity on November 29, 2003, at Green Point Stadium, Cape Town, South Africa. Via radio, television, and the internet, it was reckoned to be the most widely available live event ever, reaching 166 countries. Naturally, both the Mercury/AIDS aspect and the welcome from Mandela meant much to May and Taylor. When Queen breached the United Nations' cultural boycott by playing Sun City in 1984, Mandela had been serving the twenty-first year of his eventual twenty-seven-year imprisonment for anti-apartheid activities. Significantly, talking to

Mojo's Roy Wilkinson the following year, Taylor offered an acknowledgment of fault and his appreciation of the chance to make enduring amends: "We probably were wrong, but we did it with good intentions. . . . It was naïve though, wasn't it? It felt very good to go back for this 46664 event."

Queen's renaissance began with yet another all-star bash, when May attended the Fender Stratocaster's fiftieth anniversary gig on September 24, 2004, at Royal Albert Hall, London, along with a gang of grizzled guitar greats: David Gilmour, Ronnie Wood, Albert Lee, and Hank Marvin. May backed Paul Rodgers—who'd credited him with career revival back at the 1991 Seville Guitar Expo—on "All Right Now." "I made the first move," May told Mick Wall for *Mojo Classic* in 2005. "After the show we talked. Paul's lady, Cynthia [Kereluk, his manager and wife since September 2007], she stood between us and her eyes went back and forth and she said, 'There's something happening here, isn't there?' We said, 'Well, yes.' She said, 'All you need is a drummer?' I said, 'Well, I do know a drummer.'"

Roger appears at *We Will Rock You* the musical, Star City Lyric Theatre, Sydney, October 11, 2004. *Bob King/Redferns Collection/Getty Images*

May sent Taylor a video of the Fender show. He replied, "I wonder why we didn't think of this before?" Two months later, Queen's induction to the fledgling U.K. Music Hall of Fame at the Hackney Empire theater gave the threesome their first run-out together. May recalled that he'd wavered between encounters. "I was thinking, 'Oh God, should we really be doing this, what am I doing with my life, etc.?' he told Wall. "Then I suddenly saw Paul singing 'We Will Rock You' and I thought, 'Jesus Christ! This is something!'"

From there, as May explained to Dave Ling of *Classic Rock* in 2008, "Roger was definitely the driving force in making

this happen. He wanted to get back on the road somehow." Immediate rehearsals went so well they officially announced the new/old band as Queen + Paul Rodgers on January 25, 2005. Having listed the other members—Spike Edney, Jamie Moses, and bassist Danny Miranda (from Brooklyn, ex–Blue Öyster Cult)—they explained that Deacon had been invited to join them, but, as Taylor told Mark Blake for *Mojo Classic: Queen* that year, "He has decided to hide away—and I respect that." But Deacon OK'd their calling themselves Queen, and Taylor insisted to all comers, "You're a mug not to use your brand name."

Westfallenhalle, Dortmund, Germany, April 25, 2005. *Martin Meissner/AP Images*

Then naturally, every interviewer asked, what would Freddie think? "He would love it because Paul was genuinely one of his all-time favourite singers," said Taylor. "Obviously it's stuff we ask ourselves every day," May told Wall. "I correspond with Freddie's mum and I was anxious to know that she felt alright about it. She sent me a lovely letter confirming she did and wishing us luck. That means a lot."

Rodgers was slightly younger than both May and Taylor—perhaps surprising in that he wrote his first hit, "All Right Now," in 1970. And he came from a fathomlessly different background. Born December 17, 1949, in Middlesbrough on England's northeast coast, he grew up working-class to the marrow—son of a shipyard worker, abbreviated education—and joined three other teenagers in Free in 1968, then founded Bad Company in 1974. While experience had smoothed his roughest edges, Rodgers remained a formidable match for anything May and Taylor's conflictual work habits might throw at him.

However, the early stages seemed to lay sound foundations. Rodgers informed Paul Elliott for *Mojo Classic: Queen* that audiences could expect "Raw-edged, powerhouse, soulful rock and blues," adding a droll warning that Mercury diehards might have to live with "an absence of tights."

MEN Arena, Manchester, May 4, 2005. *Jon Super/Redferns Collection/Getty Images*

Considering how their live set might be constructed, May had no qualms about Queen operating as backing band on the Rodgers classics: "Top of my list would be 'Can't Get Enough' . . . playing it kicks your whole body into life," he told Wall. As Rodgers recalled to Mark Blake of *Mojo*, "At first Brian said, 'Let's do 50 per cent Queen material and 50 per cent your stuff.' I said, 'No, you guys haven't been on the road for a long time. We should do more of yours.'" That settled it. The shows would feature four or five Rodgers songs.

But then May and Taylor had to adjust to Rodgers' greasy R&B riffing approach to Queen's music. "Rhythmically, it's very different," May told Jonathan Wingate for *Record Collector* in 2009. "Freddie was an instinctively on-the-beat guy. His piano playing was rivetingly percussive at times and his singing was the same . . . like a machine gun. Paul is interpreting as he goes so we have to really be quite strong to provide the backdrop he needs."

Queen + Paul Rodgers debuted, appropriately, on another show in South Africa for the 46664 campaign, at Fancourt Country Club, George, home of Nelson Mandela Metropolitan University, on March 19, 2005, with Will Smith hosting. Then the band embarked on a tour that grew and grew: twenty-six dates in the U.K. and Europe; stadiums and festivals in July, the biggest back in Hyde Park, London, when sixty-five thousand attended despite a week's postponement after the London suicide bombings killed fifty-six people.

While they took a break in September, a live double CD, *Return Of The Champions*, recorded at Sheffield

Scrutinizing the newcomer, Taylor marvelled that "Paul's range is phenomenal. I wouldn't have thought he could hit those high notes, but he can" (*San Jose Mercury*, 2006). May, in pursuit of some satisfying way to "reinterpret the past," noted that "Everyone else [who covered Queen songs] has always tried to sing it like Freddie. Paul looked at the words, then did it *his* way."

Hallam Arena on May 9, reached Nos. 12 in the U.K. and 84 in America. In October they played Aruba, Japan, then Queen's first two U.S. gigs since 1982, at Meadowlands, New Jersey, and the Hollywood Bowl, Los Angeles. They returned to North America the following March for a full tour, twenty-four shows, the top-line tickets a controversial $200.

Characteristically, May sometimes worried the heavy touring might "disconnect" him again. But it didn't, and Taylor could only crow about "rejuvenation" and rediscovering "the pure delight I had when I first got into drums as a kid." And, Rodgers told Blake, when they reached Vancouver, their final gig, on April 13 (and handy for Rodgers' home in the Okanagan Valley, British Columbia), "Normally by the end of a tour everybody is ready to go home, but we weren't. We'd just played what we all felt was the best gig on the tour—we were gobsmackingly together. We all agreed the logical step was to go into the studio."

 "[My doctoral thesis is] about 96 percent done. It breaks my heart because I get no time to finish it. It's all written up, all the work's done, but I can't get that last bit done."

—Brian May, quoted by Jonh Ingham,
Sounds, 27.09.1975

But it took a while. Rodgers had solo commitments. May had developed some less usual involvements. Back in 1975 he told Jonh Ingham of *Sounds* the only trouble with rock stardom was a lack of opportunity for abstract and "erm, extrinsic" thinking. This time around he had that covered via his co-authorship of the popular science book *Bang! The Complete History Of The Universe*, published in November 2006.

In 1996, May had met his childhood astronomy hero Sir Patrick Moore and subsequently made guest appearances on his monthly BBC TV show, *The Sky At Night*, which Moore had presented since April 1957. Eventually the two decided to write the book with octogenarian Moore's young astrophysicist co-presenter Chris Lintott.

The trio's endeavours went down well and, for May, triggered another successful return to his past. He decided to resurrect his PhD thesis on interplanetary dust, thirty-six years after setting it aside when very close to completion. Luckily, studies in his speciality had barely progressed in the meanwhile, and he finally secured his Imperial College doctorate in August 2007. He even talked to scientific website earthsky.org, declaring astronomy a personal antidote to his "severe

depressions." "I would go out and look at the sky and see perhaps Orion, looking very strong and brave and always the same," he said. "Always a friend that I could come back to. I remember looking up and getting a feeling of bravery from the stars, a feeling there was something that was eternal. And that I would get through."

May's better-balanced "extrinsic" life—including by then anything-goes debates with fans via "Brian's Soapbox" on his website—must have helped him handle the comeback. From March 2007, at Taylor's Priory home studio, the three principals started writing and recording, playing all instruments themselves and together "live in the studio." Speaking to Blake, new prime motivator Taylor insisted, "We couldn't become our own tribute band. So if we were going to keep doing this, we had to have some brand-new stuff to play."

Of course, co-writing led to further discovery about one another. Rodgers told Blake: "[With Brian and Roger] it's always, 'What can I add to these songs that nobody else has ever done before?' It's kicked me up the arse. . . . And Roger, when he played me his demos, I was like, 'Who's this amazing guitarist?' He replied, 'It's me.' These men are a constant surprise to me." In their cheeriest moments, May wondered whether "we might even get Paul into a leotard, yet!"

However, Taylor brought out the trickier side of what Rodgers had to cope with: "Brian and I go to incredible lengths to get things right. He'd never met two pickier, fussier individuals," he told Ling. For instance, Rodgers had very little experience singing harmonies—certainly not Queen-style harmonies—and had to toil through some interminable rehearsals. So they had "some discussions," May told Blake, before succumbing to his innate candor: "No, OK, some arguments where we all had to go off and have a think. The last session lasted about three months, which nearly killed me." A few weeks later, he elaborated to Wingate that the mixing and mastering had been the most "stressful" test: "The difficult decisions have been left to the end . . . all sorts of stuff that kind of rankles between us has to be sorted out. It's been quite difficult—in common with every Queen album."

They sent a copy of the album to Deacon and heard nothing—which was good because, as May told David Murray of the Brisbane *Courier Mail*, "There is a tacit agreement. If he doesn't respond he likes it. If he doesn't like something, you hear straight away."

On June 27, 2008, Queen + Paul Rodgers, played Hyde Park again, for guest of honor Nelson Mandela in celebration of his forthcoming ninetieth birthday, alongside Annie Lennox, Simple Minds, Jerry Dammers, Will Smith, and Joan Baez.

The Cosmos Rocks came out in September in Europe, the following month in North America. It carried dedications to

Freddie Mercury and Paul Kossoff, Free's original guitarist who died because of drug and alcohol abuse in 1976, aged twenty-five. Reviews generally expressed indifference. Yet the diverse emotional fervor of all three participants did push through and invigorate almost every track, even if its array of resemblances to everything from Queen, Free, and Bad Company to Santana and Springsteen didn't exactly cohere. Commercially, it was big in Estonia and hit a lot of other Top 10s around Europe, including No. 5 in the U.K. (but only 47 in America).

When they toured, however, prodigious audiences made these middle-aged men very happy. May marvelled at how many teenagers showed up: "Our music seems to connect with people on a strange kind of human and spiritual level, and it seems to go across generations as well, which is incredibly lucky if you want to call it luck," he told Wingate. They opened to the biggest audience any of them had ever seen—345,000 in Freedom Square, Kharkiv, Ukraine, September 12—and journeyed onward to thirty-nine more concerts in twenty countries, among them Russia, Latvia, Serbia, Dubai, Chile, Argentina, and Brazil.

By February 2009, they had made no announcements about plans for the year. But May seemed to have eyes for nothing but the future when he told the Brisbane *Courier Mail*, "I feel it's a new band, I really do. We all bring to it what we have in our histories and what we have in our hearts, but it is a new band."

EXTRA DATES

QUEEN
+ PAUL RODGERS
—— LIVE ——

- FRIDAY 10 OCTOBER
NOTTINGHAM
TRENT FM ARENA
08444 124 624

- SATURDAY 11 OCTOBER -
GLASGOW SE&CC
0870 040 4000

- MONDAY 13 OCTOBER -
- FRIDAY 7 NOVEMBER -
LONDON O2 ARENA
0844 856 0202

- TUESDAY 14 OCTOBER -
CARDIFF
INTERNATIONAL ARENA
029 2022 4488

- THURSDAY 16 OCTOBER -
BIRMINGHAM NIA
0870 909 4114

- SATURDAY 18 OCTOBER -
LIVERPOOL ECHO ARENA
0844 8000 400

- SUNDAY 19 OCTOBER -
SHEFFIELD ARENA
0114 256 56 56

- TUESDAY 4 NOVEMBER -
NEWCASTLE
METRO RADIO ARENA
0844 493 6666

- WEDNESDAY 5 NOVEMBER -
MANCHESTER
EVENING NEWS ARENA
0844 847 8000

OFFICIAL UK TOUR HOTLINE
08700 11 26 26
www.ticketzone.co.uk
www.queenonline.com
www.queenpluspaulrodgers.com
www.paulrodgers.com

A 3DD WINTERS ENTERTAINMENT PRESENTATION

The COSMOS ROCKS!

American Idol finalist Adam Lambert (far left) and
winner Kris Allen (right) perform with Brian and
Roger during the *American Idol* Season 8 finale at
Nokia Theatre, Los Angeles, May 20, 2009.
*Kevin Winter/*American Idol *2009/Getty Images for FOX*

The Live Releases

by Gary Graff

DURING THE FIRST FULL U.S. TOUR of Queen + Paul Rodgers in 2007, drummer Roger Taylor remarked that "you know, we really *do* love performing live. Everybody goes on and on about the albums and the production and the pristine sound and all of that, but I still think we've always known how to kick some ass on stage."

There, then, is the conundrum.

Thanks to its own flair for intricate, theatrical pomp and the adept helping hands of studio savants like Roy Thomas Baker and Reinhold Mack, Queen made the kinds of albums that were difficult to reproduce on stage. The stacked harmonies, layered guitar parts, filters, baffles, and other accoutrements of the sessions—not to mention the genuinely sophisticated vision of the band and its collaborators—usually succeeded in making this four-piece rock band sound like a chamber group at the least and a small, plugged-in orchestra at the most. What happens, for instance, when Brian May is limited to just one guitar and his amp stack (though a rash of effect pedals certainly help)? How can we listen to "We Are The Champions," "Somebody To Love," or "Tie Your Mother Down" without those mountains of vocal harmonies?

But the fact of the matter is Queen was able to pull it off even when those layers were stripped away. And there's been ample evidence of that throughout the group's career—and beyond, thanks to the appetite for posthumous releases since Freddie Mercury's death in 1991.

Since 1979 Queen has released seven live albums, dating from the 1973 radio sessions on *Queen At The BBC* to *Live Magic*'s sampling of the band's last-ever concert on August 9, 1986, at the U.K.'s Knebworth Park. A fair representation of the group's performing career—though the earlier, pre-*Jazz* period is sadly unheard, at least on official releases—these titles show that even without the studio embellishments, Queen could deploy energy, cheek, and, not unimportantly, a pretty strong body of songs to validate its spot as a top worldwide live draw.

One caveat, though: Queen's concert appeal was as much visual as aural, and something's lost when you can't

Hollywood's 1995 release (*Live At The Beeb* on Band of Joy in the U.K., 1989). The cover features a Douglas Puddifoot image of the band's first photo shoot at Freddie's Kensington flat.

see Mercury preening and strutting in an assortment of provocative and occasionally ridiculous (oh, those hot pants) outfits, or the flashy light show the group carried with it. Fortunately there's a generous cadre of DVDs available (see Selected Discography), including companion pieces to some of these live albums, and the Queen experience tends to make a little more impact in that format.

This is all not to say that the live sound recordings miss the mark. Certainly not. In fact, *Queen At The BBC* (released in the U.K. in 1989 as *Live At The Beeb* and the U.S. in 1995), more than any of the other titles, is a revelation, documenting the group's earliest days. Taken from two of six BBC sessions, the set leans heavily on *Queen I* (only one track, a nascent "Ogre Battle," comes from *Queen II*), and the performances are leaner and more Spartan than their recorded counterparts—Queen hews closer to Led Zeppelin, say, than The Beatles. Stretched-out versions of "Liar" and

"Son And Daughter" in particular show off the group's improvisational skills, dynamic renditions that make any fan hunger for more than just this thirty-seven-and-a-half-minute snippet of this comparatively raw phase of Queen.

Live Killers (1979) was Queen's first released live album and holds a somewhat ambivalent position in group lore—which has improved somewhat with hindsight. A pastiche of several concerts from the band's European tour in early 1979, it was the most successful of Queen's live albums (double-platinum in the U.S. and No. 16 on the Billboard 200 chart) but, initially, the most derided. Edits are clear and plentiful; Taylor once joked that "the only thing live about *Live Killers* is the bass drum," and the bandmembers openly groused about their own mix.

> *"I'm all for live albums if they work, but I don't think you should design the normal album in that way at all. The live show is effective at a moment in time and an album has got to live forever really."*
>
> —BRIAN MAY, QUOTED BY HARRY DOHERTY,
> *Melody Maker*, 06.12.1975

With some distance, however *Live Killers* is a solid and at times striking souvenir of Queen hitting its stride as an epic arena concert act. The career-spanning (to that point) track list captures the "fast" version of "We Will Rock You" (repeated later in the set in its usual arrangement before "We Are The Champions") and fierce, extended jams during "Now I'm

Japan, 1979.

60TH ANNIVERSARY 2006

Here" and "Brighton Rock," the latter of which pushes beyond twelve minutes. The medley of "Killer Queen"/"Bicycle Race"/"I'm In Love With My Car" is somewhat unsatisfying, but the "quiet" segment comprising "Dreamer's Ball," "Love of My Life," and "'39" is an effective counter to the rest of the album's bombast. Queen openly acknowledged the use of tapes for the operatic section of "Bohemian Rhapsody" in the liner notes. (Another Queen performance from the era, at the 1979 Concerts for the People of Kampuchea, is underrepresented by a solitary track, "Now I'm Here," on an album from the benefits that came out in 1981.)

Live Magic, released in 1986 in the U.K. and 1996 in the U.S., is something of an odd curio in the Queen catalog. Recorded at four shows on the European leg of the 1986 *Magic* tour—including a pair at Wembley Stadium that would surface again later—it's a truncated single-disc set that in its vinyl incarnation severely chopped several of the songs. The CD version, at least, returned them to their regular lengths, and while some Queen fans might crave more, the compactness of the set means the energy never flags, and the full takes of "Another One Bites the Dust," "One Vision," and "Hammer To Fall" exhibit the same lusty quality that lit up Live Aid's London concert the summer before.

Following Mercury's death in 1991, *Live At Wembley '86* came along as a more satisfying document of the *Magic* tour—as evidenced by its platinum sales in the United States. Clearly energized by a hometown crowd and riding the wave of its Live Aid triumph, Queen rocks the hell out of "Tie Your Mother Down," "Tear It Up," and an oldies medley of "(You're So Square) Baby I Don't Care," "Hello Mary Lou (Goodbye Heart)," "Tutti Frutti," and "Gimme Some Lovin'." May plays a nine-minute version of his "Brighton Rock" solo leading into "Now I'm Here," and Mercury milks a campy bit of "Big Spender" as an intro to "Radio Ga Ga."

Queen pulled a back-to-the-future for a pair of other posthumous concert souvenirs, dipping into periods not yet represented on disc. *Queen On Fire: Live At The Bowl* (2004)

1979.

comes from a June 5, 1982, show at Milton Keynes, England, during the *Hot Space* tour. By all accounts it was a period of some dissension within the band, and Mercury—who, legend states, had his hand bit by a lover backstage before the group went on—seems peevish as he tries to explain the urban-flavored material from the new album, concluding that "it's only a bloody record!" May, meanwhile, steps up to infuse meatier guitar parts into *Hot Space* tracks like "Back Chat" and "Action This Day." (Listeners will also notice a short gap in May's solo segment when the cord fell out of his guitar.)

Mercury also seems a bit disgruntled with the crowd on *Queen Rock Montreal* (2008), recorded during a two-night stand on the group's 1981 tour that was also filmed for the *We Will Rock You* theater feature. He exhorts the Canadian fans to "move it you fuckers—come on!" during "Jailhouse Rock" and seems put off when they don't sing along to "Love Of My Life." The set dips into the then-current *Flash Gordon* soundtrack for "Flash's Theme" and "The Hero" (neither of which made the film or the subsequent DVD release), but there's more energy evident in performances of still-fresh hits

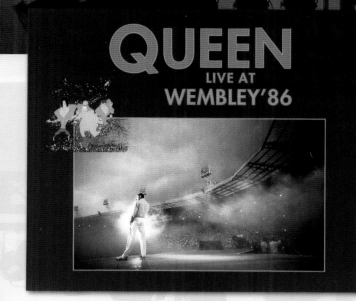

1992.

from *The Game* ("Crazy Little Thing Called Love" and "Another One Bites The Dust") and the usual well-worn favorites.

The Queen + Paul Rodgers era was launched not in the studio but on stage, so it's fitting that the first recording of the line-up followed suit. *Return Of The Champions* (2005) hails from a May 9, 2005, performance in Sheffield, England, and can't help but sound a bit jarring with Rodgers' soulful attack standing in for Mercury's theatrics. The familiarity of the songs ultimately carries the day, particularly with everybody in good form—and May and Taylor sounding rejuvenated to be playing live again, and also getting more shots at singing lead, both on their own and in tandem with Rodgers. But it's perhaps telling that it's the renditions of songs by Rodgers' previous groups, Free ("Wishing Well," "All Right Now") and Bad Company ("Can't Get Enough," "Feel Like Makin' Love"), that sound most natural. ⚜

China, 2004.

2007.

2005.

Carry On, Carry On

259

The Cosmos Rocks

by Daniel Nester

QUEEN
+ PAUL RODGERS
the cosmos rocks

2008.

WHAT'S IN A ROCK BAND'S NAME? Does Axl Rose engage in false advertising when he calls himself Guns N' Roses as the band's sole original member? Is Journey still Journey as it soldiers on with replacement-for-the-replacement singers? Or how about Van Halen, which begat Van Hagar, which then begat Van Gary Cherone-of-Extreme?

So that which we call Queen by any other name, would it rock just as hard? Sure it would. Then why did drummer Roger Taylor and guitarist Brian May, minus lead singer Freddie Mercury and bassist John Deacon (retired since 1997) still call themselves Queen when they teamed up with Paul Rodgers, former frontman for Free, Bad Company, and the Firm? Why didn't they call themselves May, Taylor, and Rodgers?

Because that wouldn't be the Queen way, that's why. From the outset, Queen was always more than the sum of its parts, always about outsized, rafter-reaching ambition—or inflated egos, some might say. To call any outing with "all the active members" of the band involved anything other than the band's name, as Roger Taylor explained in an interview, would be foolish. It wouldn't reach to as many people as possible, which is the whole point of being Queen.

So when Queen—er, Roger and Brian—set out to tour for the first time in nineteen years with Paul Rodgers, bandmembers dubbed themselves "Queen + Paul Rodgers." There was noise from orthodox corners of the Queen fan base, but the shows went on. The noise stepped up, however, when the trio announced they would record new songs as Queen + Paul Rodgers. Even with the plus sign affixed after the Queen name, one that indicated Rodgers as a separate-but-equal post-Freddie entity, the very idea of new material seemed a beyond-the-pale sacrilege to many fans, a sullying of the Queen legacy.

Critics were also skeptical. "Have you always wanted to hear the 'Feel Like Making Love' guy try to sing the greatest hits of Queen?" Kelefah Sanneh wrote in the *New York Times* after an October 2005 New Jersey gig. "Actually, don't bother answering. It's happening, regardless."

If you can get past all the snark and listen to 2008's *The Cosmos Rocks* with open ears, the result isn't half bad. The initial chemistry that attracted the trio to play live around the world rears up most on the rockers, and there are plenty of those. Opener "Cosmos Rockin'" unblushingly plows through meat-and-potatoes progression fun and comic lyrics ("We got the cosmos rockin'!/We got the universe rockin'!"). "C-Lebrity," the album's first and only single, features Roger Taylor drumming most like his hero John Bonham since *News Of The World*, all over behemoth Brian May riff-o-rama. Two Rodgers tracks, "Warboys (A Prayer For Peace)" and "Voodoo," are able readings of solo songs the frontman had sung live, and prove that lyrics aren't the strong suit of either camp.

Speaking of camp, "Call Me" challenges this reviewer's sensibility most. As long as Roger and Brian kept it bluesy hard rock, as they wisely did on tour, mention of Freddie

Mercury's absence was mostly avoided. One BBC reviewer called "Call Me" "Can't Get Enough Of Your Crazy Little Thing Called Love," which is pretty apt. The track's shortcomings speak more to the absence of Freddie's white leather shorts worldview, how he used to giggle tracks such as these to let us in on the joke. Maybe the inclusion of the iTunes-only bonus track "Runaway," their so-wrong-it's-right cover of Del Shannon's 1961 hit, on the album proper would have reached some tongue-in-cheek equilibrium. Still, that track's a keeper: Brian May's guitar version of Max Crook's immortal organ line simply transcends.

An unexpected standout is the mid-tempo "Small," which builds up to the minor revelation that perhaps it's Roger Taylor, and not May or Rodgers, who can best write material suited for this "most peculiar supergroup," as *Mojo* called them. The track reprises as the final track, and it's a welcome slight return.

There have been plenty of incongruous hybrid projects in the history of rock: Bing Crosby and David Bowie sing a duet for "Little Drummer Boy" (not to mention an ascendant Queen and a descendant Bowie in 1980 for "Under Pressure); Elvis Costello singing with Fall Out Boy and Burt Bacharach; the White Stripes' Jack Black and Alicia Keys collaborating on a Bond flick theme. For full-album collaborations, none other than Freddie Mercury and Montserrat Caballé's *Barcelona* has to be up there for unexpected incongruity. And then there's Queen + Paul Rodgers. Maybe *The Cosmos Rocks* fits into the audacious Queen discography after all. ❧

Tour Dates
Queen + Paul Rodgers

19.03.2005	Fancourt	George, ZAF
28.03.2005	Brixton Academy	London, GBR
30.03.2005	Le Zenith	Paris, FRA
01.04.2005	Palacio De Deportes	Madrid, ESP
02.04.2005	Paulau Sant Jordi	Barcelona, ESP
04.04.2005	Palalottomatica	Rome, ITA
05.04.2005	Forum	Milan, ITA
07.04.2005	Nelson Mandela Forum	Firenze, ITA
08.04.2005	BPA Palas	Pesaro, ITA
10.04.2005	St. Jakobshalle	Basel, CHE
13.04.2005	Stadthalle	Vienna, AUT
14.04.2005	Olympiahalle	Munich, DEU
16.04.2005	Sazka Arena	Prague, CZE
17.04.2005	Arena	Leipzig, DEU
19.04.2005	Festhalle	Frankfurt, DEU
20.04.2005	Sportspaleis	Antwerpen, BEL
23.04.2005	Arena	Budapest, HUN
25.04.2005	Westfallenhalle	Dortmund, DEU
26.04.2005	Ahoy Hall	Rotterdam, NLD
28.04.2005	Color Line Arena	Hamburg, DEU
30.04.2005	Globen	Stockholm, SWE
03.05.2005	Metro	Newcastle, GBR
04.05.2005	MEN Arena	Manchester, GBR
06.05.2005	NEC Arena	Birmingham, GBR
07.05.2005	International	Cardiff, GBR
09.05.2005[1]	Hallam	Sheffield, GBR
11.05.2005	Wembley Pavillion	London, GBR
13.05.2005	Odyssey Arena	Belfast, GBR
14.05.2005	The Point	Dublin, IRL
02.07.2005	Estádio Restelo	Lisbon, PRT
06.07.2005	Rhein-Energie Stadion	Cologne, DEU
10.07.2005	Gelredome	Arnhem, NLD
15.07.2005	Hyde Park	London, GBR
08.10.2005	Aruba Entertainment Center	Oranjestad, ABW
16.10.2005	Continental Airlines Arena	East Rutherford, NJ
22.10.2005	Hollywood Bowl	Los Angeles, CA
26–27.10.2005	Saitama Arena	Saitama, JPN
29–30.10.2005	Yokohama Arena	Yokohama, JPN
01.11.2005	Nagoya Dome	Nagoya, JPN
03.11.2005	Fukuoka Dome	Fukuoka, JPN
03.03.2006	American Airlines Arena	Miami, FL
05.03.2006	Veterans Coliseum	Jacksonville, FL
07.03.2006	Gwinett Center	Duluth, GA
09.03.2006	MCI Center	Washington, DC
10.03.2006	Digital Credit Union Center	Worcester, MA
12.03.2006	Nassau Coliseum	Uniondale, NY
14.03.2006	Wachovia Spectrum	Philadelphia, PA
16.03.2006	Air Canada Centre	Toronto, CAN
17.03.2006	HSBC Arena	Buffalo, NY
20.03.2006	Mellon Arena	Pittsburgh, PA

21.03.2006	Quicken Loans Arena	Cleveland, OH
23.03.2006	Allstate Arena	Rosemont, IL
24.03.2006	Palace at Auburn Hills	Auburn Hills, MI
26.03.2006	Xcel Energy Center	St. Paul, MN
27.03.2006	Bradley Center	Milwaukee, WI
31.03.2006	Glendale Arena	Glendale, AZ
01.04.2006	Cox Arena	San Diego, CA
03.04.2006	Arrowhead Pond	Anaheim, CA
05.04.2006	HP Pavilion	San Jose, CA
07.04.2006	MGM Garden Arena	Las Vegas, NV
10.04.2006	Key Arena	Seattle, WA
11.04.2006	Rose Garden	Portland, OR
13.04.2006	Pacific Coliseum	Vancouver, CAN
25.05.2006	Mandalay Bay Events Center	Las Vegas, NV
27.06.2008	Hyde Park	London, GBR
03.09.2008	Elstree Film Studio	London, GBR
12.09.2008	Freedom Square	Kharkov, UKR
15–16.09.2008	Olympic Sports Complex	Moscow, RUS
19.09.2008	Arena	Riga, LVA
21.09.2008	Velodrom	Berlin, DEU
23.09.2008	Sportspaleis	Antwerp, BEL
24.09.2008	Bercy	Paris, FRA
26.09.2008	Palalottomatica	Rome, ITA
28.09.2008	Datch Forum di Assago	Milan, ITA
29.09.2008	Hallenstadion	Zurich, CHE
01.10.2008	Olympiahalle	Munich, DEU
02.10.2008	SAP Arena	Mannheim, DEU
04.10.2008	TUI Arena	Hanover, DEU
05.10.2008	Color Line Arena	Hamburg, DEU
07.10.2008	Ahoy Hall	Rotterdam, NLD
08.10.2008	Rockhal	Luxembourg, LUX
10.10.2008	Arena	Nottingham, GBR
11.10.2008	SECC	Glasgow, GBR
13.10.2008	O2 Arena	London, GBR
14.10.2008	Arena	Cardiff, GBR
16.10.2008	NIA	Birmingham, GBR
18.10.2008	Echo Arena	Liverpool, GBR
19.10.2008	Arena	Sheffield, GBR
22.10.2008	Palau Sant Jordi	Barcelona, ESP
24.10.2008	Estádio Municipal	Murcia, ESP
25.10.2008	Palacio De Deportes	Madrid, ESP
28.10.2008	Arena	Budapest, HUN
29.10.2008	Belgrade Arena	Belgrade, SER
31.10.2008	O2 Arena	Prague, CZE
01.11.2008	Stadthalle	Vienna, AUT
04.11.2008	Arena	Newcastle, GBR
05.11.2008	MEN Arena	Manchester, GBR
07.11.2008	O2 Arena	London, GBR
8.11.2008	Wembley Arena	London, GBR
14.11.2008	Racecourse	Dubai, UAE
19.11.2008	San Carlos de Apoquindo Stadium	Santiago De Chile, CHL
21.11.2008	Estádio Vélez Sarsfield	Buenos Aires, ARG
26–27.11.2008	Via Funchal	Sao Paulo, BRA
29.11.2008	HSBC Arena	Rio de Janeiro, BRA

Note

1. Provided the material for the *Return Of The Champions* CD and DVD.

Tour dates and tickets courtesy Martin Skala, QueenConcerts.com

12 QUEEN FOREVER

"A NEW BAND?" That's how Brian May described Queen + Paul Rodgers. Yet the Rodgers hybrid ended only a few months later in 2009 with the release of *Live in Ukraine* double-CD and DVD, an honorable monument to that gargantuan gig in Kharkiv. In 2013, probably veiling irritation about May's and Taylor's micro-controlling instincts, Rodgers told this writer, "I wanted to get back to my solo career."

Clearly, Queen could have retired, disappeared.

Instead, they did anything but. On the one hand, the Queen nostalgia industry boomed, much of it with May's and Taylor's support—especially 2011's *Stormtroopers in Stilettos*, an early-days exhibition in London (and then Dresden) and *Queen: Days of Our Lives*, a BBC TV documentary.

Of course, that was all alongside their evidently perennial musical, *We Will Rock You*. After years of chasing round Toronto, Milan, Oslo, Copenhagen, and such, when the London Dominion Theatre run ended after twelve years on May 31, 2014, Taylor did start to admit what he really felt about it, artistically. He referred to it as "a terrible idea" (to Kate Mossman, the *Guardian*, 2014) and said "Brian really embraces musical theatre, but I truly don't" (to James McNair, the *Independent*, 2013).

However, the drummer got his retaliation by producing and musical-directing a taste challenge which May didn't like, *The Queen Extravaganza*. Taylor told McNair, "There are an awful lot of bands out there doing our old act. An awful lot of fake moustaches and underwhelming performances. We thought, 'Wouldn't it be great to have a tribute act that does Queen justice?'" This novel concept, an official tribute band, toured America in 2012–2013, the U.K. in 2014, and, at time of writing, seemed a going concern.

During a Queen hiatus, which lasted a while, Taylor and May explored their late-middle-aged lives.

A better ease-taker than May, father-of-five Taylor married for the second time (to Sarina Potgieter, August 26, 2010) and took a bow at the unveiling of a (happily non-posthumous) statue called *The Drummer* in his old hometown, Truro, on June 10, 2011.

Brian May and Brian Justin Crum perform onstage with the cast of *We Will Rock You* at the Hippodrome Theater on October 15, 2013, in Baltimore, Maryland. *J. Countess/Getty Images*

Brian May and Roger Taylor with their Ambassadors of Rock award during the O2 Silver Clef Awards 2009 in London, England. *Jon Furniss/WireImage/Getty Images*

Richard Jones, Brian May, Sophie Ellis-Bextor, and Anita Dobson attend the private view of *Queen: Stormtroopers in Stilettos* on February 24, 2011, in London, England. *Nick Harvey/WireImage/Getty Images*

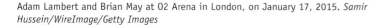
Adam Lambert and Brian May at O2 Arena in London, on January 17, 2015. *Samir Hussein/WireImage/Getty Images*

Still, he wasn't exactly a complacent celebrity. He got down to finishing *Fun on Earth*, his first solo album since 1998, released in November 2013, and reworked all his "solos" into a twelve-CD box called *The Lot*—both collection and new album proving his oddly unrecognized compositional/multi-instrumental/vocal substance.

While his haloed hair turned white in acceptance of the advance of age, May put himself about as never before. From 2010–2013, you could say he did enough to fill a book, but that would sell him short since he wrote four of them during those years. There was *A Village Lost & Found* (with Elena Vidal), a study of T. R. Williams pioneering 1850s stereoscopic photography (early 3-D); a related volume, *Diableries: Stereoscopic Adventures in Hell* (with Denis Pellerin), revisiting a genre of nineteenth-century Parisian satire; *The Cosmic Tourist*, a verbal and visual tour of "the 100 most awe-inspiring destinations in the universe" (with his *Bang! The Complete History of the Universe* co-authors Chris Lintott and doyen/father figure Sir Patrick Moore—who died soon afterwards, aged 89); and *Brian May's Red Special* (with Simon Bradley), the story of the homemade guitar he'd played from schoolkid to pensioner.

He did plenty more in his spare time as well. May had always admired Kerry Ellis, a renowned singer/actress who played Meat in the 2002 original London cast of *We Will Rock You*. So it was no surprise when he produced her 2011 album, *Anthems*, and played live with her over a three-year period.

As a side effect of all the above, the superstar guitar hero frequently found himself in small towns across the U.K., talking to local people in intimate, unglamorous settings, be it Letchworth and Cheltenham talking stereoscopy or Bury St. Edmunds and Buxton playing Kerry Ellis songs. Perhaps this had something to do with May's opinions and personal philosophy; he had a desire to connect with ordinary life during these years.

His most notable involvement in this time was undoubtedly his campaigns to protect wild animals. It started in response to the badger cull, proposed and fragmentarily executed starting in 2010 by the U.K.'s Conservative/Liberal Democrat coalition government. Fundamentally horrified, May deployed his cool, scientific mind to argue against the prevalent notion that badgers infected farmers' cattle with TB, in favor of vaccination rather than slaughter.

Committing head, heart, and soul to the cause—and cooperating with national organizations such as the Royal Society for the Prevention of Cruelty to Animals—he spent weeks at public enquiries, took part in rural demonstrations against the cull, and lobbied MPs. Eventually, he became a familiar figure around the Houses of Parliament (although he was careful to remain unattached to any Party and advocate no ideology other than "common decency"). He learned about the political process and, in due course, engaged with wider social issues such as the government's commercialization of the National Health Service and economic injustice.

Come December 2014, when the *Guardian*'s Mossman asked him for a "Christmas Message" six months ahead of the next U.K. General Election, May had nothing seasonal to offer: "We need a change of government, and if there isn't one, I think we will all slit our wrists."

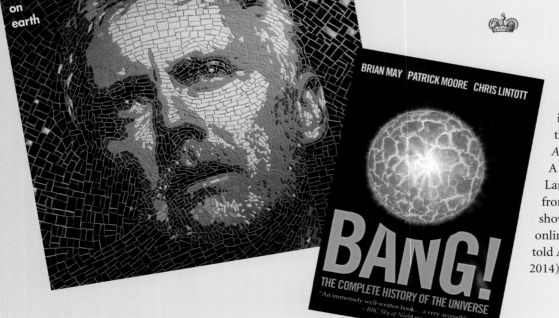

Coming back to Queen, May and Taylor hadn't forgotten Lambert. In fact, it turned out he'd been on their minds even before the *American Idol* encounter. A friend of Taylor's spotted Lambert as a Queen candidate from his first appearance on the show. Taylor then found a clip online. "I was just like, 'Wow,'" he told Andy Greene (*Rolling Stone*, 2014). "[Adam] had this slight Elvis

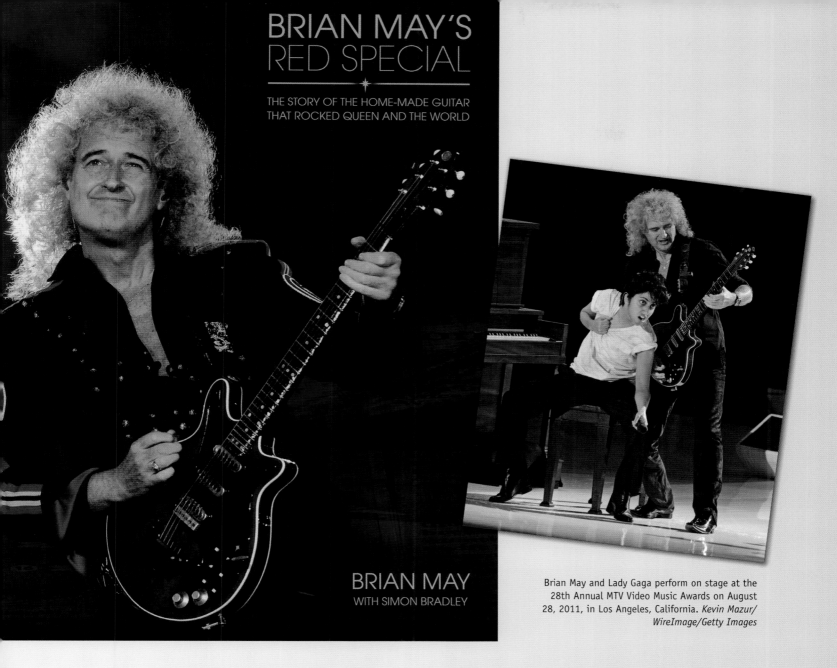

BRIAN MAY'S RED SPECIAL

THE STORY OF THE HOME-MADE GUITAR
THAT ROCKED QUEEN AND THE WORLD

BRIAN MAY
WITH SIMON BRADLEY

Brian May and Lady Gaga perform on stage at the
28th Annual MTV Video Music Awards on August
28, 2011, in Los Angeles, California. *Kevin Mazur/
WireImage/Getty Images*

look going on. I just thought, 'What a voice! Those octaves!'"

Before that grand finale, Lambert ran into trouble. Although he'd never been closeted, a picture of him kissing a man conspicuously "outed" him and resulted in a hate campaign. The betting favorite, he ended up finishing second to Kris Allen. The two shared the stage for the finale's Queen-accompanied blast through "We Are The Champions."

That very night, May and Taylor mentioned to Lambert the possibility of working together, but vaguely. Then all went quiet while Queen changed labels, leaving EMI after almost forty years and joining Island/Universal. This shift resulted in the conflicting releases of assorted remasters, singles, and "rarities" compilations by both companies to nobody's fascination (bar want-it-all collectors).

Lambert understandably went about his business. Born on

January 29, 1982, in Indianapolis, he'd sung in musicals since he was ten until the frontman bug bit around 2006. *Idol* followed, and in November 2009, *For Your Entertainment*, his million-selling U.S. No. 3 solo album was released after that. So in autumn 2011, when Queen finally called, as he told Greene, "It felt like the right time, since I'd established my solo career." (That's the cool version. He also said to Lisa Verrico (*Sunday Times*, 2011), "Was I scared? Hell, yeah. Freddie's are fuckin' big shoes.")

Nonetheless, he filled them. On his debut as part of Queen + Adam Lambert, on November 6, 2011, at the MTV Music Awards in Belfast, Ireland, he swaggered through "The Show Must Go On," "We Will Rock You," and, again, "We Are The Champions." May told Greene he'd never doubted. "A singer is full-on in every respect . . . the sound, the look, the animal magnetism. Adam's performing from his heart."

Brian May performs alongside Jessie J during the Closing Ceremony on Day 16 of the London 2012 Olympic Games at Olympic Stadium. *Stu Forster/Getty Images*

teasers . . . such as a July 2013 note about working on "some Queen/Freddie/Michael Jackson tapes."

Then they played a one-off with Lambert that September at the iHeartRadio Music Festival in Las Vegas before plunging into a big Queen + Adam Lambert year in 2014: a thirty-five-date world tour, June to September, taking in the United States, Canada, Japan, Australia, South Korea, and New Zealand. Still, when Mercury came up on the screens, people hollered "We love you, Freddie!", meaning no harm, but asking the obvious question—echoed by many an interviewer.

"I'm not replacing him," Lambert told Nick Hasted for *Classic Rock* (February 2015). "I'm trying to keep the memory alive and remind people how amazing he was . . . I'm trying to share with the audience how much he inspired me." May backed him up: "Adam has that range and that affinity for things on the edge of camp that Freddie had . . . it's a Queen show as much as it ever was. I don't think Freddie would mind me saying that or that I'm being disloyal—it's nice to feel Freddie's part of it without being swamped by nostalgia."

Then came the new Queen material on *Queen Forever*, released November 2014, and yet another compilation: swathes of '80s love songs largely embellished by three tracks from the archive, revamped and reworked, including a Mercury duet with Michael Jackson called "There Must Be More To Life Than This." William Orbit, who mixed the album version, told BBC Radio 4's *Front Row*, "The Jackson vocal was kind of a throwdown. He came in and did one take and you could actually hear Freddie saying things like 'Middle 8! Bridge! Chorus repeat!' —which of course I chopped." Even so, whatever terrible turns their lives had taken, two late greats, their voices almost becoming one in their gentle fragility . . .

Apart from the three tracks, though, Taylor told Hasted *Queen Forever* was "a rather odd mixture," "bloody miserable," and "a record-company confection. It's not a full-blooded Queen album." It sold and charted modestly: No. 38 in the United States and No. 5 in the U.K.

But playing live felt right. They announced a U.K. and European tour for January–February 2015, starting with a New Year around-midnight show in Westminster Hall—part of the Houses of Parliament—and televised to the nation.

The Queen veterans proceeded, if with measured tread. In June 2012, just after Lambert's second solo album, *Trespassing*, hit No. 1 in the United States and No. 3 in the U.K., May's *Soapbox* blog reported Queen + Adam Lambert rehearsing along with Spike Edney and bassist Neil Fairclough. They put in ten days, preparing for six European dates . . . and Lambert made his full Queen debut in front of 300,000 Ukrainians in Kiev on June 30, 2012, though he did miss out on the perhaps even more boggling Olympic Closing Ceremony on July 12, where the nature of the event demanded a showcase appearance from May and Taylor.

And just as May relished his live, no-safety-net performance in the Olympic Stadium, Lambert loved Queen's old-fashioned, high-wire approach. "This is pure," he told Greene. "We're not playing to a click. We're not playing to tracks. This is all live instruments. I'm singing all the vocals. This is the real deal."

Then they took a break. Lambert played solo around the world. Meanwhile, May's *Soapbox* dropped occasional Queen

"All I know is, we're going to be right next to Big Ben," Lambert chortled to Mossman. "Maybe we can scale him. Maybe Brian can climb him!" Getting to know them, he'd acquired a new "Q" tattoo on his right arm and pisstaking rights with regard to his venerable employers: "They love each other and bicker like an old married couple. It's totally passive aggressive and great," he observed.

What next then for *this* new "new band?"

Or bands, given that Queen and Queen + Adam Lambert remain separate entities?

The Freddie Mercury biopic continues slow gestation—John Deacon–approved, by the way, because "John's given his blessing to whatever Brian and I might do with the brand" (Taylor told McNair). Early title-role choice Sacha Baron Cohen faded away to be replaced by Ben Whishaw, up for anything as demonstrated by a CV including Hamlet at the Old Vic and the movie voice of Paddington Bear.

Meanwhile, May—surely not just to get Taylor's goat—says he's developing a *We Will Rock You* sequel with original writer Ben Elton.

And what about a new Queen album? There's no question May and Taylor will play on. "I love making a racket in a big, loud rock band," Taylor told Hasted, and May affirmed, "When Queen calls everything else takes a back seat."

Of course, when Hasted asked whether they'd do a studio album with Lambert, cautious responses ensued. Taylor said, "If we have the material, then I wouldn't go into making a record with any other singer than Adam." And Lambert said, "[This is] a limited engagement . . . creating new music and calling ourselves Queen is a different situation."

So keep an eye on Brian's *Soapbox* for the latest, such as his enthusiasm about rehearsals with the "GFG" (Gift from God, referring to Lambert) and a mention of "astonishing work in new songs."

As Queen folk often remark, "Any way the wind blows . . ."

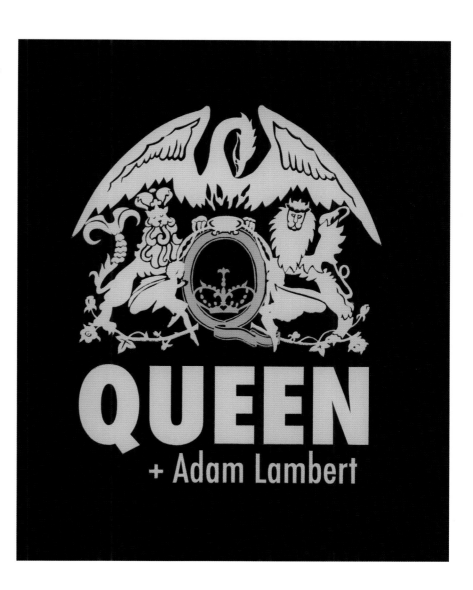

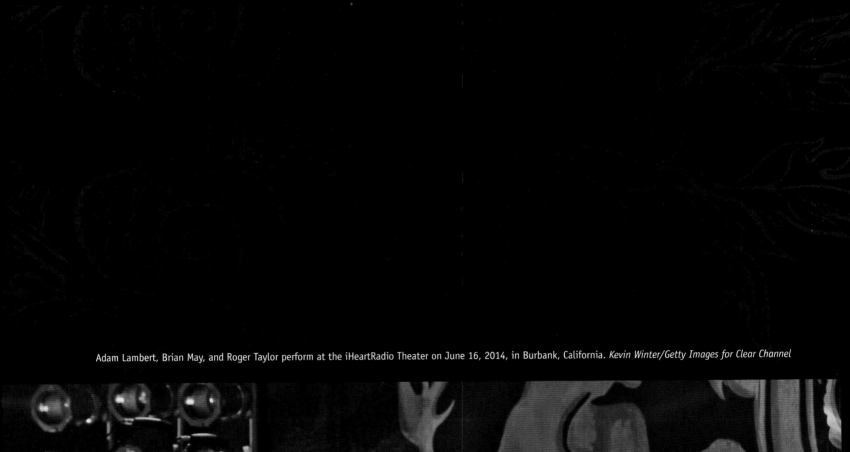

Adam Lambert, Brian May, and Roger Taylor perform at the iHeartRadio Theater on June 16, 2014, in Burbank, California. *Kevin Winter/Getty Images for Clear Channel*

Adam Lambert, Brian May, and Roger Taylor at the Zenith arena in Paris on January 26, 2015. *Thomas Samson/AFP/Getty Images*

SELECTED DISCOGRAPHY & MORE (ALSO SELECTIVE)

BY PHIL SUTCLIFFE

"My songs are like Bic razors.
... You listen to it, like it, discard it, then on to the next. Disposable pop."

—FREDDIE MERCURY

ALBUMS

This listing, with notes, includes only band albums—not "solo" efforts—and works from the basis of the initial U.S. album track listings with any U.K. variants and later edition variants like bonus tracks shown in annotations. In chronological order, all original studio albums are included, along with selected compilations and live albums. The label for the U.K. (and, broadly, the rest of the world, bar North America) is shown as "EMI" until, with *The Miracle*, CD takes over as the main album format when it becomes "Parlophone" (another label under the EMI corporate umbrella).

QUEEN

Recorded: Fall 1971 to January 1972, Trident, London, except for "The Night Comes Down," De Lane Lea, London, fall 1971
Released: EMI, July 13, 1973 (U.K.); Elektra, September 4, 1973 (U.S.)
Producers: John Anthony, Roy Thomas Baker, and Queen (except Louie Austin co-produced "The Night Comes Down")

"Keep Yourself Alive" (May); "Doing All Right" (May/Staffell); "Great King Rat" (Mercury); "My Fairy King" (Mercury); "Liar" (Mercury); "The Night Comes Down" (May); "Modern Times Rock 'n' Roll" (Taylor); "Son And Daughter" (May); "Jesus" (Mercury); "Seven Seas Of Rhye" (Mercury)

CD bonus tracks, 1991 Hollywood reissue (U.S. only): "Mad The Swine" (Mercury) and versions of "Keep Yourself Alive" and "Liar"

Notes: The Queen sleeve credited "Deacon John" on bass and "Roger Meddows-Taylor" on drums, but neither the inversion nor the hyphenation survived to their second album.
The long gap between recording and release arose because Queen recorded at its then-management Trident's studio before they'd signed to any record company, and it then took more than a year before bandmembers secured EMI's interest and signature.
May co-wrote "Doing All Right" with Tim Staffell in 1969 while May, Staffell, and Taylor were in Smile.

QUEEN II

Recorded: August 1973, Trident, London
Released: EMI, March 8, 1974 (U.K.); Elektra, April 4, 1974 (U.S.)
Producers: Roy Thomas Baker and Queen (except Robin G. Cable and Queen produced "Nevermore" and "Funny How Love Is")

"Procession" (May); "Father To Son" (May); "White Queen (As It Began)" (May); "Some Day One Day" (May); "The Loser In The End" (Taylor); "Ogre Battle" (Mercury); "The Fairy Feller's Master-Stroke" (Mercury); "Nevermore" (Mercury); "The March Of The Black Queen" (Mercury); "Funny How Love Is" (Mercury); "Seven Seas Of Rhye" (Mercury)

CD bonus tracks, 1991 Hollywood reissue (U.S. only): "See What A Fool I've Been" (May) and remixes of "Ogre Battle" and "Seven Seas Of Rhye"

Notes: The truly iconic Mick Rock cover shot later became the visual basis for the "Bohemian Rhapsody" video.
Queen divided the original vinyl LP into "The White Side" (mainly May songs) and "The Black Side" (Mercury songs). They didn't know CDs were on the way.

SHEER HEART ATTACK

Recorded: July 1974 to September 1974, Rockfield, Wales; and Trident, Wessex, and Air, London.
Released: EMI, November 8, 1974 (U.K.); Elektra, November 12, 1974 (U.S.)
Producers: Roy Thomas Baker and Queen

"Brighton Rock" (May); "Killer Queen" (Mercury); "Tenement Funster" (Taylor); "Flick Of The Wrist" (Mercury); "Lily Of The Valley" (Mercury); "Now I'm Here" (May); "In The Lap Of The Gods" (Mercury); "Stone Cold Crazy" (May, Mercury, Taylor, Deacon); "Dear Friends" (May); "Misfire" (Deacon); "Bring Back That Leroy Brown" (Mercury); "She Makes Me (Stormtrooper In Stilettos)" (May); "In The Lap Of The Gods . . . Revisited" (Mercury)

CD bonus track, 1991 Hollywood reissue (U.S. only): a remix of "Stone Cold Crazy"

Notes: "Brighton Rock" borrowed its name from a Graham Greene novel as well as the renowned stick of seaside confectionery. On "Bring Back That Leroy Brown," May played a "genuine George Formby ukulele-banjo"; comedian and movie actor Formby was Britain's premier ukulele hero from the '30s to the '50s and probably the first British musician to refuse to play racially segregated shows in apartheid South Africa (on his 1946 tour).

A NIGHT AT THE OPERA

Recorded: July to November 1974, Rockfield, Wales; and Sarm, Olympic, Scorpio, and Lansdowne, London
Released: EMI, November 21, 1975 (U.K.); Elektra, December 2, 1975 (U.S.)
Producers: Roy Thomas Baker and Queen

"Death On Two Legs (Dedicated To . . .)" (Mercury); "Lazing On A Sunday Afternoon" (Mercury); "I'm In Love With My Car" (Taylor); "You're My Best Friend" (Deacon); "'39" (May); "Sweet Lady" (May); "Seaside Rendezvous" (Mercury); "The Prophet's Song" (May); "Love Of My Life" (Mercury); "Good Company" (May); "Bohemian Rhapsody" (Mercury)

CD bonus tracks, 1991 Hollywood reissue (U.S. only): remixes of "I'm In Love With My Car" and "You're My Best Friend"

Notes: Queen concluded their severance from Trident management—who, they made clear, in no way inspired "Death On Two Legs (Dedicated To . . .)"—in August 1974, shortly after they'd begun work on the album.
Taylor's rich pickings from "I'm In Love With My Car" via the B-side of the "Bohemian Rhapsody" single provoked bitterness in the band, but Deacon's "You're My Best Friend" (probably inspired by wife Veronica) was the first Queen A-side not written by Mercury or May. Diversifying, May played harp on "Love Of My Life" and toy Koto—a small version of Japan's zither-like national instrument—on "The Prophet's Song."

A DAY AT THE RACES

Recorded: July to November 1976, The Manor, Oxfordshire, Wessex; and Sarm East, London
Released: EMI, December 10, 1976 (U.K.); Elektra, December 18, 1976 (U.S.)
Producers: Queen

"Tie Your Mother Down" (May); "You Take My Breath Away" (Mercury); "Long Away" (May); "The Millionaire Waltz" (Mercury); "You And I" (Deacon); "Somebody To Love" (Mercury); "White Man" (May); "Good Old-Fashioned Lover Boy" (Mercury); "Drowse" (Taylor); "Teo Torriate (Let Us Cling Together)" (May)

CD bonus tracks, 1991 Hollywood reissue (U.S. only): remixes of "Tie Your Mother Down" and "Somebody To Love"

Notes: In the U.K., this was the first Queen album to be TV-advertised—using scenes from their September 18 Hyde Park free concert for which they'd interrupted the album sessions. This is the only Queen album produced solely by the band. As a thank you for the welcome Queen received in Japan, Mercury sang a verse of "Teo Torriate" in Japanese, translated by their "friend and interpreter" Chika Kujiraoka, who'd helped them in Tokyo.

NEWS OF THE WORLD

Recorded: June to September 1977, Basing Street and Wessex, London
Released: EMI, October 28, 1977 (U.K.); Elektra, November 1, 1977 (U.S.)
Producers: Queen, assisted by Mike Stone

"We Will Rock You" (May); "We Are The Champions" (Mercury); "Sheer Heart Attack" (Taylor); "All Dead, All Dead" (May); "Spread Your Wings" (Deacon); "Fight From The Inside" (Taylor); "Get Down, Make Love" (Mercury); "Sleeping On The Sidewalk" (May); "Who Needs You" (Deacon); "It's Late" (May); "My Melancholy Blues" (Mercury)

CD bonus tracks, 1991 Hollywood reissue (U.S. only): remix of "We Will Rock You"

Notes: The cover illustration is a variation by Frank Kelly Freas of his own artwork for the cover of a 1953 issue of Astounding Science Fiction *magazine, spotted by sci-fi fan Roger Taylor.*
Apart from being the scene of the fabled Mercury/Sid Vicious encounter, Wessex was also where May met his boyhood skiffle hero, Lonnie Donegan, and played on a couple of tracks on his new album.
This version of "Sleeping On The Sidewalk" is a first run-through when, according to the band, they didn't even know the tape was running, but it turned out "right" so they kept it.

JAZZ

Recorded: July to October 1978, Mountain, Montreux, Switzerland; and Super Bear, near Nice, France
Released: EMI, November 10, 1978 (U.K.); Elektra, November 14, 1978 (U.S.)
Producers: Queen and Roy Thomas Baker

"Mustapha" (Mercury); "Fat Bottomed Girls" (May); "Jealousy" (Mercury); "Bicycle Race" (Mercury); "If You Can't Beat Them" (Deacon); "Let Me Entertain You" (Mercury); "Dead On Time" (May); "In Only Seven Days" (Deacon); "Dreamer's Ball" (May); "Fun It" (Taylor); "Leaving Home Ain't Easy" (May); "Don't Stop Me Now" (Mercury); "More Of That Jazz" (Taylor)

CD bonus tracks, 1991 Hollywood reissue (U.S. only): remixes of "Fat Bottomed Girls" and "Bicycle Race"

Notes: Two birthday parties interrupted recording in Montreux. At Taylor's on July 26, Mercury actually swung from a hotel chandelier—his (unsourced) quote on the experience: "I have always wanted to swing from a chandelier, and when I saw this exquisite cut crystal thing dangling there I just could not resist it!" Then at his own do on September 5, while all about him stripped naked and jumped in the pool, Mercury sang Gilbert & Sullivan duets with his friend Peter Straker.
Rumors abound about the composition of "Bicycle Race": that Mercury was inspired by watching the lean riders of the Tour De France zoom past his Nice hotel and that he even had a fling with one of them. But the race that year never went near Nice . . . maybe he just watched it on TV?
In King Lear mode, May walked out into a Montreux storm with a tape recorder to capture real thunderclaps for "Dead On Time."

LIVE KILLERS

Recorded: European Jazz tour, January 17 to March 1, 1979; mixed at Mountain, Montreux
Released: EMI, June 22, 1979 (U.K.); Elektra, June 26, 1979 (U.S.)
Producers: Queen

DISC ONE

"We Will Rock You" (May); "Let Me Entertain You" (Mercury); "Death On Two Legs (Dedicated To . . .)" (Mercury); "Killer Queen" (Mercury); "Bicycle Race" (Mercury); "I'm In Love With My Car" (Taylor); "Get Down, Make Love" (Mercury); "You're My Best Friend" (Deacon); "Now I'm Here" (May); "Dreamer's Ball" (May); "Love Of My Life" (Mercury); "'39" (May); "Keep Yourself Alive" (Mercury)

DISC TWO

"Don't Stop Me Now" (Mercury); "Spread Your Wings" (Deacon); "Brighton Rock" (May); "Bohemian Rhapsody" (Mercury); "Tie Your Mother Down" (May); "Sheer Heart Attack" (Taylor); "We Will Rock You" (May); "We Are The Champions" (Mercury); "God Save The Queen" (Trad. Arr. May)

Notes: For their first double-LP, Queen chose tracks from sixteen different concerts.
Queen bought Mountain Studios around the time they mixed Live Killers *there (April 1979).*

THE GAME

Recorded: June to July 1979 and February to May 1980, Musicland, Munich, Germany
Released: EMI, June 30, 1980 (U.K.); Elektra, June 30, 1980 (U.S.)
Producers: Queen, engineered and co-produced by Mack

"Play The Game" (Mercury); "Dragon Attack" (May); "Another One Bites The Dust" (Deacon); "Need Your Loving Tonight" (Deacon); "Crazy Little Thing Called Love" (Mercury); "Rock It (Prime Jive)" (Taylor); "Don't Try Suicide" (Mercury); "Sail Away Sweet Sister (To The Sister I Never Had)" (May); "Coming Soon" (Taylor); "Save Me" (May)

CD bonus track, 1991 Hollywood reissue (U.S. only): remix of "Dragon Attack"

Notes: The cover shot finds Mercury's look in transit—hair cropped, but upper lip still shaved.
The first Queen album not to bear some form of the "no synthesizers" disclaimer. Brian May's account is that they first used the Oberheim OB-X on Flash Gordon, *although it was released later.*
Queen firsts: U.S. No. 1 album; album released on CD; "urban" chart-topping single with "Another One Bites The Dust."

FLASH GORDON

Recorded: (in part, probably) June to July 1979 and February to May 1980, Musicland, Munich; and (mainly) October to November 1980, Town House, Music Centre, Advision, and Utopia, London
Released: EMI, December 8, 1980 (U.K.); Elektra, January 27, 1981 (U.S.)
Producers: Brian May and Mack

"Flash's Theme" (May); "In The Space Capsule (The Love Theme)" (Taylor); "Ming's Theme (In The Court Of

Ming The Merciless)" (Mercury); "The Ring (Hypnotic Seduction Of Dale)" (Mercury); "Football Fight" (Mercury); "In The Death Cell (Love Theme Reprise)" (Taylor); "Execution Of Flash" (Deacon); "The Kiss (Aura Resurrects Flash)" (Mercury); "Arboria (Planet Of The Tree Men)" (Deacon); "Escape From The Swamp" (Taylor); "Flash To The Rescue" (May); "Vultan's Theme (Attack Of The Hawkmen)" (Mercury); "Battle Theme" (May); "The Wedding March" (May); "Marriage Of Dale And Ming (And Flash Approaching)" (May/Taylor); "Crash Dive Of Mingo City" (May); "Flash's Theme Reprise" (May); "The Hero" (May)

CD bonus track, 1991 Hollywood reissue (U.S. only): remix of "Flash's Theme"

Notes: Queen interwove work on this soundtrack with The Game *sessions.*
As well as synthesizer, Queen used a full orchestra for the first time on some tracks.
With its mix of music and dialogue snippets, the original soundtrack fulfilled Queen's desire "to write the first rock 'n' roll soundtrack to a non-music film," according to Taylor (Mark Blake, Mojo, 2008).

GREATEST HITS

Released: EMI, November 2, 1981 (U.K.); Elektra, November 3, 1981 (U.S.)

"Another One Bites The Dust" (Deacon); "Bohemian Rhapsody" (Mercury); "Crazy Little Thing Called Love" (Mercury); "Killer Queen" (Mercury); "Fat Bottomed Girls" (May); "Bicycle Race" (Mercury); "Under Pressure" (Queen/Bowie); "We Will Rock You" (May); "We Are The Champions" (Mercury); "Flash" (May); "Somebody To Love" (Mercury); "You're My Best Friend" (Deacon); "Keep Yourself Alive" (May); "Play The Game" (Mercury)

Notes: U.K. version included "Save Me," "Don't Stop Me Now," "Now I'm Here," "Good Old Fashioned Lover Boy," and "Seven Seas Of Rhye" but not "Keep Yourself Alive" and "Under Pressure"—and the running order was completely different. Better buys than this 1981 U.S. Greatest Hits *are the 1994 Hollywood reissue of the same name that follows the seventeen-track running order of the original U.K. release, or the 2002 EMI version with "Teo Torriate (Let Us Cling Together)" as a bonus track added to the original U.K.* Greatest Hits, *Queen's most consistent seller domestically, shifting well over three million and charting in the Top 75 for nearly 500 weeks.*

HOT SPACE

Recorded: September (officially, but quite possibly June and July) 1981 (by no means nonstop) to March 1982, Mountain, Montreux; and Musicland, Munich
Released: EMI, May 21, 1982 (U.K.); Elektra, May 25, 1982 (U.S.)
Producers: Queen and Mack

"Staying Power" (Mercury); "Dancer" (May); "Back Chat" (Deacon); "Body Language" (Mercury); "Action This Day" (Taylor); "Put Out The Fire" (May); "Life Is Real (Song For Lennon)" (Mercury); "Calling All Girls" (Taylor); "Las Palabras De Amor (The Words Of Love)" (May); "Cool Cat" (Deacon, Mercury); "Under Pressure" (Queen/Bowie)

CD bonus track, 1991 Hollywood reissue (U.S. only): remix of "Body Language"

Notes: Breaks in recording Hot Space *included Queen's ill-starred tours of Venezuela and Mexico, and two concerts in Montreal, Canada, specifically set up for filming.*
Notes demanding urgent response, which Winston Churchill habitually attached to his memos during World War II, gave Taylor his title for "Action This Day."
"Calling All Girls," released in the U.S. on July 1982, was Taylor's first A-side single track as a songwriter—anywhere in the world!

THE WORKS

Recorded: August 1983 to January 1984, Record Plant, Los Angeles; and Musicland, Munich
Released: EMI, February 27, 1984 (U.K.); Capitol, February 28, 1984 (U.S.)
Producers: Queen and Mack

"Radio Ga Ga" (Taylor); "Tear It Up" (May); "It's A Hard Life" (Mercury); "Man On The Prowl" (Mercury); "Machines (Back To Humans)" (May/Taylor); "I Want To Break Free" (Deacon); "Keep Passing The Open Windows" (Mercury); "Hammer To Fall" (May); "Is This The World We Created?. . ." (May/Mercury)

CD bonus tracks, 1991 Hollywood reissue (U.S. only): reissue "I Go Crazy" (May) and extended versions of "Radio Ga Ga" and "I Want To Break Free"

Notes: Keyboardist Fred Mandel became the first outside musician to make a major contribution to a Queen album, playing piano or synthesizers on "Radio Ga Ga," "Man On The Prowl," "I Want To Break Free," and "Hammer To Fall."

The big hits came from Taylor and Deacon. The drummer's worldwide smash with "Radio Ga Ga" meant that all four bandmembers had written big hits. "Ga Ga" started life as "kaka" because that's what Taylor's little son Felix thought of what he heard on the radio. Mercury's false boobs in the "I Want To Break Free" video and on stage upset North and South America for opposite reasons—the North because it was too conservative to accept a man in drag as popular entertainment, the South because the cross-dressing desecrated what had become a revolutionary freedom anthem.

Queen attracted some media opprobrium by releasing all nine tracks on singles.

A KIND OF MAGIC

Recorded: November 1985 to April 1986, Musicland, Munich, Germany; Mountain, Montreux, Switzerland; and Townhouse, London
Released: EMI, June 2, 1986 (U.K.); Capitol, June 3, 1986 (U.S.)
Producers: Queen and Mack on tracks 1, 3, 4, 5, 9; Queen and David Richards on tracks 2, 6, 7, 8, 10

"One Vision" (Queen); "A Kind Of Magic" (Taylor); "One Year Of Love" (Deacon); "Pain Is So Close To Pleasure" (Deacon/Mercury); "Friends Will Be Friends" (Deacon/Mercury); "Who Wants To Live Forever?" (May); "Gimme The Prize (Kurgan's Theme)" (May); "Don't Lose Your Head" (Taylor); "Princes Of The Universe" (Mercury); "Forever" (May)

CD bonus tracks, 1991 Hollywood reissue (U.S. only): extended version of "One Vision"

Notes: Original U.K. LP did not include "Forever" (an instrumental version of "Who Wants To Live Forever?"), whereas the CD did, along with versions titled "A Kind Of 'A Kind Of Magic'" and "Friends Will Be Friends Will Be Friends . . ."
It may be the song credits indicated the start of a move toward the more sharing attitude manifested from The Miracle onward. Bandmembers' new openness to using other musicians in the studio saw tour keyboardist Spike Edney widely featured, Steve Gregory playing sax on "One Year Of Love," Joan Armatrading singing backing vocals on "Don't Lose Your Head," and the National Philharmonic Orchestra featuring on "Who Wants To Live Forever?" Four tracks—"Who Wants To Live Forever?" "Gimme The Prize (Kurgan's Theme)," "Don't Lose Your Head," and "Princes Of The Universe"—were written for the Highlander movie and appeared in some form on the soundtrack.

LIVE MAGIC

Recorded: July 11 and 12, Wembley Stadium, London; July 27, Népstadion, Budapest, Hungary; August 9, 1986, Knebworth, England
Released: EMI, December 1, 1986 (U.K.); Hollywood, August 1996 (U.S.)
Producers: Queen and Trip Khalaf (longtime concert soundman)

"One Vision" (Queen); "Tie Your Mother Down" (May); "Seven Seas Of Rhye" (Mercury); "A Kind Of Magic" (Taylor); "Under Pressure" (Queen/Bowie); "Another One Bites The Dust" (Deacon); "I Want To Break Free" (Deacon); "Is This The World We Created" (Mercury/May); "Bohemian Rhapsody" (Mercury); "Hammer To Fall" (May); "Radio Ga Ga" (Taylor); "We Will Rock You" (May); "Friends Will Be Friends" (Deacon/Mercury); "We Are The Champions" (Mercury); "God Save The Queen" (trad. arr. May)

Notes: All but three tracks were edited for length on the LP version. The CD restored some of the cuts.
Knebworth was the last concert Queen ever played.
Live At Wembley '86, released in 1992 and referred to below in connection with the DVD, is an extended version of the same Wembley shows featured here.

THE MIRACLE

Recorded: January 1988 to January 1989, Olympic and Townhouse, London; and Mountain, Montreux
Released: Parlophone, May 22, 1989 (U.K.); Capitol, June 6, 1989 (U.S.)
Producers: Queen and David Richards

"Party"; "Khashoggi's Ship"; "The Miracle"; "I Want It All"; "The Invisible Man"; "Breakthru"; "Rain Must Fall"; "Scandal"; "My Baby Does Me"; "Was It All Worth It"

Original CD version bonus tracks (U.S. and U.K.): "Hang On In There," "Chinese Torture," 12-inch single version of "The Invisible Man"
CD additional bonus track, 1991 Hollywood reissue (U.S. only): 12-inch single version of "Scandal"

Notes: From The Miracle onward, to the great benefit of in-band harmony, all songwriting was credited to "Queen" unless otherwise stated. Interruptions to recording abounded: a tour by Taylor's hobby band, The Cross; Deacon's restorative family vacations; Mercury's remaining Montserrat Caballé activities; May's suddenly hectic schedule of sessions for other artists.

Queen At The Beeb

Recorded: February 5 and December 3, 1973, BBC Langham 1, London
Released: Band of Joy, December 4, 1989 (U.K.); Hollywood, March 7, 1995 (U.S.)
Producer: Bernie Andrews

"My Fairy King" (Mercury); "Keep Yourself Alive" (May); "Doing All Right" (May/Staffell); "Liar" (Mercury); "Ogre Battle" (Mercury); "Great King Rat" (Mercury); "Modern Times Rock 'N' Roll" (Taylor); "Son And Daughter" (May)

Notes: Hollywood called it Queen At The BBC.
This is one of a seemingly endless series of "At The Beeb" albums drawn from BBC radio archives. These tracks aren't exactly live but recorded to a strict timetable for a Radio 1 program called Sounds Of The '70s. *The aim was artistic, but also to avoid using up "needle time," restricted by the Beeb's agreement with the Musicians' Union. A quirky digression from the band's otherwise ultra-pro catalog.*

Innuendo

Recorded: March (officially, but May by Jim Hutton's account) 1989 to November 1990, Metropolis, London; and Mountain, Montreux
Released: Parlophone, February 4, 1991 (U.K.); Hollywood, February 5, 1991 (U.S.)
Producers: Queen and David Richards

"Innuendo"; "I'm Going Slightly Mad"; "Headlong"; "I Can't Live Without You"; "Don't Try So Hard"; "Ride The Wild Wind"; "All God's People" (Queen/Mike Moran); "These Are The Days Of Our Lives"; "Delilah"; "The Hitman"; "Bijou"; "The Show Must Go On"

Notes: Mercury asked his bandmates to carry on recording after they'd finished The Miracle *and then told them the reason for his urgency—that he was dying of AIDS.*
In the U.S., Queen launched the album with a party aboard the old British liner Queen Mary, *permanently docked in Long Beach, California.*
Steve Howe from Yes played "Additional Wandering Minstrel Spanish Guitar—Somewhere In The Middle" on the title track.
The LP version had to be shorter, so Queen chose to edit four tracks: "I'm Going Slightly Mad," "Don't Try So Hard," "Bijou," and "The Hitman."

Greatest Hits II

Released: Parlophone (U.K.-only release), October 28, 1991 (U.K.)

"A Kind Of Magic" (Taylor); "Under Pressure" (Queen/ Bowie); "Radio Ga Ga" (Taylor); "I Want It All" (Queen); "I Want To Break Free" (Deacon); "Innuendo" (Queen); "It's A Hard Life" (Mercury); "Breakthru" (Queen); "Who Wants To Live Forever" (May); "Headlong" (Queen); "The Miracle" (Queen); "I'm Going Slightly Mad" (Queen); "The Invisible Man" (Queen); "Hammer To Fall" (May); "Friends Will Be Friends" (Deacon/Mercury); "The Show Must Go On" (Queen); "One Vision" (Queen)

Notes: This single-CD includes some edits for length—the double-LP version is uncut.
Its release preceded Mercury's death by a month.
This collection of hits dating 1981–1991, with no duplication from the first Greatest Hits, *signals the start of consumer-choice problems for any latecomer to Queen who wants to catch up via compilations. The 1992 U.S. release* Classic Queen *is a consciously post-Mercury set, a big hit at the time and fair enough but not necessarily a solid-gold "best of"—and missing* Made In Heaven *tracks, of course. The 1997 May/Taylor selection* Rocks Vol. 1 *(*Queen Rocks *in the U.K.) offers a narrow range of material as indicated by the title. So the best buy, if affordable, would be* The Platinum Collection *(released by EMI in the U.K. in 2000 and by Hollywood in the U.S. in 2002); it simply boxes up the three* Greatest Hits *volumes, which are all detailed in this selective discography and cover Queen's entire career before the "+ Paul Rodgers" era, without duplication and including solo and guest artist snippets (these last items being what you'd miss if you bought* Greatest Hits I and II, *Hollywood's 1995 repackaging of the first two British collections).*

Made In Heaven

Recorded: May to November 1991 and spring 1994 to October 1995, Mountain, Montreux; and Metropolis, London
Released: Parlophone, November 6, 1995 (U.K.); Hollywood, November 7, 1995 (U.S.)
Producers: Queen, David Richards, Justin Shirley-Smith, and Joshua J. Macrae

"It's A Beautiful Day" (Queen); "Made In Heaven" (Mercury); "Let Me Live" (Queen); "Mother Love" (May/ Mercury); "My Life Has Been Saved" (Queen); "I Was Born To Love You" (Mercury); "Heaven For Everyone" (Taylor); "Too Much Love Will Kill You" (May/Frank Musker/ Elizabeth Lamers); "You Don't Fool Me" (Queen); "A Winter's Tale" (Queen); "It's A Beautiful Day (Reprise)" (Queen); "Untitled" (hidden track)

Notes: The Mercury piano on "It's A Beautiful Day" is said to have been recorded as far back as 1980 at Musicland, Munich.
"Made In Heaven" and "I Was Born To Love You" use Mercury vocals from his 1985 solo album Mr. Bad Guy; *"Heaven For Everyone" his*

guest vocal from The Cross' 1986 album Shove It; and "Too Much Love Will Kill You" his vocal from an unreleased track recorded for The Miracle—all with freshly created backings by Queen.

On "Mother Love," the snatch of Carole King and Gerry Goffin's "Goin' Back" is taken from the B-side of the single Mercury recorded as Larry Lurex in 1972.

The song "My Life Has Been Saved" appeared previously as the B-side to Queen's 1989 single "Scandal." This version uses the same Mercury vocal with a new band backing.

The moods of the closing twenty-two-minute hidden track have been read as reflecting the ups and downs of the twenty-two years between Queen and Made In Heaven—which is a nice thought. It's uncredited because this mainly instrumental elegy was initiated by David Richards and embellished by May and Taylor. For length, it had to be cut from LP and cassette versions.

GREATEST HITS III

Released: Parlophone, November 8, 1999 (U.K.), Hollywood, November 9, 1999 (U.S.)

"The Show Must Go On" (Queen; perf. by Queen w/ Elton John); "Under Pressure (Rah Mix)" (perf. and written by Queen w/ David Bowie); "Barcelona" (Mercury/Moran; perf. by Mercury w/ Montserrat Caballé); "Too Much Love Will Kill You" (May/Musker/Lamers); "Somebody To Love" (Mercury; perf. by Queen w/ George Michael); "You Don't Fool Me" (Queen); "Heaven For Everyone" (Taylor); "Las Palabras De Amor (The Words Of Love)" (May); "Driven By You" (perf. and written by May); "Living On My Own" (perf. and written by Mercury); "Let Me Live" (Queen); "The Great Pretender" (Buck Ram; perf. by Mercury); "Princes Of The Universe" (Mercury); "Another One Bites The Dust" (Deacon; perf. by Queen w/ Wyclef Jean feat. Pras & Free); "No-One But You (Only The Good Die Young)" (May); "These Are The Days Of Our Lives" (Queen); "Thank God It's Christmas" (May/Taylor)

Notes: The cover credits "Queen +" because of the solo and guest artist material. In the U.S. this was titled Greatest Hits, Vol. 3 *because, in 1995, Hollywood had belatedly issued the first two U.K. compilations boxed together as* Greatest Hits, Vols. 1 & 2.

Unlike the previous two Hits *collections,* III *stretches the title by including several non-hits.*

The opening track comes from Queen and Elton John's live spot at the Paris premiere of Maurice Béjart's Mercury-referencing Ballet For Life.

"Somebody To Love" comes from the Concert For Life EP Five Live. "Another One Bites The Dust," re-recorded and remixed with Wyclef Jean, hit No. 5 in the U.K. singles chart in 1998.

Queen recorded "No-One But You (Only The Good Die Young)" as a new (and quiet) track on the 1997 Rocks Vol. 1 (*U.K.* Queen Rocks) compilation.

QUEEN FOREVER

Released: Virgin EMI, November 10, 2014 (U.K.), Hollywood (U.S.)

"Let Me In Your Heart Again" (May); "Love Kills" (Mercury/Giorgio Moroder); "There Must Be More To Life Than This" (Mercury); "It's A Hard Life" (Mercury); "You're My Best Friend" (Deacon); "Love Of My Life" (Mercury); "Drowse" (Taylor); "Long Away" (May); "Lily Of The Valley" (Mercury); "Don't Try So Hard" (Mercury); "Bijou" (Mercury/May); "These Are The Days Of Our Lives" (Taylor); "Las Palabras De Amor (The Words of Love)" (May); "Who Wants To Live Forever" (May); "A Winter's Tale" (Mercury): "Play The Game" (Mercury); "Save Me" (May); "Somebody To Love" (Mercury); "Too Much Love Will Kill You" (May/Frank Musker/Elizabeth Lamers); "Crazy Little Thing Called Love" (Mercury)

Notes: Collector's point is "There Must Be More To Life Than This," the Mercury/Michael Jackson duet (see Chapter 8) on a song from Mercury's 1985 solo album Mr. Bad Guy. In interviews, Taylor expressed chagrin that the Jackson estate permitted only the one track to be used from several the duo recorded.

The other tracks are slightly unpredictable compilation fodder, remasters from the slower, sweeter side of the Queen repertoire apart from largely new recordings of The Works outtake "Let Me In Your Heart Again" (previously released on a solo album by May's wife, Anita Dobson) and "Love Kills" (previously released as Mercury's first solo single in 1984–and, incidentally, a nominee for Worst Original Song from a movie soundtrack at the 5th Golden Raspberry Awards, an acknowledgment Mercury would no doubt have treasured).

A "deluxe" double-CD version carried another 17 tracks.

QUEEN + PAUL RODGERS

RETURN OF THE CHAMPIONS

Recorded: May 9, 2005, live at Hallam FM Arena, Sheffield, England
Released: Parlophone, September 19, 2005 (U.K.); Hollywood, September 13, 2005 (U.S.)
Recorded by: Justin Shirley-Smith and Peter Brandt

"Reaching Out" (Andy Hill/Don Black); "Tie Your Mother Down" (May); "I Want To Break Free" (Deacon); "Fat Bottomed Girls" (May); "Wishing Well" (Rodgers/Paul Kossoff/John Bundrick/Tetsu Yamauchi/Simon Kirke); "Another One Bites The Dust" (Deacon); "Crazy Little Thing Called Love" (Mercury); "Say It's Not True" (Taylor); "'39" (May); "Love Of My Life" (Mercury); "Hammer To Fall" (May); "Feel Like Makin' Love" (Rodgers/Mick Ralphs); "Let There Be Drums" (Sandy Nelson/Richard Podolor); "I'm In Love With My Car" (Taylor); "Guitar Solo" (May); "Last Horizon" (May); "These Are The Days Of Our Lives" (Queen); "Radio Ga Ga" (Taylor); "Can't Get Enough" (Ralphs); "A Kind Of Magic" (Taylor); "I Want It All" (Queen); "Bohemian Rhapsody" (Mercury); "The Show Must Go On" (Queen); "All Right Now" (Andy Fraser/Rodgers); "We Will Rock You" (May); "We Are The Champions" (Mercury); "God Save The Queen" (trad. arr. May)

Notes: Released as a double-CD. DVD version includes additional tracks: a remix of "It's A Beautiful Day" and "Imagine" live from their concert in Hyde Park, London, July 15, 2005, a week after the London bombings.
"Reaching Out" was originally released in 1996 as a three-track charity single for the Nordoff-Robbins Musical Therapy Centre. The single featured May and Rodgers, Charlie Watts, Lulu, and Sam Brown billed as "Music Therapy," and it included the single version of the song, as well as acoustic and instrumental versions.
Onstage, "Bohemian Rhapsody" began with Mercury singing from the big screen, then Rodgers took over.
"Let There Be Drums" was a 1961 hit single when Taylor was twelve.

THE COSMOS ROCKS
Recorded: March 2007 to early summer 2008, Taylor's Surrey home studio known as The Priory
Released: Parlophone, September 15, 2008 (U.K.); Hollywood, October 28, 2008 (U.S.)
Producers: May, Rodgers, and Taylor; co-producers Joshua J. Macrae, Justin Shirley-Smith, and Kris Fredriksson
Songwriting: all tracks May, Rodgers, and Taylor

"Cosmos Rockin'"; "Time To Shine"; "Still Burnin'"; "Small"; "Warboys"; "We Believe"; "Call Me"; "Voodoo"; "Some Things That Glitter"; "C-lebrity"; "Through The Night"; "Say It's Not True"; "Surf's Up . . . School's Out"; "Small (Reprise)"

Notes: All instruments played by the three principals, with May and

Rodgers alternating on bass. The only additional musician is Foo Fighters' Taylor Hawkins singing backups on "C-lebrity."
A limited edition of the CD was packaged with a fifteen-song edit of the DVD Super Live In Japan.

LIVE IN UKRAINE
Recorded: September 12, 2008, live in Freedom Square, Kharkiv, Ukraine
Released: Parlophone (U.K.), Hollywood (U.S.) June 15, 2009
Producers: Joshua J. Macrae, Justin Shirley Smith, Kris Fredriksen

"One Vision" (Queen); "Tie Your Mother Down" (May); "The Show Must Go On" (Queen); "Fat Bottomed Girls" (May); "Another One Bites The Dust" (Deacon)/"Hammer To Fall" (May)/"I Want It All" (Queen); "I Want To Break Free" (Deacon); "Seagull" (Rodgers/Mick Ralphs); "Love Of My Life" (Mercury); "'39" (May); "Drum Solo" (Taylor); "I'm In Love With My Car" (Taylor); "Say It's Not True" (Taylor); "Shooting Star" (Rodgers); "Bad Company" (Simon Kirke/Rodgers); "Guitar Solo" (May); "Bijou" (Queen); "Last Horizon" (May); "Crazy Little Thing Called Love" (Mercury); "C-lebrity" (Taylor); "Feel Like Makin' Love" (Rodgers/Ralphs); "Bohemian Rhapsody" (Mercury); "Cosmos Rockin'" (Taylor); "All Right Now" (Andy Fraser/Rodgers); "We Will Rock You" (May); "We Are The Champions" (Mercury); "God Save The Queen" (trad. arr. May)

Notes: Double CD packaged with a DVD of the concert—crucial in order to get the magnitude of the event: 350,000, Queen's biggest ever audience (10 million Ukrainian homes tuned in to live TV coverage too).
David Mallet filmed and directed the DVD, as usual.
The digital download version carried two Taylor compositions as bonus tracks: "A Kind Of Magic" and "Radio Ga Ga."

ANOTHER MATTER OF INTEREST
Of course, "true fans" may want to acquire everything Queen ever recorded and all the members' solo and even session work too. Really, for the fond but less than fanatical newcomer to Queen, the choice may lie between buying your preferred albums or *The Platinum Collection*—the three Greatest Hits volumes boxed together.

But there is one Queen-related compilation deserving the consideration of Freddie Mercury fanatics (and appreciative wonderment from other interested onlookers): the *Solo Collection* (released October 23, 2000, on Parlophone, U.S. and U.K.). The full version comprises ten CDs and two DVDs: all his completed solo studio recordings (including the Barcelona album with Montserrat Caballé, of course), plus all manner of rarities, offcuts, and outtakes (even a singsong 'round the old Joanna with *la* Caballé back home at Garden Lodge), as well as a series of interview clips, promo videos, and documentary film. Credit for this labor of love goes to Queen archivist Greg Brooks, with compilation, coordination, and remaster craftsmanship by Justin Shirley-Smith, Peter Mew, and Kris Fredriksson.

Meanwhile, by the time this book is published, vinyl-fancying Queen buffs may already be deep into the Hollywood reissues of all the band's albums on black plastic, announced in November 2008 and due to be spread over two years.

45s/Singles, EPs

Despite their heavy rock side, Queen earned their reputation as a classic singles band seeking album sales in the time-honored way: via radio and chart hits. Mostly it worked to some degree, though less so in the U.S. than the rest of the world. Listed here are their single releases in the U.S. and U.K. with chart positions (where a " — " indicates "didn't chart"). Because format shifting from the '70s onward led to multiple B-sides on every release, with variations from one country to another, only A-sides are noted, except where intent or event created a "double-A." Release dates are by consensus of established reference sources or by arithmetic where that fails; mostly correct, no doubt, but don't bet your shirt on them.

"Keep Yourself Alive" (May)
EMI, July 6, 1973 (U.K.), — ; Elektra, October 9, 1973 (U.S.), — (re-released July 1975, —)

"Liar" (Mercury)
Elektra, February 14, 1974 (U.S.), —

"Seven Seas Of Rhye" (Mercury)
EMI, February 23, 1974 (U.K.), 10; Elektra, June 20, 1974 (U.S.), —

"Killer Queen" (Mercury)
EMI, October 11, 1974 (U.K.), 2; Elektra, October 21, 1974 (U.S.), 12

"Now I'm Here" (May)
EMI, January 17, 1975 (U.K.), 11

"Bohemian Rhapsody" (Mercury)
EMI, October 31, 1975 (U.K.), 1; Elektra, December 2, 1975 (U.S.), 9

"You're My Best Friend" (Deacon)

EMI, May 18, 1976 (U.K.), 7; Elektra, June 10, 1976 (U.S.), 16

"Somebody To Love" (Mercury)
EMI, November 12, 1976 (U.K.), 2; Elektra, December 10, 1976 (U.S.), 13

"Tie Your Mother Down" (May)
EMI, March 4, 1977 (U.K.), 31; Elektra, March 8, 1977 (U.S.), 49

"Good Old Fashioned Lover Boy" (Mercury)/"Death On Two Legs" (Mercury)/"Tenement Funster" (Taylor)/"White Queen" (May) EP
EMI, May 20, 1977 (U.K.), 17

"Long Away" (May)
Elektra, June 7, 1977 (U.S.), —

"We Are The Champions" (Mercury)/"We Will Rock You" (May)
EMI, October 7, 1977 (U.K.), 2; Elektra, December 10, 1976 (U.S.), 4

"Spread Your Wings" (Deacon)
EMI, February 10, 1978 (U.K.), 34

"It's Late" (May)
Elektra, April 25, 1978 (U.S.), 74

"Bicycle Race" (Mercury)/"Fat Bottomed Girls" (May)
EMI, October 13, 1978 (U.K.), 11; Elektra, October 24, 1978 (U.S.), 24

"Don't Stop Me Now" (Mercury)
EMI, January 26, 1979 (U.K.), 9; Elektra, February 20, 1979 (U.S.), 86

"Jealousy" (Mercury)
Elektra, April 27, 1979 (U.S.), —

"Love Of My Life (Live)"
EMI, June 29, 1979 (U.K.), 63

"We Will Rock You (Live)" (May)
Elektra, August 24, 1979 (U.S.), —

"Crazy Little Thing Called Love" (Mercury)
EMI, October 5, 1979 (U.K.), 2; Elektra, December 7, 1979 (U.S.), 1

"Save Me" (May)
EMI, January 25, 1980 (U.K.), 11

"Play The Game" (Mercury)

EMI, May 30, 1980 (U.K.), 14; Elektra, June 1980 (U.S.), 42

"Another One Bites The Dust" (Deacon)
EMI, August 22, 1980 (U.K.), 7; Elektra, August 12, 1980 (U.S.), 1

"Need Your Loving Tonight" (Deacon)
Elektra, November 18, 1980 (U.S.), 44

"Flash" (May)
EMI, November 24, 1980 (U.K.), 10; Elektra, January 27, 1981 (U.S.), 42

"Under Pressure" (Queen/Bowie)
EMI, October 26, 1981 (U.K.), 1; Elektra, October 27, 1981 (U.S.), 29

"Body Language" (Mercury)
EMI, April 19, 1982 (U.K.), 25; Elektra, April 19, 1982 (U.S.), 11

"Las Palabras De Amor (The Words Of Love)" (May)
EMI, June 1, 1982 (U.K.), 17

"Calling All Girls" (Taylor)
Elektra, July 19, 1982 (U.S.), 60

"Back Chat" (Deacon)
EMI, August 9, 1982 (U.K.), 40; Elektra, November 23, 1982 (U.S.), —

"Radio Ga Ga" (Taylor)
EMI, January 23, 1984 (U.K.), 2; Capitol, February 7, 1984 (U.S.), 16

"I Want To Break Free" (Deacon)
EMI, April 2, 1984 (U.K.), 3; Capitol, April 13, 1984 (U.S.), 45

"It's A Hard Life" (Mercury)
EMI, July 16, 1984 (U.K.), 6; Capitol, July 16, 1984 (U.S.), 72

"Hammer To Fall" (May)
EMI, September 10, 1984 (U.K.), 13; Capitol, October 12, 1984 (U.S.), —

"Thank God It's Christmas" (May/Taylor)
EMI, November 26, 1984 (U.K.), 21

"One Vision" (Queen)
EMI, November 4, 1985 (U.K.), 7; Capitol, November 20, 1985 (U.S.), 61

"A Kind Of Magic" (Taylor)
EMI, March 17, 1986 (U.K.), 3; Capitol, June 4, 1986 (U.S.), 42

"Princes Of The Universe" (Mercury)
Capitol, April 7, 1986 (U.S.), —

"Friends Will Be Friends" (Deacon/Mercury)

EMI, June 9, 1986 (U.K.), 14

"Pain Is So Close To Pleasure (Remix)" (Deacon/Mercury)
Capitol, August 26, 1986 (U.S.), —

"Who Wants To Live Forever" (May)
EMI, September 15, 1986 (U.K.), 24

"I Want It All" (Queen)
Parlophone, May 2, 1989 (U.K.), 3; Capitol, May 10, 1989 (U.S.), 50

"Breakthru" (Queen)
Parlophone, June 19, 1989 (U.K.), 7; Capitol, June 28, 1989 (U.S.), —

"The Invisible Man" (Queen)
Parlophone, August 7, 1989 (U.K.), 12

"Scandal" (Queen)
Parlophone, October 9, 1989 (U.K.), 25; Capitol, October 11, 1989 (U.S.), —

"The Miracle (Remix)" (Queen)
Parlophone, November 29, 1989 (U.K.), 21

"Innuendo" (Queen)
Parlophone, January 14, 1991 (U.K.), 1

"I'm Going Slightly Mad" (Queen)
Parlophone, March 4, 1991 (U.K.), 22

"Headlong" (Queen)
Parlophone, May 13, 1991 (U.K.), 14; Hollywood, January 17, 1991 (U.S.), —

"These Are The Days Of Our Lives" (Queen)
Hollywood, September 5, 1991 (U.S.), —

"The Show Must Go On" (Queen)
Parlophone, October 14, 1991 (U.K.), 16

"Bohemian Rhapsody (Reissue)" (Mercury)
Parlophone, December 9, 1991 (U.K.), 1; Hollywood, February 6, 1992 (U.S.), 2

"We Will Rock You" (May)/"We Are The Champions (Reissue)" (Mercury)
Hollywood, August 1992 (U.S.), 52

Five Live EP (live, George Michael and Queen w/ Lisa

Stansfield): "Somebody To Love" (Mercury)/"These Are The Days Of Our Lives" (Queen)/"Killer" (Adam Tinley/Seal Henry-Samuel)/"Papa Was A Rolling Stone" (Norman Whitfield/Barrett Strong)/"Calling You" (Bob Telson)/"Dear Friends" (May)
Parlophone, April 19, 1993 (U.K.) 1; Hollywood, May 1, 1993 (U.S.), 46
Note: The last track features a snippet of the Queen original from Sheer Heart Attack with Mercury singing.

"Somebody To Love" (from *Five Live* EP, Queen w/ George Michael)
Hollywood, May 1993 (U.S.), 30

"Heaven For Everyone" (Taylor)
Parlophone, October 23, 1995 (U.K.), 2; Hollywood, October 1995 (U.S.), —

"A Winter's Tale" (Queen)
Parlophone, December 11, 1995 (U.K.), 6

"Too Much Love Will Kill You" (May/Musker/Lamers)
Parlophone, February 26, 1996 (U.K.), 15; Hollywood, February 1996 (U.S.), —

"Let Me Live" (Queen)
Parlophone, June 17, 1996 (U.K.), 9

"You Don't Fool Me" (Queen)
Parlophone, November 18, 1996 (U.K.), 17; Hollywood, November 1996 (U.S.), —

"No-One But You (Only The Good Die Young)" (May)
Parlophone, January 5, 1998, (U.K.), 13

"Another One Bites The Dust (Re-recording w/ Wyclef Jean feat. Pras & Free)" (Deacon)
Dreamworks, November 14, 1998 (U.K.), 5

"Under Pressure (Rah Mix)" (Queen/Bowie)
Parlophone, December 6, 1999 (U.K.), 14

"We Will Rock You (Re-recording w/ Five + Queen)" (May)
RCA, July 17, 2000 (U.K.), 1

"Flash (Vanguard Remix)" (May)
Parlophone, March 17, 2003 (U.K.), 15

"Another One Bites The Dust (The Miami Project Mix)" (Deacon)
Parlophone, December 11, 2006 (U.K.), 31

Queen + Paul Rodgers
"Say It's Not True" (May/Rodgers/Taylor)
queenonline.com (download), December 1, 2007; Parlophone CD single, December 31, 2007 (U.K.), 90

"C-lebrity" (May/Rodgers/Taylor)
Parlophone, September 8, 2008 (U.K.), 33

"Keep Yourself Alive (Long-Lost Retake)"/"Stone Cold Crazy (Remastered)"
Universal, February 27, 2011 (U.K.); Hollywood, April 16, 2011 (U.S.)

"Let Me In Your Heart Again (William Orbit Mix)"
Virgin EMI, November 3, 2014 (U.K.), 102; Hollywood, November 3, 2014 (U.S.)

DVD'OGRAPHY

This selective DVD videography lists Queen's best/most significant performance films and also the two main promo compilations, in chronological order of the events they portray or relate to (the promo compilations are dated here by the last promo featured on each). Worth considering, though found only on video at the time of this writing, are the Rudi Dolezal and Hannes Rossacher documentaries *The Magic Years, Volumes I to III*, covering pre-Queen days to 1986 (on MPI, released in 1991).

GREATEST VIDEO HITS 1

Released: Parlophone, October 14, 2002 (U.K.); Hollywood, October 15, 2002 (U.S.)

DISC ONE
"Bohemian Rhapsody"; "Another One Bites The Dust"; "Killer Queen"; "Fat Bottomed Girls"; "Bicycle Race"; "You're My Best Friend"; "Don't Stop Me Now"; "Save Me"; "Crazy Little Thing Called Love"; "Somebody To Love"; "Spread Your Wings"; "Play The Game"; "Flash"; "Tie Your Mother Down"; "We Will Rock You"; "We Are The Champions"

DISC TWO
"Now I'm Here (Live)"; "Good Old Fashioned Lover Boy";

"Keep Yourself Alive"; "Liar"; "Love of My Life (Live)"; "We Will Rock You (Live Fast Version)"

Notes: This compilation includes Queen promos from the start through "Flash" (January 1981), along with a documentary, old interviews, and new commentary from May and Taylor added for the DVD version.
There has been a gripe about the technique used for conversion from the original 1981 Greatest Flix *video compilation to DVD, since it involved some cropping to the top and bottom of the frame.*
"Good Old Fashioned Lover Boy" is from BBC TV's Top Of The Pops, *June 1977.*

QUEEN ROCK MONTREAL & LIVE AID

Recorded: November 24 and 25, 1981, The Forum, Montreal, Canada; July 13, 1985, Wembley Stadium, London (plus documentary material before and after)
Released: Parlophone, October 29, 2007 (U.K.); Eagle Vision, October 30, 2007 (U.S.)
Director: Saul Swimmer (Queen Rock Montreal only)

DISC ONE (MONTREAL)

"Intro"; "We Will Rock You"; "Let Me Entertain You"; "Play the Game"; "Somebody to Love"; "Killer Queen"; "I'm in Love With My Car"; "Get Down, Make Love"; "Save Me"; "Now I'm Here"; "Dragon Attack"; "Now I'm Here (Reprise)"; "Love Of My Life"; "Under Pressure"; "Keep Yourself Alive"; "Drum And Tympani Solo"; "Guitar Solo"; "Crazy Little Thing Called Love"; "Jailhouse Rock"; "Bohemian Rhapsody"; "Tie Your Mother Down"; "Another One Bites The Dust"; "Sheer Heart Attack"; "We Will Rock You"; "We Are The Champions"; "God Save The Queen"

DISC TWO (LIVE AID)

"Bohemian Rhapsody"; "Radio Ga Ga"; "Hammer To Fall"; "Crazy Little Thing Called Love"; "We Will Rock You"; "We Are The Champions"; "Is This The World We Created?. . ."

Notes: This digitally remastered version of Queen Rock Montreal *came out in October 2007 but adds a lot of value with the twenty minutes of show-stealing perfection from Live Aid.*
May and Taylor's (optional) commentary on Queen Rock Montreal *makes it plain they really did not get on with director Swimmer. The Live Aid disc includes rehearsal scenes and interviews.*
The concert double CD, Queen Rock Montreal, *has two tracks not on the DVD: "Flash" and "The Hero."*

QUEEN ON FIRE: LIVE AT THE BOWL

Recorded: June 5, 1982, Milton Keynes Bowl, England (additional material from Stadthalle, Vienna, Austria, May 12, 1982, and Seibu Lions Stadium, Tokorozawa, Japan, November 3, 1982)
Released: Parlophone, October 25, 2004 (U.K.); Hollywood, November 9, 2004 (U.S.)
Director: Gavin Taylor (Milton Keynes)

DISC ONE

"Flash"; "The Hero"; "We Will Rock You"; "Action This Day"; "Play The Game"; "Staying Power"; "Somebody To Love"; "Now I'm Here"; "Dragon Attack"; "Now I'm Here (Reprise)"; "Love Of My Life"; "Save Me"; "Back Chat"; "Get Down, Make Love"; "Guitar Solo"; "Under Pressure"; "Fat Bottomed Girls"; "Crazy Little Thing Called Love"; "Bohemian Rhapsody"; "Tie Your Mother Down"; "Another One Bites The Dust"; "Sheer Heart Attack"; "We Will Rock You"; "We Are The Champions"; "God Save The Queen"

DISC TWO

Vienna concert excerpts: "Another One Bites the Dust"; "We Will Rock You"; "We Are the Champions"; "God Save the Queen"
Tokyo concert excerpts: "Flash"/"The Hero"; "Now I'm Here"; "Impromptu"; "Put Out the Fire"; "Dragon Attack"; "Now I'm Here (Reprise)"; "Crazy Little Thing Called Love"; "Teo Torriate (Let Us Cling Together)"

Notes: These discs feature Queen in the thick of their often successful, yet fractious, diversion into disco, funk, and so on, touring Hot Space *but already, to May's delight, shifting some arrangements in a rockier direction live. Apart from other concert excerpts from the same year, Disc Two also features contemporary interviews with the band (except for Deacon) and a photo gallery.*
At Milton Keynes, May had a troubled show, snapping two strings during "We Will Rock You" and disconnecting his guitar lead during the "Guitar Solo," which was interrupted for about twenty seconds while he and a roadie fixed it.
After the Tokyo show, Queen didn't played live again for twenty-one months.

LIVE AT WEMBLEY STADIUM

Recorded: Wembley Stadium, London, July 12, 1986 (plus excerpts from July 11)
Released: Parlophone, June 9, 2003 (U.K.); Hollywood, June 17, 2003 (U.S.)
Director: Gavin Taylor

DISC ONE

"One Vision"; "Tie Your Mother Down"; "In The Lap Of The Gods . . . Revisited"; "Seven Seas Of Rhye"; "Tear It Up"; "A Kind Of Magic"; "Under Pressure"; "Another One Bites The Dust"; "Who Wants To Live Forever"; "I Want To Break Free"; "Impromptu"; "Guitar Solo"; "Now I'm Here"; "Love Of My Life"; "Is This The World We Created?. . ."; "(You're So Square) Baby I Don't Care"; "Hello Mary Lou (Goodbye Heart)"; "Tutti Frutti"; "Gimme Some Lovin'"; "Bohemian Rhapsody"; "Hammer To Fall"; "Crazy Little Thing Called Love"; "Big Spender"; "Radio Ga Ga"; "We Will Rock You"; "Friends Will Be Friends"; "We Are The Champions"; "God Save The Queen"

DISC TWO

Excerpts from the previous night at Wembley: "A Kind Of Magic"; "Freddie Singalong"; "Another One Bites The Dust"; "Tutti Frutti"; "Crazy Little Thing Called Love"; "We Are The Champions (Finale)"/"God Save The Queen"
Pre-*Magic* tour rehearsals (most songs incomplete): "Tie Your Mother Down"; "Seven Seas Of Rhye"; "Tear It Up"; "A Kind Of Magic; "Now I'm Here"; "I Want To Break Free"; "Piano Introduction"; "Bohemian Rhapsody"

Notes: The entire concert from what turned out to be Queen's final tour. As well as music from the previous night's concert and the preceding rehearsals, Disc Two features interviews with May, Taylor, tour manager Gerry Stickells, and video director Gavin Taylor, plus a real bonus in the Rudi Dolezal/Hannes Rossacher thirty-minute documentary about the event, A Beautiful Day.
This film previously appeared as a video, Live At Wembley, *and is available as a CD,* Live At Wembley 1986.

GREATEST VIDEO HITS 2

Released: Parlophone, November 3, 2003 (U.K.); Hollywood, November 25, 2003 (U.S.)

DISC ONE

"A Kind Of Magic"; "I Want It All"; "Radio Ga Ga"; "I Want To Break Free"; "Breakthru"; "Under Pressure"; "Scandal"; "Who Wants To Live Forever"; "The Miracle"; "It's A Hard Life"; "The Invisible Man"; "Las Palabras De Amor"; "Friends Will Be Friends"; "Body Language"; "Hammer To Fall"; "Princes Of The Universe"; "One Vision"

DISC TWO

Interview and documentary with track excerpts, apart from complete versions of "Piano Solo"; "Staying Power" (live at

Milton Keynes); "One Vision (Extended Version)"; "Who Wants To Live Forever (Ian And Belinda Version)"; "Back Chat"; and "Calling All Girls"

Notes: Straightforwardly, the promos 1982 to 1989 are on Disc One. Disc Two features an assortment of documentary excerpts, interviews (including Deacon!), and music relating to Hot Space, The Works, A Kind Of Magic, *and* The Miracle. *Again, the star turn is by Dolezal and Rossacher: sixteen minutes of their 1984 Musicland Studios interview with Freddie Mercury, called "A Musical Prostitute" (how Mercury described himself on that occasion).*
Sadly, Disc One is minus four tracks from Innuendo *that did feature on the video version of this release,* Greatest Flix II. *However, Disc Two does include a "Who Wants To Live Forever" promo that is not mentioned on the box.*

THE FREDDIE MERCURY TRIBUTE CONCERT FOR AIDS AWARENESS: SPECIAL 10TH ANNIVERSARY REISSUE

Recorded: April 20, 1992, Wembley Stadium, London
Released: Parlophone, May 13, 2002 (U.K.); EMI, November 26, 2002 (U.S.)
Director: David Mallett

DISC ONE

"Tie Your Mother Down" (feat. Joe Elliott, May, Slash); "Heaven And Hell"/"Pinball Wizard" (feat. May, Tony Iommi); "I Want It All" (feat. Roger Daltrey, Iommi); "Las Palabras De Amor" (feat. Zucchero); "Hammer To Fall" (feat. Gary Cherone, Iommi); "Stone Cold Crazy" (feat. James Hetfield, Iommi); "Thank You" (from edited medley)/"Crazy Little Thing Called Love" (feat. Robert Plant); "Too Much Love Will Kill You" (feat. May, Spike Edney); "Radio Ga Ga" (feat. Paul Young); "Who Wants To Live Forever" (feat. Seal); "I Want To Break Free" (feat. Lisa Stansfield); "Under Pressure" (feat. Annie Lennox, David Bowie); "All The Young Dudes" (feat. Ian Hunter, Mick Ronson, Bowie); "Heroes" (feat. Bowie, Ronson); "'39" (feat. George Michael); "These Are The Days Of Our Lives" (feat. Michael, Stansfield); "Somebody To Love" (feat. Michael, London Gospel Choir); "Bohemian Rhapsody" (feat. Elton John, Axl Rose); "The Show Must Go On" (feat. John, Iommi); "We Will Rock You" (feat. Rose); "We Are The Champions" (feat. Liza Minelli and the entire cast); "God Save The Queen" (tape)

DISC TWO

Documentary, rehearsals, picture gallery, and information.

Notes: Much edited concert coverage plus a disc of documentary, for the benefit of the Mercury Phoenix Trust.

The earlier U.K. two-tape video version cut parts of the first-half sets by Extreme, Def Leppard, Spinal Tap, and Robert Plant (who requested the removal of "Innuendo" because he didn't think he did justice to himself or the song). The U.S. version also dropped Zucchero and Bob Geldof singing "Too Late God." But this DVD drops the whole first half, when artists played their own sets, and delivers only the part of the concert where Queen backed other artists singing their songs (apart from Bowie who did his own compositions). The cropping of the picture in translation from video to DVD was another cause of dissatisfaction.

QUEEN + PAUL RODGERS

RETURN OF THE CHAMPIONS

Recorded: May 19, 2005, Hallam FM Arena, Sheffield, England (one track, "Imagine," recorded July 15, 2005, Hyde Park, London)
Released: Parlophone, October 31, 2005 (U.K.); Hollywood, October 18, 2005 (U.S.)
Directors: David Mallet (Sheffield) and Aubrey Powell (Hyde Park)

"Reaching Out"; "Tie Your Mother Down"; "I Want To Break Free"; "Fat Bottomed Girls"; "Wishing Well"; "Another One Bites The Dust"; "Crazy Little Thing Called Love"; "Say It's Not True"; "'39"; "Love of My Life"; "Hammer To Fall"; "Feel Like Makin' Love"; "Let There Be Drums"; "I'm In Love With My Car"; "Guitar Solo"; "Last Horizon"; "These Are The Days Of Our Lives"; "Radio Ga Ga"; "Can't Get Enough"; "A Kind Of Magic"; "I Want It All"; "Bohemian Rhapsody"; "The Show Must Go On"; "All Right Now"; "We Will Rock You"; "We Are The Champions"; "God Save The Queen"; "It's A Beautiful Day (Remix)" (Mercury vocal "flown in"); "Imagine"

Notes: Very early in Queen's "comeback" tour with Paul Rodgers they recorded and filmed this warm and powerful concert for CD (see above) and DVD.
The CD doesn't have the last two bonus tracks that weren't recorded live in Sheffield.
Mercury and Queen played "Imagine" at Wembley Arena, London, on December 9, 1980, the night after they heard of John Lennon's murder. This time, it was for the victims of the London bombings, killed and injured by terrorists on July 7, 2005.

ACKNOWLEDGMENTS

TO QUEEN for all that wildly disciplined music down the years. A belief-beggaring banquet of aural imagination, wouldn't you say?

And appreciation to all the other writers and the photographers whose work adorns this handsome tome. Please check out their curricula vitae in the "Contributors" section.

Additional thanks to those parties who came through with stunning visual materials, including AP Worldwide Images, Paul Bird, Voyageur Press photo researcher Krystyna Borgen for help locating early images, Robert Brabant, Corbis, Jason Cullen, The Everett Collection, Ferdinand Frega (Queenmuseum.com), Debra Senske and Getty Images/Redferns, Christian Lamping, The Mad Peck, Photofest, Retna, Jay Allen Sanford at Re-Visionary Press (Revolutionary Comics), Joel Schnell in Quayside Publishing Group's Minneapolis photo studio for photography of much of the memorabilia included herein, Martin Skala (QueenConcerts.com), Michael Spleet, Tate Images, and Brannon Tommey (photosets.net).

Very special thanks to Peter Hince for unselfishly sharing his collection and his expertise, and to Billy Squier and Reinhold Mack for sharing their incredible memories and insights.

To Dennis Pernu, the man at Voyageur Press who diligently picked out loads of errors, left hardly any in (we hope), and added very few of his own as far as I could see, while remaining cool at all times—that is, from where I sit, thanks to a paragon among editors. Also to Melinda Keefe and Carmen Nickisch at Voyageur for their expert editorial support, and to Katie Sonmor for keeping the creative end on track. If you Queen fans think you've found any mistakes or even misinterpretations (and you apply strict standards, we know), please don't shoot off anything other than a corrective email—we're doing our best here.

And to my wife, Gaylee, who also read the whole thing, even before Mr. Pernu. Hope she said "This sentence is too long, you should break it up into three parts" and suchlike often enough and that I responded well enough to suit your taste and reading pleasure.

All the best,

Phil Sutcliffe

SOURCES

Although they disliked the press, Queen always seemed to encounter excellent interviewers and give a good account of themselves—too bright to hold back, I guess. Just a few of the quotes in this book are acknowledged as unsourced, usually because they turned up in some obscure fan-compiled corner of the web—they got in because I thought they sounded right regardless (judgment call! could be wrong, of course). Appreciation to all the interviewers here for illuminating the story:

Martin Aston (*Mojo Classic*); Simon Bates (BBC Radio 1); Mark Blake (*Mojo*); Bob Coburn (*Rockline* radio); Caroline Coon (*Melody Maker*); Harry Doherty (*Melody Maker*); Daryl Easlea (*Mojo Classic*); Ian Fortnam (rocksbackpages.com); Andy Greene (*Rolling Stone*); Kevin Greening (BBC Radio 1); Nick Hasted (*Classic Rock*); Rosie Horide (*Disc*); Mick Houghton (*Sounds*); John Ingham (*Sounds*); Adam Jones (*Rhythm*); Jim Ladd (KMET radio); Dave Ling (*Classic Rock*); James McNair (the *Independent*); Mark Mehler (*Circus*); Kate Mossman (the *Guardian*); Ron Ross (*Circus*); Don Rush (*Circus*); Robin Smith (*Record Mirror*); Tony Stewart (*NME*); Wesley Strick (*Circus*); Tim Teeman (*The Times*); David Thomas (*Mojo*); Jon Tiven (*Circus*); Martin Townsend (*The Hit*); Mary Turner (Westwood 1 radio); Lisa Verrico (the *Sunday Times*); Mick Wall (*Mojo Classic*); Julie Webb (*NME*); Chris Welch (*Melody Maker*); Roy Wilkinson (*Mojo*); and Jonathan Wingate (*Record Collector*).

Other interview sources with no byline shown include izotope.com; *Music Star*; and Radio KKLZ, Las Vegas.

Book sources of background information and/or quotes were:

Evans, David, and David Minns, editors. *More Of The Real Life . . . Freddie Mercury*. London: Britannia, 1992.

Freestone, Peter, with David Evans. *Freddie Mercury*. London: Omnibus, 1998.

Gunn, Jacky. *The Official International Queen Fan Club Biography*. London: Queen Productions, 1989.

Gunn, Jacky, and Jim Jenkins (written in cooperation with Queen). *Queen: As It Began*. London: Pan IMP, 1993.

Hodkinson, Mark. *Queen: The Early Years*. London: Omnibus, 1995.

Hutton, Jim, and Tim Wapshott. *Mercury And Me*. London: Bloomsbury, 1994.

Jackson, Laura. *Queen: The Definitive Biography*. London: Piatkus, 1999.

———. *Brian May: The Definitive Biography*. London: Piatkus, 2007.

Sky, Rick. *The Show Must Go On: The Life Of Freddie Mercury*. London: Harper Collins, 1994.

Website sources of reference and data:

www.allmusic.com

www.queenonline.com (the band's official site)

www.ultimatequeen.co.uk/homepage.htm

en.wikipedia.org/wiki/Queen_(band) (It's fantastic on Queen—honest!)

CONTRIBUTORS

"But to be frank I'm not that keen on the British music press, and they've been pretty unfair to us.... we want to play good music, no matter how much of a slagging we get."

—FREDDIE MERCURY, *quoted by Chris Welch,*
MELODY MAKER, *09.11.1974*

Detroit's **ROBERT ALFORD** is a thirty-five-plus-year veteran rock 'n' roll photographer. The list of more than five hundred acts he has photographed reads like a who's who of popular music, ranging from AC/DC to ZZ Top and including such stalwarts as Led Zeppelin and The Rolling Stones. His photographs have been featured prominently in magazines (*Rolling Stone*, *People*, *Time*, *Creem*, and *Classic Rock*), on album covers, in liner notes, on television (VH1 and A&E), and in music documentaries.

Born in Liverpool in 1964, **MELISSA BLEASE** has been writing about music, food, dogs, and boys since the early 1980s. She has worked for a range of publications, including *Company* magazine and the *Guardian* newspaper. Today, she lives in Bath, mainly writing for local lifestyle magazine *Venue* and teaching aspiring young journalists at the Bath Theatre Royal. She also maintains a regular blog (theanimaldisco. blogspot.com) and enjoys the fact that, the older she gets, the more like Freddie Mercury she becomes.

JON BREAM has covered popular music for the *Minneapolis Star Tribune* since 1974, giving him the second-longest tenure of any current daily newspaper pop-music critic in the United States. He has published reviews and features in countless newspapers, from the *Boston Globe* to the *Los Angeles Times*, and in various magazines, including *Rolling Stone*, *Billboard*, *Creem*, *Entertainment Weekly*, *Vibe*, and *TV Guide*. Bream is the author of *Prince: Inside The Purple Reign*, *Whole Lotta Led Zeppelin: The Illustrated History Of The Heaviest Band Of All Time*, and *Diamond Is Forever*. As a longtime voter for the Rock and Roll Hall of Fame, Bream cast his ballot for Queen.

JOHN BUCCIGROSS has been an ESPN *SportsCenter* anchor since 1996 and an ESPN.com columnist since 2001. He is the author of the book *Jonesy*, about the life of former NHL player Keith Jones. Buccigross was born in Pittsburgh, Pennsylvania, and graduated from Steubenville Catholic Central High School in Ohio and Heidelberg University in Tiffin, Ohio. He lives in Connecticut with his wife, Melissa, and children, Brett, Malorie, and Jackson. His three favorite Queen songs are "Radio Ga Ga," "Somebody To Love," and "Play The Game."

New Zealand–born, South London–based, and oft' wandering **GARTH CARTWRIGHT** is an award-winning journalist and critic who regularly contributes to the *Guardian*, the *Sunday Times*, *fRoots*, and the BBC's website. He is the author of *Princes Amongst Men: Journeys With Gypsy Musicians* and the forthcoming *More Miles Than Money: Journeys In Wild America*.

STEPHANIE CHERNIKOWSKI (stephaniecherphoto. com) moved to New York City from her native Texas in 1975. Her images have been commissioned and included in CDs by such diverse artists as R.E.M., the Ramones, Stevie Ray Vaughan, Waylon Jennings, Alex Chilton, and Roky Erickson. Stephanie is also the author of the critically acclaimed book *Dream Baby Dream: Images from the Blank Generation* (1996), and her work has appeared in numerous other books and publications, including *The Village Voice*, the *New York Times*, *Rolling Stone*, *New Music Express*, *Melody Maker*, and *Mojo*.

STEPHEN DALTON began his journalistic career twenty years ago at Britain's longest-running rock weekly, the *New Musical Express*. He has since written about music and film for dozens of publications around the world. He is currently a regular writer for the *London Times* and the U.K. rock monthly *Uncut*. A lifelong Queen fan, he now believes the weight of scientific evidence proves beyond doubt that fat-bottomed girls do indeed make the rocking world go around.

JIM DEROGATIS (jimdero.com) is the pop music critic at the *Chicago Sun-Times*; the co-host of *Sound Opinions* (soundopinions.org), "the world's only rock 'n' roll talk show," originating at Chicago Public Radio and syndicated nationally by American Public Media; and the author of several books about music and culture, including *Let It Blurt: The Life And Times Of Lester Bangs, America's Greatest Rock Critic, Staring At Sound: The True Story Of Oklahoma's Fabulous Flaming Lips*, and *The Velvet Underground: A Walk On The Wild Side With Lou Reed, John Cale, Andy Warhol, Nico, And More.*

HARRY DOHERTY was a staff writer with *Melody Maker* through the 1970s, associated with artists like Queen, Thin Lizzy, Kate Bush, and Blondie. Later, he was the founding editor of the English-language edition of *Metal Hammer* and was the creator and founding editor of the video magazine *Hard 'N' Heavy*, which is in the record books for having three volumes in the *Billboard* Top 20 video chart simultaneously. He is currently media editor of Nielsen Book in the U.K.

DAVID DUNLAP JR. is a contributing writer for the *Washington City Paper*. To this day, he regrets burning his first copy of Queen's *Flash Gordon* soundtrack in the backyard. He had just returned from a lecture delivered by the author of *The God Of Rock: A Christian Perspective of Rock Music* and was temporarily convinced that Queen was sending him a pro-drug message through the backward masking on "Another One Bites The Dust." Nonetheless, he thought *The Game* was too awesome to burn, so *Flash* took the heat.

Writer and humorist **ANDREW EARLES** (failedpilot.com) has contributed to *Spin, Vice, Paste, Harp, Magnet, Washington City Paper, Philadelphia Weekly, Memphis Flyer*, and other publications. Additionally, his writing and editorial work can be found in several books, including *Whole Lotta Led Zeppelin: The Illustrated History Of The Heaviest Band Of All Time, The Rock Bible Unholy Scripture For Fans & Bands, Mock Stars: Indie Comedy And The Dangerously Funny, The Overrated Book*, and *Lost In The Grooves: Scram's Capricious Guide To The Music You Missed*. Andrew makes his home in Memphis, Tennessee.

CHUCK EDDY is the author of the books *Stairway* and *The Accidental Evolution of Rock 'n' Roll*, and has se as music editor at *The Village Voice* and as a senior edito *Billboard*. He has written thousands of pieces over the ye *Creem, Rolling Stone, Spin, Blender*, rhapsody.com, and o publications and websites. He lives in Queens, New York.

GARY GRAFF is an award-winning music journalist based in Detroit. He is a regular contributor to the *New Yo Times* Features Syndicate, *Billboard*, UPI, the *Cleveland Pla Dealer*, the *Oakland Press* and *Journal Register* Company Newswire, *Revolver*, Red Flag Media, and other publications, as well as United Stations Radio Networks and radio stations in Detroit and Milwaukee. He is the editor of *The Ties That Bind: Bruce Springsteen A To E To Z* and the series editor of th MusicHound Essential Album Guide series.

PETER HINCE (www.peterhince.co.uk) first met Queen in 1973 while working for Mott The Hoople, whom Queen was supporting on a U.K. tour. "They'll never make it," he recalls thinking. Peter subsequently became a roadie to Freddie and John, then head of the Queen crew while retaining his original role. He worked full-time for the band until 1986. Today he is a successful advertising photographer based in the U.K. with top clients around the globe. He is also a writer and has a completed set of humorous and unique observational memoirs from his unrivalled time with Queen, and several works of fiction too.

DAVE HUNTER is an author, musician, and journalist. He is the presenter and co-author of the *Totally Interactive Guitar Bible* and its two follow-ups, *Interactive Fender Bible* and *Interactive Gibson Bible*. Among his other books are the popular *The Guitar Amp Handbook, Guitar Rigs*, and *Guitar Effects Pedals*, and he contributes regularly to *Guitar Player* and *Vintage Guitar* magazines.

GREG KOT (gregkot.com) has been the *Chicago Tribune*'s rock music critic since 1990. He co-hosts the nationally syndicated rock 'n' roll talk show *Sound Opinions* (soundopinions.org) on public radio and is the author of *Wilco: Learning How To Die* and *Ripped: The Digital Music Revolution*.

REINHOLD MACK, aka "Mack," first worked with Queen co-producing the 1980 LP *The Game* with the band. He went on to co-produce the *Flash Gordon* soundtrack, *Hot Space*, *The Works*, and *A Kind Of Magic*, as well as Roger Taylor's *Strange Frontier* and Freddie Mercury's *Mr. Bad Guy*. Mack, who recorded four of Queen's live releases, has also produced or engineered Billy Squier, Black Sabbath, and Electric Light Orchestra.

ROBERT MATHEU has been a music photographer since his teenage years in Detroit, where he attended the earliest shows of the Stooges, MC5, Alice Cooper, Led Zeppelin, Cheap Trick, Pretenders, Clash, Stevie Ray Vaughan, and the likes. His work has appeared in *Playboy*, *Rolling Stone*, *Creem*, and *Mojo*, and on more than 200 albums. He oversaw the 2001 return of *Creem*, the 2007 hardcover anthology *CREEM: America's Only Rock 'n' Roll Magazine*, and *The Stooges: Authorized And Illustrated Story*.

JAMES MCNAIR is a Glasgow-born music journalist who lives in London. A regular contributor to *Mojo* magazine and the U.K. broadsheet *The Independent*, he counts Keith Richards, Björk, Brian Wilson, and the late James Brown among his favorite interviewees. "I have fond memories of seeing Queen play 'Seven Seas Of Rhye' on *Top Of The Pops* in 1974," says McNair. "I was nine years old and much taken with Freddie's chainmail glove."

JEFFREY MORGAN has been the Canadian editor of *Creem* since 1975. He is also the author of the definitive authorized biography of Alice Cooper, *The Life and Crimes of Alice Cooper*. His award-winning newspaper column, "Jeffrey Morgan's Media Blackout," appears weekly in Detroit's *Metro Times*.

DANIEL NESTER (danielnester.com) is the author of *God Save My Queen: A Tribute* and *God Save My Queen II: The Show Must Go On*, experimental essay collections addressing his obsession with Queen, as well as *The History Of My World Tonight* (poems) and *How To Be Inappropriate*, a collection of humorous nonfiction. His work appears in *The Morning News*, *Open City*, *The Daily Beast*, *Time Out New York*, *Nerve*, and *Bookslut*, and has been anthologized in places like *The Best American Poetry*, *The Best Creative Nonfiction*, and *Third Rail: The Poetry Of Rock And Roll*. He teaches writing at The College of Saint Rose in Albany, New York, and owns a Burns Red Special replica guitar, among countless other Queen-associated memorabilia.

"The Man Who Shot the '70s," **MICK ROCK** (mickrock.com) launched his photography career in 1972 with an unknown named David Bowie. His career continued to soar during the decade when he created iconic images of figures like Lou Reed, Iggy Pop, the Sex Pistols, and, of course, Queen. Mick moved to New York from his native U.K. in the 1970s and quickly became involved in the underground scene. He has produced several highly acclaimed retrospectives of the glam era and more recently has worked with such stars as Kate Moss, Michael Stipe, the Strokes, and the Raconteurs.

ROCK 'N' ROLL COMICS and **HARD ROCK COMICS** were launched by Todd Loren to spin illustrated (and unlicensed) biographies of rock stars. Some of those stars were supportive, while others sued. Loren was convinced the First Amendment to the U.S. Constitution protected his "illustrated articles," and the California Supreme Court agreed. In June 1992, Loren was found murdered in his San Diego condo. The comics continued for two more years, with Jay Allen Sanford serving as managing editor and with KISS participating in the bio series. The company closed its doors in 1994. In 2005, BulletProof Film released the documentary *Unauthorized and Proud of It: Todd Loren's Rock 'N' Roll Comics*, featuring interviews with Loren's family, friends, and adversaries. Loren's murder remains unsolved.

SYLVIE SIMMONS (sylviesimmons.com) was born in London and lives in San Francisco. She's been writing about rock since 1977, first as L.A. correspondent for U.K. weekly *Sounds*, then for *Kerrang!*, legendary U.S. magazine *Creem*, and *Mojo*. Her writing has also appeared in *Q*, *Rolling Stone*, and *Blender*, as well as the *Guardian* and the *San Francisco Chronicle*. Her own books include the cult fiction of *Too Weird For Ziggy* and biographies of Neil Young and Serge Gainsbourg.

Among rock fans, **BILLY SQUIER** (billysquier.com) requires no introductions. He has recorded nine solo LPs, as well as two with his acclaimed mid-1970s outfit, Piper. Born and raised in Boston, Massachusetts, he has played with talent as diverse as the Grateful Dead, Steve Miller, Jimi Hendrix, and future New York Doll Jerry Nolan, and toured alongside fellow heavyweights like KISS, Alice Cooper, Foreigner, and, of course, Queen.

INDEX

QUEEN

OVERLEAF: The last U.S. concert date, *Hot Space* tour, Forum, Inglewood, September 15, 1982. © *Robert Matheu*

"We're pretty proud of what we've done as a whole. We took chances. Some of the things we did set the world alight, and some didn't. But at least we made our own mistakes. We did what we wanted to do."
—BRIAN MAY